T0376662

AFRICAN ETHNOGRAPHIC STUDIES
OF THE 20TH CENTURY

Volume 59

THE GURAGE

THE GURAGE

A People of the Ensete Culture

WILLIAM A. SHACK

Routledge
Taylor & Francis Group

LONDON AND NEW YORK

First published in 1966 by Oxford University Press for the International African Institute.

This edition first published in 2018
by Routledge
2 Park Square, Milton Park, Abingdon, Oxon OX14 4RN

and by Routledge
711 Third Avenue, New York, NY 10017

Routledge is an imprint of the Taylor & Francis Group, an informa business

British Library Cataloguing in Publication Data
A catalogue record for this book is available from the British Library

ISBN: 978-0-8153-8713-8 (Set)
ISBN: 978-0-429-48813-9 (Set) (ebk)
ISBN: 978-1-138-59804-1 (Volume 59) (hbk)
ISBN: 978-0-429-48664-7 (Volume 59) (ebk)

Publisher's Note
The publisher has gone to great lengths to ensure the quality of this reprint but points out that some imperfections in the original copies may be apparent.

Disclaimer
The publisher has made every effort to trace copyright holders and would welcome correspondence from those they have been unable to trace.

A Gurage elder

THE GURAGE

A People of the Ensete Culture

WILLIAM A. SHACK

Published for the
INTERNATIONAL AFRICAN INSTITUTE
by the
OXFORD UNIVERSITY PRESS
LONDON   NEW YORK   NAIROBI

Oxford University Press, Ely House, London W.1

GLASGOW NEW YORK TORONTO MELBOURNE WELLINGTON
CAPE TOWN SALISBURY IBADAN NAIROBI LUSAKA ADDIS ABABA
BOMBAY CALCUTTA MADRAS KARACHI LAHORE DACCA
KUALA LUMPUR SINGAPORE HONG KONG TOKYO

First published 1966
Reprinted 1969

Printed in Great Britain by
Hazell Watson & Viney Ltd., Aylesbury, Bucks

To
HAILU ARAYA

Oğama təyud dar žäk^{u}årä yəkär bōdä; gam^{w}ə qəraç yəkär.

Until the tale-bearer has related (his story), he seems like an elephant; after he has related (it) he seems a flea.

A Gurage proverb

recorded by W. LESLAU

Contents

Illustrations

PLATES

FIGURES

TABLES

MAPS

Preface

THIS study is based on field research among the Gurage of Shoa Province in South-West Ethiopia, carried out intermittently between September 1957 and July 1959. The research was made possible by employment with the Imperial Ethiopian Ministry of Education and the Administrative Staff of Tafari Makonnen Secondary School. In all, extended stays of six to eight weeks on four occasions in two Gurage villages and several shorter visits provided the only basis for direct observation of Gurage life. Field data were supplemented by extensive interviews with migrant and resident Gurage in Addis Ababa.

The circumstances under which field work was conducted, combining field trips with teaching commitments, were obviously less than ideal. But whatever measure of success I achieved I owe to the co-operation, goodwill, and patience of the Gurage, who allowed me to impose my anthropological interests upon them. Hence my deepest gratitude of all is to the Gurage people whose hospitality and show of kindness have made an unforgettable impression. *Balabbatt* Täsämä Amärga,Chief of the Chaha Gurage, and *Abba* François Markos, Head of the Catholic Mission in Endeber, stand foremost among those who afforded me many pleasurable moments and through them my investigations were greatly facilitated. They introduced me to Gurage society.

I am also indebted to several of my teachers who helped to shape my interests in social anthropology. In this regard, I owe more than a word of thanks to Professor Fred Eggan whose teaching, guidance, and encouragement prepared me as a graduate student to conduct field research. At the London School of Economics, Ford Foundation Fellowships in 1959–60 and 1960–1 provided me with financial support to prepare an earlier version of this study which was presented as a doctoral thesis. And to the Foundation, I am indeed thankful. Professor I. Schapera supervised my writing and he was a whetstone against which I could sharpen my tools of social anthropological inquiry; I am profoundly indebted to him. I lack sufficient literary skills adequately to describe the intellectual stimulus received in the Graduate Seminars conducted by Professor Raymond Firth, where much of the material in this study was first examined under his theoretical guidance. This has made an indelible imprint upon my thinking.

It will be obvious to the reader that this study of Gurage social structure has been greatly influenced by the writings of Professors Radcliffe-Brown, Evans-Pritchard, and Fortes, especially in my analysis of Gurage lineage and political systems; and by Professor Gluckman and his colleagues of the 'Manchester School' in my efforts to utilize the concepts of 'cross-cutting ties' in the analysis of certain Gurage rituals.

The revisions to the original manuscript, upon which this book is based, were made in Ethiopia between 1962–3. This fortunately afforded me several opportunities to recheck my data by revisiting the Gurage. Several of my colleagues at the University College of Addis Ababa assisted at various stages in the final preparation of the manuscript. Woizerit Tsedala Marayam Bayu has skilfully drawn many of the charts, diagrams, and the land-use map; my friend, Ato Hapte Mariam Markos, upon whom I have leaned heavily for linguistic assistance, made the orthographic corrections; Mr. Georges Savard gave useful suggestions regarding the prehistoric material; Mr. Patrick Hutton read the entire draft and shaped my anthropological barbarisms into readable English, and Mrs. Rose Bender typed the final copy. The first chapter benefited from the comments of Professor Edward Ullendorff; Dr. A. J. Drewes read with critical attention the entire manuscript from the vantage point of his rich knowledge of the Eastern Gurage, and this has been of immense value in making final revisions. I wish also to thank my wife whose moral support has been expressed immeasurably in patience and forbearance. Finally, as with all other anthropologists whose field studies the International African Institute has undertaken to publish, I too am deeply grateful for the assistance of the Director, Professor Daryll Forde, and the Editorial Secretary, Miss Barbara Pym.

W. A. S.

Haile Sellassie I University
University College
Addis Ababa, September 1964

A Note on Orthography

THE following orthography has been adopted for the spelling of Guraginä words which appear in this book; all vernacular terms are in the Chaha dialect. The consonantal signs used are roughly with English phonetic values, but there are some sounds in Chaha which do not occur in English. They are: the palatal series, gʸ kʸ; labiovelars, gʷ kʷ; rounded labials, bʷ fʷ mʷ; emphatics, ṭ q č; affricates, ǧ č; sibilants, ž š. The phonemic values of the Chaha vowels according to English equivalents are roughly as follows: ä, as in 'up'; a, somewhat similar to 'father'; e, as in 'say'; ə, as in 'er'; i, as in 'see'; o, as in 'go'; u, as in 'fool'. No distinction has been made between long and short vowels. Amharic words which appear in the text have not been rendered phonetically, they follow accepted usage of transcription. For easier reading of Gurage tribal names they are spelled without phonetic notation. In general, the orthography, though greatly simplified, is consistent with that used by W. Leslau in *Ethiopic Documents: Gurage*.

CHAPTER I

Introductory

THIS book is a study of the social institutions and modes of livelihood of the Gurage of South-West Ethiopia. In this first chapter I put down what is known of Gurage origins. In later sections I attempt to throw into relief the salient features of Gurage culture against a background of those political and religious factors of Ethiopian history which have played so enormous a role in shaping Gurage society. But now I summarize briefly the ethnographic field of this study.

The Gurage tribal grouping, a small linguistic and ethnographic enclave, occupies a portion of the southernmost range of the Central Ethiopian Plateau. The people speak a Semitic language, and are sedentary agriculturalists, clustered in numerous small, densely settled, kin-group villages. The distinguishing feature of these village settlements is the extensive growth of towering banana-like plants, called *'ensete'* that command attention immediately. Properly termed *Ensete edulis*, these plants look very much like the common variety of banana (*Musa spp.*) which is cultivated throughout East and Central Africa.[1] But unlike Musa, the true banana, *Ensete edulis* does not bear edible fruit; in fact, tribes who do not cultivate ensete refer to it, as do foreigners, as the 'false banana tree'. Ensete is the staple subsistence crop of the Gurage, intensively cultivated, and a complex of cultural traits has evolved connected with its mode of production. Ensete dominates Gurage modes of thought and interests, and moulds their livelihood. The cultivation of ensete is the prominent cultural feature of nearly the whole of South-West Ethiopia; I term this region the 'Ensete Culture Complex Area' and say more about it later.[2]

The structural features of Gurage society are typical of those found in the many small-scale 'segmentary' societies in Africa. In

---

[1] See for example, Read, 1956; Fallers, 1956.

[2] The ecological and cultural features distinguishing South-west Ethiopia from the plough cultivating-grain producing areas, and from the cattle-keeping zone, of Ethiopia are described in Shack, 1963a. See also Chap. III below.

terms of the typological framework within which African Political Systems have been classified, Gurage society is on that end of the continuum of tribes lacking centralized institutional political leadership.[3] Gurage society is one in which there is a low degree of specialization of roles and in which local groups recruited by unilineal descent form the core. Local agnatic kin-based groups are distinguished by their corporateness. Social, political, and economic relations are more or less consistent with the principles of genealogical ties between local descent groups. Social grouping based on lineages is reflected in their territorial distribution. Political power, authority, and wealth are vested in the lineage structure, and in theory, though not in actuality, constituent lineages of the total structure are politically and economically equal. Conversely, ritual power, authority, and wealth are vested in the lineages directly associated with the principal Gurage religious cults: the Male Cult, *Čəšt*, the Female Cult, *Däm^{w}am^{w}it*, and the Cult of the Thunder God, *Božä*. Gurage religious congregations comprising the total aggregate of local descent groups over-ride the genealogical and territorial principles of grouping.

In Chapters IV and V it will be seen that the small descent groups of shallow genealogical depth upon which Gurage political units are built compare structurally with such tribes as the Konkomba, Amba, and Tallensi.[4] Here, I only introduce summarily the structural features of the Gurage political and ritual systems. The Gurage political system is characterized by its segmentary form; the religious system by its centralized form. This structural asymmetry, with ritual dominating, is the distinguishing feature of Gurage political and religious organization. Political units are relatively independent and positions with political authority are attached to fields of clanship. Ritual officials sanction the authority of political leaders, give mythical and ritual validation to the principles of descent, and counterbalance the exercise of secular power. The network of interlocking ties within the total system, essentially expressed in ritual terms, makes for cohesion at the level of agnatic kin ties and in the wider field of political relations between larger descent group structures.

[3] Fortes and Evans-Pritchard, 1940, pp. xi–23 *passim*.
[4] See Middleton and Tait, 1958, pp. 1–31 *passim*, and the typology of segmentary societies suggested by the writer's Group II category. Cf. also Fortes, 1945.

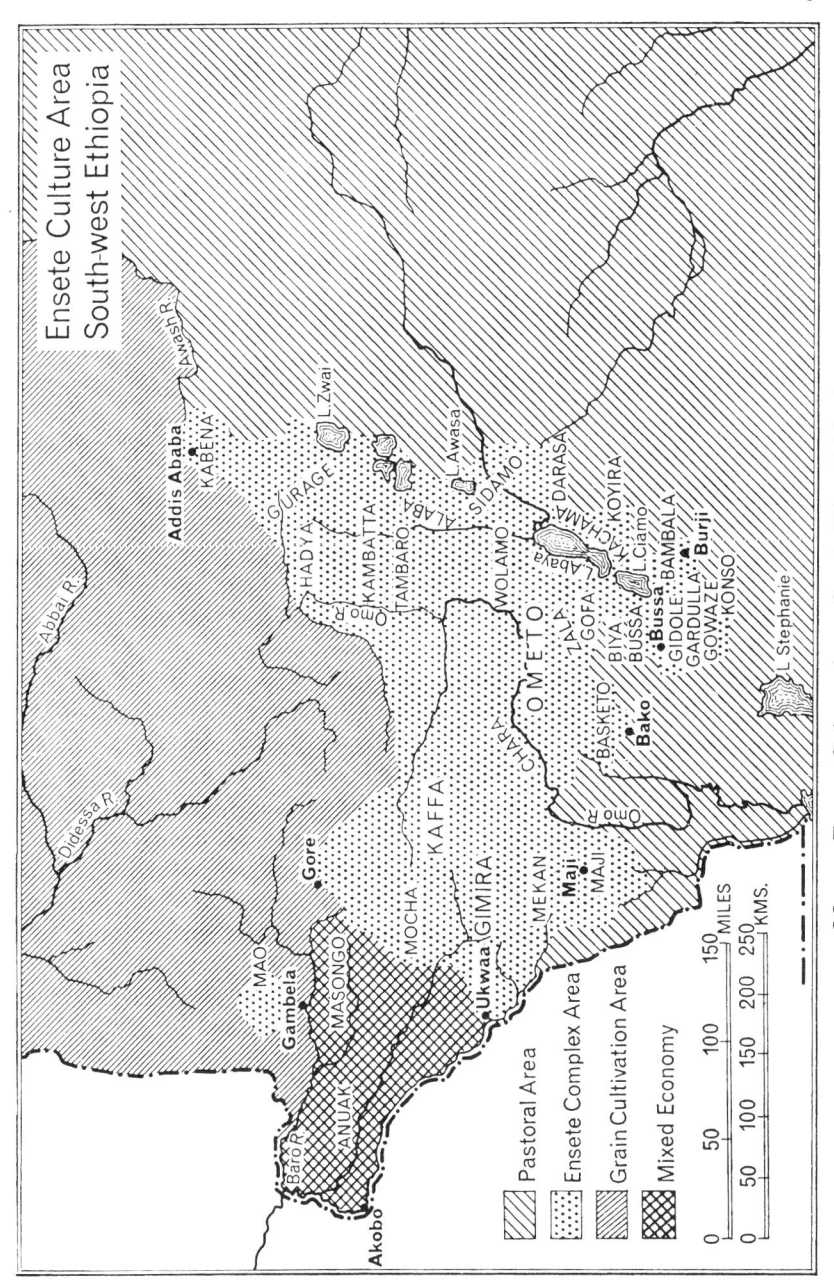

Map 1. Ensete Culture Area: South-West Ethiopia.

The Gurage tribal grouping is called by the Gurage as well as by other tribes, '*Yä säbat bet Gurage*', 'Gurage of the. . . Seven Houses (Tribes). The Chaha, Ezha, Geyto, Muher, Ennemor, Akilil, and Walani—Woriro tribes comprise the seven houses. Since the fourteenth century the *säbat bet* have undergone a slow process of change. They have been bordered by warring tribes such as the Sidamo,[5] and the Mača and the Arussi Galla, all have threatened their existence and prevented tribal movements. And when hostilities could not be completely exhausted externally, they were turned inwards and internecine strife became a common feature of Gurage tribal life. The Gurage have faced squarely the crusades and prophets of both Ethiopic Christianity and Islam. They have incorporated into their own indigenous beliefs and practices chosen tenets of these faiths which best suited them. They shared a problem common to the whole of Ethiopia in the nineteenth century: the beginning of Amhara rule.

THE ETHNO-HISTORICAL FIELD:
SOUTH-WEST ETHIOPIA

I

I turn now to discuss broadly the human and cultural features of South-West Ethiopia. Here Gurageland is situated. It is here that several culturally similar and dissimilar groups have been historically in contact, giving up ground in one place, holding fast in other areas, and adapting to various ecological conditions generally.[6] It is in South-West Ethiopia, and under similar circumstances, that the Gurage and their culture have evolved.

South-West Ethiopia is a vast area defined roughly as lying between the Rift Valley lake chain and the international boundaries of the Sudan with Ethiopia. (Map 1.) It borders the northern frontier of Kenya; the 8·5° longitude is about its northern limit. It is traversed by two great rivers, the Ghibie and the Gojeb, neither of which is navigable. In the East and in part of the South-East the terrain is mountainous with many valleys and plains, some

---

[5] 'Sidamo' is used throughout in a broad linguistic and ethnographic sense to refer to the Sidamo Language Group, consisting of the tribes known as the Gudella (Hadya), Kambatta, Jambaro, Alaba, and the Sidamo proper. Cf. also Fn. 11, p. 6, below.

[6] The ethnic and linguistic configuration of South-West Ethiopia has been termed by Bryan, 'A Linguistic No-Man's Land', *Africa*, XV, 4, 1945, pp. 188–205.

fertile, others barren, while most of the high country is dotted with patches of heavy forest growth. Towards Lake Rudolph in the South, where tribes keep cattle and practise rudimentary agriculture, the terrain is less fertile. Much of the land round Lakes Rudolph and Stephanie is barren.

On racial and cultural grounds, South-West Ethiopia distinguishes itself from Northern Ethiopia. Today, the South-west is inhabited by representatives of Negroid and Prenilotic branches of mankind, as well as by a Caucasoid element which is a Cushitic subfamily of the Hamitic stock.[7] The predominant Semitic influence characteristic of the North has penetrated southwards, being strikingly preserved in the physical features of the people known collectively as 'Sidamo', a people who have had a profound influence on the shaping of Gurage culture. The Sidamo possess a significant Negroid strain and speak a Cushitic language, as do many tribes in this region. They are sedentary cultivators of ensete, tilling the soil by hoe, and though cattle are kept their use is mainly as a source of food and fertilizer. Near the Sudan border are the Prenilotes, people speaking languages of the Sudanic stock, some of these specifically of the Nilotic subdivision.[8] The Anuak, Mao, Koma, and Gumuz are representatives of this group, all depending for subsistence primarily upon agriculture. In the far south, many elements of the 'East African Cattle Complex', such as the milking-complex and age-grade cycling, obtain in modified form among the sedentary Konso, and the semi-nomadic Reshiat tribes. But in its more representative form, the cattle complex dominates the culture of the Borana Galla who occupy nearly the whole of Southern Ethiopia, extending over into the Northern Frontier District of Kenya.[9] In the main, however, intensive cultivation of *Ensete edulis* is by far the most characteristic mode of livelihood in South-West Ethiopia.

II

The Gurage are basically of Sidamo stock, and their territory, which I term 'Gurageland', was once inhabited by Sidamo tribes who formerly occupied the whole of Western and Southern Ethiopia. In a later epoch the Sidamo were decimated, or absorbed, in part by 'Aksumites', the 'Semitized' Hamites, who pushed

[7] Murdock, 1959, p. 187   [8] *Ibid*, p. 170.
[9] Ernesta Cerulli, 1956. See also Murdock, op. cit., pp. 196–203.

southwards about the seventh century A.D., after the fall of the Aksum kingdom, and in part by hordes of Galla invaders who began their move Westwards and Northwards in the early thirteenth century.[10] In consequence, the Sidamo were subsequently reduced to small groups, such as now exist in and around the Ghibie River valley; they speak kindred languages and are racially, culturally, and physically homogeneous.[11] During the fourteenth century the Sidamo were once again invaded by other waves of Semitic Ethiopians from the northern highlands; the descendants are the present-day Gurage. Through the centuries the Sidamo and Semitic invaders intermarried to produce the Gurage, whose physical characteristics resemble, in general, those of the Sidamo.

The Semitic element in the Gurage peoples came from the same basic stock that provided the nucleus of the Semitic peoples in the Horn of Africa. The migration of Semites from Southern Arabia to Ethiopia is held to have taken place between 1,000 to 400 B.C. These people, who at some time during the first millennium before Christ, crossed the Red Sea to colonize the highlands of the Horn, were an off-shoot of the Semitic Sabean civilization, which flourished in South-western Arabia. The physical appearance of this Ethiopian-Semite is generally Caucasian, where it has not been modified by Negroid or Hamitic mixtures, the colour ranging from brown to black. These physical characteristics, together with those acquired through Hamitic influences, are observable in Gurage communities, the Semitic characteristics predominating.

Whatever their physical appearance, the Gurage generally recognize an ideal type which to them is distinctively characteristic of the 'purest' stock. The attributes of this ideal are lightness of

[10] On the question of 'early proto-Hamitic' expansion in East Africa, from which the Sidamo are believed to be descended, see Clark, 1954, p. 232 *passim*; Cole, 1954, pp. 275–78; Honea, 1958, p. 98.
An excellent searching account of the Aksumite period in ancient Ethiopian history is given by Pankhurst, 1961, pp. 1–62. For the Galla invasions consult Beckingham and Huntingford, 1954; Cf. also, Huntingford, 1955, pp. 19–22.

[11] Linguistic classification of the Cushitic-speaking groups is still a matter of considerable controversy as indicated by the following sources. Tucker and Bryan, 1956, p. 123, classify the 'Sidamo Language Group' as Cushitic, consisting of the Sidamo, Hadya, Kambatta, Alaba, Darasa, and perhaps the Bambala. Murdock, op. cit., p. 187, considers the Sidamo as members of the 'Western' branch of the Cushitic subfamily of the 'Hamitic' stock; the Darasa and Kambatta belonging to the 'Eastern' branch. Greenberg, 1955, places Sidamo in the Cushitic subfamily of the 'Afroasiatic' stock.

skin colour, a long straight nose, thin lips, and delicate bone structure. Although these features are seldom found together in one
individual Gurage, the high esteem in which the tribe, as a whole,
holds them has contributed to ethnic consciousness and pride. The
Gurage are considered by other Ethiopians as well as by foreigners
to be the handsomest of Ethiopian peoples. Gurage women,
perhaps more widely known for their beauty than for any other
quality, usually come closer to the ideal than do the men.

III

Guraginä, as the Gurage term their language, is a Semitic language. It has been influenced considerably by Sidamo, a Cushitic
substratum language of South Ethiopic.[12] The numerous Sidamo
elements in the Gurage language cluster, in the phonology,
morphology, syntax, and mainly in vocabulary, on the one hand,
and the North Ethiopic (Semitic) features in the morphology and
vocabulary on the other hand, are evidence put forward by lin-
guists to support the accepted theory of Gurage origins reviewed
above. *Guraginä* is classified as belonging to the South Ethiopic
group of languages.[13]

Gurage linguistic groupings are divided into three categories
which roughly correspond to the political and geographical divisions of Gurage tribes. Usually the tribal name is also the name of
the dialect spoken by that tribe. The major linguistic groupings
and their corresponding subdivisions are these:[14]

Eastern	*Western*	*Northern*
Selti	Chaha	Aymellel
Wolane (Walani)	Ezha	
Ulbarag (Urbarag)	Ennemor	
Innek'or	Endegen	
Zeway	Gyeto	
	Muher	
	Masqan	
	Gogot	

---

[12] This problem is discussed by Leslau, 1945. He also gives several succinct
descriptions of linguistic influences on *Guraginä*; See Leslau, 1952, and 1956.

[13] Cohen, 1910–11, pp. 39–46, 1931; pp. 55–241; Ullendorff, 1950, 1955;
Mondon-Vidailhet, 1902, 1913.

[14] Tucker and Bryan, op. cit., p. 136. 'Zeway' dialect is spoken by the fishermen on the island of Lake Zeway. Note also that the writers classify the speakers
of *Guraginä* as forming a 'Dialect Cluster'.

Each Gurage dialect is usually understood only by its own speakers, and there is a rough correlation between the contiguity of dialect groups and the extent to which their dialects are mutually intelligible. On the other hand, contact with neighbouring peoples has also had its effect on Gurage dialects. In contrast with the Western Gurage, there is a close linguistic relationship between the Eastern Gurage and the Harari, owing to their spatial and cultural proximity, and the vocabulary of the Eastern Gurage shows considerable infiltration of Arabic. The influence of Sidamo on *Guraginä* has already been mentioned, and the effects that Amharic, the *lingua franca* for most of Ethiopia's non-Amhara people, has had on the Gurage should also be borne in mind. The Gurage have developed a number of interlingual taboos about words having phonetic correspondence in both languages, particularly words concerned with sex.[15] Other linguistic changes in *Guraginä* are due to the mobility of certain sections of the population and, as the trend toward geographical mobility appears to be increasing, especially owing to labour migration, linguistic changes will most probably occur concomitantly.

IV

Among the Gurage, as among several other tribal societies in Ethiopia, there exists a low-caste occupational group of hunters, artisans, and ritual specialists who are, according to tenable theories, believed to be remnants of earlier inhabitants of the Horn. They are known generally as *Watta* though each tribe ascribes a name to its group: among the Amhara they are known as *Wayto*, to the Galla as *Watta*, to the Kafa as *Manjo*, to the Somali as *Midgaan*, *Tumaal*, and *Yibir*, and to the Gurage as *Fuga*.[16]

Fuga is the generic name given to that portion of the Central group of Watta who inhabit the region of the Gurage.[17] Although

---

[15] Leslau, 1952, p. 275. See also p. 127 below where the use of interlingual taboos in relationship to Gurage co-wife behaviour is discussed.

[16] The most complete survey of the *Watta* is given by Enrico Cerulli 1922, pp. 200–14. Cf. also Isenberg and Krapf, 1843, p. 181 *passim*; Bianchi, 1884, pp. 303–13; among the Somali see in particular Lewis, 1961, pp. 11–14; on the prehistorical aspects of the problem consult Clark and Honea, loc. cit. On the characteristics of the *Fuga* caste see Shack, 1964.

[17] I use *Fuga* here in the general sense to refer to all artisans, clarifying this usage on p. 11 below.

there is some variation in their physical characteristics, Fuga mainly resemble the Bantu Negro. As with the Wayto and Manjo of similar status, the Fuga also have adopted the language of the dominant group, while retaining their own 'language' or 'jargon', which in certain ritual observances is highly esoteric, being understood only by those belonging actually or symbolically to their caste. Fuga relationships with the wider society in social and economic activities are institutionalized and reinforced by supernatural sanctions. The ritual language of Fuga ritual experts is called *Fedwät*, which only they and the Gurage women speak; it is kept carefully guarded from Gurage men and strangers, for it forms an integral part of the initiation rites for girls. This is described later in Chapter VI on Gurage religious organization.

The religion of the Fuga most probably has had some effect on the beliefs and practices of the Gurage since certain magical practices and sorcery are in the hands of Fuga. As we show subsequently, they take part, and play an important role in Gurage ceremonials. Fuga rituals and beliefs, apparently, have been completely merged with the religious organization of the Gurage. If the Fuga have ritual observances of their own, I uncovered no evidence of this, but the Gurage believe that Fuga ritual experts possess rich powers of magic and their sorcery and malediction are greatly feared.[18]

Marriage between Fuga and Gurage is forbidden; this ban being enforced and backed by ritual sanctions. Fuga marry 'close' kin, 'even brothers and sisters', it has been reported. They are landless, forbidden to till soil or herd cattle, and only in very recent times have Fuga been permitted to enter Gurage households without permission. In the past, during times of warfare, it is reported that Fuga remained in the village lest their presence, which is commonly associated with the 'evil eye', should bring defeat to Gurage warriors; neither could they carry spears, considered to be the weapons of the Gurage warriors.[19] Before Gurage took to firearms for fighting, the weapon of the Fuga was the bow and arrow, which he used for hunting such game as gazelle, and especially hippo-

---

[18] A similar account of the Ari and other tribes in the Ensete Complex and occupational castes is given by Jensen, 1959.

[19] Gurage use the term *Oze* to refer to anyone possessed by the 'evil eye'; even Gurage can be so cursed.

potami round Lake Zeway and the Ghibie River valley.[20] Nowadays, the spear is chiefly used, the head being poisoned with an alkaloid; but both the killing and eating of these animals are still considered by the Gurage to be ignoble. Other occupations of the Fuga, woodworking, tanning, and smithing, are held by Gurage to be associated with evil spirits.

Gurage hold strongly to the belief that Fuga can destroy the fertility of soil, injure the breeding capabilities of cattle, and change their milk to blood or urine. For those reasons Fuga are never permitted to assist in ensete cultivation or to tend cattle. A widespread belief in Ethiopia credits the hyena with possessing the 'evil-eye', and the Gurage believe that Fuga take the form of hyenas at night, attacking children and eating their entrails, and consuming all the domestic animals that have died in the village.

Nowadays Fuga are usually paid in cash for their labours but at festival times they still receive food as payment for their services to the village, such as cutting wood and constructing essential sections of a new house. Each is given the 'Fuga's share' of any animal that is slaughtered by the villagers, to be eaten alone and apart from the homesteads. The Fuga's share of the animal consists of the lower part of the back and the feet.[21]

In other ways, status differences between Gurage and Fuga are expressed in speech idioms. Fuga address Gurage as *'abiya'* which means 'master', to which a Gurage replies 'kill the animal'; to the greeting of a female Fuga, a Gurage replies 'may he kill the animal for you and may you eat it'.[22]

Fuga cannot be bought or sold as property as slaves were formerly. Legal matters concerning Gurage-Fuga relations are dealt with by the corporate body of the village polity and, in some cases, with the help of a ritual functionary. But Fuga behaviour to one another is governed by their own separate legal codes and Gurage do not intervene in these affairs. A Gurage, regardless of his standing in the community, is subject to penalties usually in the form of fines of money or cattle, or both, for grievously harming a Fuga. The strongest punishment imposed is a ritual curse that entails an illness which is often incurable. Furthermore, the severity of punishment depends on the importance of the Fuga in the

---

[20] If Father Fernandez's account of the Gurage in the seventeenth century is correct, they also fought with bow and arrow. See also p. 17 below.

[21] Leslau, 1950, pp. 61–62.   [22] *Ibid.*, p. 62.

ritual system. If the Fuga concerned was an agent of a ritual dignitary, the punishment imposed could be considerable.

Fuga are settled throughout every tribal region in Gurageland. The size of their settlements vary, the larger clusters of Fuga settling in villages near the principal Gurage markets. In former times Fuga could not enter the market areas, their crafts being bought by Gurage traders and later resold. In poorer regions Fuga are more dispersed. Fuga are not found in every village; none were in the village I surveyed, but in the villages of ritual chiefs there are always several Fuga clients who act as agents for them. Of the various estimates I obtained from Gurage on the size of the Fuga population the average is about 5,000, inclusive of men, women, and children.

In later chapters, the importance of the role Fuga play in Gurage ritual life is dealt with: the use of *Fedwät*, the language of the Fuga in the rituals of Gurage women; the role of Fuga in circumcision rites; their participation in Gurage burials; all are examples of this. As ritual agents of the chief representatives of Gurage deities, Fuga are important intermediaries between Gurage and the supernatural world. Rituals apart, worth noting here is the client relationship obtaining between Gurage and Fuga, as well as other occupational castes of blacksmiths, *Näfʷrä*, and tanners *Gəžä*.[23] Gurage consider work employing wood, metal, and leather despicable and they despise the people who perform it. Since these craft specialists, regardless of their occupational skills, together form an endogamous caste, what has been described above for Fuga holds true for smiths and tanners as well. But only the Fuga have dual roles as craftsmen and ritual specialists.

The knowledge and skills of the Fuga serve most of the technical requirements of Gurage life. They construct the *äčba*, the centre mainstay of the Gurage house, cut wood for the walls, and fit together the rafters and beams with precision and accuracy. Their technical role is symbolized by the *äčba*; the focus from which the social, ritual, and economic life of the homestead radiates.[24] Fuga are a centre of ramification of technical relations for the village and tribe. Of no less importance, they reinforce the aesthetic

---

[23] Some Gurage men and women supplement their farming income with pottery, basketry and woven crafts; no superstitious beliefs are associated with these activities, nor do Gurage engaged in such work form a despised or low-status group.

[24] See Chapter II, p. 42 below.

values of the tribe through their art which is an extension of their craft activity. Gurage technology is based on the Fuga and the most important Gurage economic activities depend upon this technology. Gurage commonly repeat a phrase which graphically summarizes this relationship: 'a Fuga is the one who knows'.

V

It has already been noted (p. 5) that the Sidamo region was invaded during the fourteenth century by waves of Semitic peoples from the northern highlands of Ethiopia. These Christianized-pagan Ethiopians (and I take the position that they were originally Christian though a contrary view is equally plausible) became the nucleus of the Gurage tribes. They underwent many changes in forms of culture and social organization before they later came to be known as Gurage. But what modifications actually did take place are not a part of their recorded history which is reviewed in the next section. Barely enough historical threads exist, and these must be woven in several places, to patch together various pieces of ethnography in an attempt to reconstruct the pattern of ecological and social adaptation of these highland Ethiopians to the general environmental conditions of South-west Ethiopia.

It is not without conjecture that we assume the following changes in the social system of the migrating 'bands' who later came to be known as Gurage.[25] Less speculative is the fact that the Gurage system of reckoning kin has retained its basic Semitic feature of descriptive cousin terminology; the trend of change has been away from the bilateral descent system of the northern highland kinship pattern, and in a unilineal patrilineal direction, the feature of kinship common among the Sidamo tribes. This is also witnessed in the system of naming, land tenure, and inheritance, and the development of agnatic descent groups and clan structures, features of social organization which are not found among

[25] I use 'band' here for the lack of a better term to describe a population movement, which perhaps did not assume the sociological form of migrating families, clans, or tribal sections. Women were most probably present, since the composition of Ethiopian armies in historical times has been described as partly consisting of female servants for preparing food and for making beer and mead drinks. But whether the Gurage bands moved with their wives is doubtful; the early 'marriages' with Sidamo women might have been a form of concubinage.

For good accounts of the general cultural and land features of highland Ethiopia, see Nadel, 1946, Trimingham, 1952, Ch. I; a more substantive report is given by Messing, 1957; also Simoons, 1960.

the Tigre and Amhara. The thin veneer of monophysite Christianity over older, more deeply rooted forms of traditional religious ideas and ritual practices was soon rubbed off by the stronger Cushitic religion as practised by the Sidamo. Furthermore, Galla migrations in the sixteenth and seventeenth centuries, flanking the northern frontier of the Gurage, isolated them from the cultural and religious mainstreams of Christianity, as it developed and emerged as the politically dominant force on the Central plateau after the founding of the Solomonoid Dynasty in 1270 A.D. Some features of the incorporation of Sidamo rituals and beliefs that are observed in Gurage religion have been described as an amalgam constituting 'Hamitic' conceptions, neo-Sudanese beliefs in divine Kingship and ideas absorbed from Christian Ethiopians. Of this, Trimingham writes that 'their chief deity is the sky-god, in addition to whom flourishes a supernatural realm of local nature-spirits associated with natural features such as mountain peaks, streams, and trees'.[26] Moreover, the structure and organization of traditional rituals became the focal point where the important social and political aspects of Gurage life crystallized. It is not unreasonable to assume that Christian rituals became most probably incompatible with other features of the developing social system. This seems especially true in view of the segmentary political system of the Gurage and Sidamo tribal grouping, wherein political leaders are legitimatized by ritual powers held in trust by religious dignitaries who, themselves, are representatives of tribal deities. The Christian hierarchy of the Solomonoid Dynasty, represented by the Emperor of Ethiopia, being under strict religious, as well as political, obligations could only ritually legitimate those political leaders on whom it depended for support, namely those of the highland plateau peoples, the Amhara and Tigre, in the main. It was a political system with a dynasty founded on Biblical traditions.

The final significant change was ecological. The systems of cultivation and land-use as practised by the Sidamo were taken over by the Gurage. They adapted the use of the digging stick to the horticulture of ensete, the indigenous staple crop of this region, apparently growing in abundance, for the cultivation of which the plough is unsuitable. They formed village settlements according to the ecological conditions; they developed a series of traits that

[26] Trimingham, op. cit., pp. 17–18.

are characteristic of the ensete culture. These features of Gurage life are described in Chapters II and III. The Gurage today, apart from their Semitic language, cannot be distinguished readily in other social and cultural features from the Sidamo, the people their ancestors set out to colonize five centuries ago.

THE GURAGE: 1342–1889

The preceding sections have outlined the essential human and geographical features of South-West Ethiopia as they relate to the origins of Gurage culture. In the following sections I put down what is known of Gurage history; but as already indicated, Gurage history cannot be set apart entirely from the history of Ethiopia proper, in which environmental, religious, and political factors have helped to condition especially the cultural and social life of the highland plateau peoples. Gurage history has been tempered by the centuries-old, often changing, political climate of the Ethiopian Plateau.

Recorded history of the Gurage dates back no farther than the fourteenth century. Most of Gurage history is related in matter-of-fact accounts within the oral tradition of the people who are rich in oral traditions. Even though Gurage oral traditions lack documentation, and should not be disregarded, the history of such traditions often show that the facts have been altered in the process of being handed down from generation to generation. People tend to smuggle into historical narratives a personal element. An alteration is thus made to coincide closely with particular events that are of immediate concern to each generation of tale-tellers. Gurage oral history can be manipulated and often is; and this is true of Gurage genealogies.

An historical background for the Gurage based on documentary material can be drawn from Ethiopian chronicles relating to the reign of the Ethiopian king Amda Syon I (1312–42). From this period to the beginning of direct rule over all Gurage tribes, conquered finally by Emperor Menilek II in 1889, their political position varied from what was apparently one of total autonomy to one of semi-domination, involving the payment of tribute to maintain some degree of autonomy, to one of complete subjugation. We have arbitrarily chosen 1889 as the date marking the final phase of early Gurage history; a date that is as well the starting point of the contemporary phase of their history, and from which can be seen the effective changes in their social structure as a consequence of domination by Amhara-Ethiopian rule.[27]

The name 'Gerawege' appears to be first mentioned in the Ethiopian Chronicles relating the *Histoire des guerres d'Amda Syon*: 1312–42.[28] Highland Christian armies spreading out under the initiative of Syon I, who may well be called the founder of the Ethiopian state, moved south to colonize the Muslim and 'heathen' unbelievers. During Amda Syon's reign one of the Ethiopian armies under Azmač Səbhat left the Tigrean town of Gur'a, in the province of Akkulo Gəzay, came to Aymellel, now a district in northern Gurageland, and settled there. According to the Ethiopian historian Aleqa Tayye, the name of the country and the people is said to be derived from the word 'Gurage', the people or the country of Gur'a.[29]

This popular etymology of the Gurage's origin, for which there is some historical foundation, is more widely accepted than other suggestions that have been put forward. Isenberg, for instance, in attempting to correlate linguistic expressions with geographical place names, observed that 'Gurage' is so called on account of its situation, that is, being on the left, if one looks to the west from Gondar, a province in the north; 'gera' means the left, and 'gie' signifies side; hence 'on the left side'.[30] In the version preferred by Cecchi, who travelled through Gurageland in the last half of the nineteenth century, some of the Gurage people are said to have

[27] Although the unification of Ethiopia by Menilek resulted in the military-political dominance of the Amhara, nevertheless, representatives of non-Amhara tribes also filled prominent administrative positions in both Menilek's, and the present, government. Its cultural and political form was not exclusively 'Amhara'; rather it was built upon Amhara and Tigre Christian cultural complexes. Hence, it seems inappropriate to speak of 'Amhara rule' when referring to that system of government. And 'Abyssinian' as currently used by some writers seems antiquated. I find the term 'Ethiopian', as used throughout this book, acceptable since it describes more adequately the socio-cultural amalgam of the Ethiopian political system. I use 'Amhara' when referring specifically to Gurage-Amhara intertribal relationships.

[28] J. Perruchon, 1889. For the boundaries of the old Muslim Kingdom which extended to Gurage see the maps in Crawford, 1955.

[29] Ullendorff, 1950, quotes Aleqa Tayye, 1927, p. 49.

[30] Isenberg and Krapf, *op. cit.*, p. 97. This version cannot be totally disregarded since some Gurage clans apparently have historical origins of this kind; it is conceivable that the authors based their assumption on the history of one, or a few, such clans. Gurage clan origins are discussed in Chapter VI, pp. 101–2 *passim.*

claimed descent from other parts of Gurage country from which they had fled during the sixteenth-century wars with Mohammed Gran, when they are said to have been under the rule of 'Chiefs'.[31] In the seventeenth century they sent an embassy to Gondar asking Susneyos (1604–32), the reigning king of Ethiopia, for help against the constant attacks from surrounding hostile Galla tribes. Susneyos sent an army from Tigre under Azmač Sebeate who, after putting down the Galla incursions, settled in the country and made himself 'king', establishing himself on an island in Lake Zeway. His immediate descendants ruled until Sahla Sellasie (1813–47), King of Shoa, overthrew the dynasty sometime between 1832 and 1840.[32] Two other views should also be mentioned; that of Marcel Cohen, who holds that there was an independent settlement of South Arabian peoples in the Lake Zeway region; and that of *Pere* Azais, of more doubtful validity, who holds that there was an immigration of fanatical Muslims fleeing from Harar during the war with Gran, and settling in the region of Gurage.[33]

The Gurage are next mentioned in the narrative of Father Alvarez of the *Portuguese Embassy to Abyssinia*: 1520–7, written during the reign of Lebna Dengel (1508–40), more commonly known to the western world as Prester John. In this rich account of Ethiopian political, religious, and economic life appears the first description of the religious condition of the Gurage, their attitude toward Ethiopian rule and the degree to which they offered resistance. According to Alvarez, Ethiopians described the region of 'Gorages' as a 'country of pagans',

a people (as they say) who are very bad, and of these there are no slaves, because they say that they sooner allow themselves to die than serve Christians. As it appears and as the Abyssinians say, these Gorages dwell under ground.[34]

By the first part of the sixteenth century, the conflict between Christianity and Islam for political domination of the plateau peoples had had considerable effect on the Gurage and neighbouring Sidamo tribes.[35] Some indication of the way in which small

---

[31] Cecchi, 1886, p. 89.   [32] Beckingham and Huntingford, op. cit., p. ixix.
[33] Cohen, 1931, p. 244; Azais, 1926, p. 21. Both versions have some validity as to the origins of the 'Eastern' Gurage.
[34] p. 293. The meaning of the last statement is unclear.
[35] For a good summary of the conflict of Christianity and Islam in Ethiopia consult J. S. Trimingham, op. cit., Chapter II.

independent groups like the Gurage attempted to maintain their independence can be seen in the accounts given in the *Futuh el-Habacha*. The province of Hadiya, for instance, which borders on the west of Gurage was required, in addition to other forms of tribute exacted, to hand over to the Ethiopian court, each year, 'a maiden who had to become a Christian'.[36] During the reign of Galawdewos (1540–59),[37] Gurage paid an annual tribute in gold figurines, hides, and 1,000 head of cattle, in order to retain some measure of political autonomy; this in effect meant that Gurage were under the suzeranity of Negus Galawdewos and that this relationship could be dissolved whenever the Gurage withheld their payment of tribute. This characteristic pattern of Ethiopian rule, extending through the reign of Sarsa Dengel (1563–96), continued into the seventeenth century.

The Gurage-Ethiopian relationship was obviously tenuous and the weak bonds of tribute which attempted to maintain it were apparently often broken. Gurage resistance to Ethiopian domination is seen in the writings of Father Fernandez (1613–14) who records that 'there are a people called Gurages who do not obey the Emperor Susneyos, and that they fought on horseback as well as with bow and arrow'.[38] But neither the strength of this resistance nor the type of weapons used was sufficient to sustain the Gurage's quasi-political independence, and when Susneyos appointed Abyssinian *Shums* (Chiefs) to rule over the Gurage, an already modest measure of autonomy was further reduced. Little is known of the rule Azmač Sebeate established or what effect it had on Gurage social and political organization. His abortive attempts to found a petty kingdom within the political boundaries of the powerful Shoan dynasty were, as we have noted, ineffectual in the face of the overwhelming and inexorable armies of Sahla Selassie.

The collapse of Sebeate's kingdom had far-reaching effects on the eventual fate of the Gurage, the Sidamo states, and the whole of South-West Ethiopia. For coincident with a successful Shoan political domination of South-West Ethiopia was control over its vast economic resources, which did not stop at the exploitation of such material resources as gold, ivory, cattle, and valuable hides, but included as well a seemingly endless supply of slaves, the trade

---

[36] Ibid., pp. 78–79, quoting from the *Futuh*.
[37] Rene Basset, 1897, p. 223.
[38] Beckingham and Huntingford, op. cit., p. 162.

in which extended as far west as the Nile.[39] Trade routes passing through these former independent principalities were being governed and taxed directly either by appointed Shoan officials, or by local political heads who were retained in subordinate positions on agreeing to co-operate and to implement the imposed Ethiopian system of indirect rule.

Gurage tribes waged war, at times independently and sometimes as a federation, in resisting wholesale Ethiopian domination. Often they joined forces with Sidamo and Arussi Galla tribes who, when not being threatened by external forces themselves, were constantly making attacks on the Gurage.[40] Although the Gurage had not been completely subjected by 1840, nevertheless, Sahla Sellassie began to call himself 'King of Gurage'. But it was under Menilek, as King of Shoa (1865) and later as Emperor of Ethiopia (1889–1911), that the complete and final conquest of Gurage between 1875 and 1889 was undertaken, putting an end to their frequent uprisings and attempts to throw off the Ethiopian yoke.

THE POLITICS OF CONQUEST: MENILEK; THE ITALIANS; THE RESTORATION

The conquest of the Gurage brought them under the centuries-old Ethiopian system of rule. The object of Menilek was the permanent occupation of conquered territory. When tribes yielded without resistance, unlike some Gurage tribes, the Chaha Gurage for example, he left them a measure of local autonomy and promised fair treatment, as in the case of the Jimma Galla; but when they opposed him, his policy was one of ruthless extermination.

Many tribesmen were sold into slavery. The vast majority of conquered tribesmen were, however, reduced to the status of *gäbär*. This widely interpreted Amhara term describes the serf-like status of the peasantry who, being reduced to tenants on their own land, supported the feudal structure of the military colonies of conquerors with food and services. Wherever Ethiopian military colonies settled, Christianity soon followed and was established in

[39] See the appendix on slavery in Guebre Sellassié, 1932, Vol. II. I describe in Chapter V, pp. 143–4, p. 147 the effects of the slave trade on Gurage political organization.

[40] On the folk literature of the wars between Galla and Gurage see Cerulli, 1922, loc. cit.

many areas of Gurage. Churches that had fallen into ruin during the long period of conflict between Islam and Christianity, were rebuilt, and many new ones were founded to provide places of worship for the conquerors. The hierarchy of Coptic clergy came, and occupied a privileged position in the feudal administration. Armed with the Psalter, and possessing the powers of excommunication, priests were held to be especially in charge of the spiritual welfare of the conquerors, and of those conquered who heretofore had not been baptized. Priests could exact special fees for offering prayers for souls. Many conquered souls often needed prayers.

The Menilek policy showed tolerance to Islam. Islamic courts were recognized as part of the political and judicial structure of Muslim tribes; recognition was necessary and politically expedient. The alternative, the suppression of Islam, would have incited additional political turmoil, encouraging powerful Muslim leaders to declare *jihads* against the 'Christian infidels'. Holy wars waged in the early stages of the Menilek conquests in the South-west by the Arussi Galla,[41] Somali, and other Muslim tribes, often rendered Abyssinian forces helpless, and further delayed attainment of the Menilek goal. Moreover, a *jihad* declared by one Muslim tribe had the effect of rallying other Muslim tribes, even those normally hostile to one another, to form a monolithic front against the oppressors of Islam.

The effect of this tolerant policy toward Islam provided, as it were, an unwritten clause, the provisions of which many Muslims sought to claim. This situation encouraged powerful Muslim leaders to found independent groups under their guidance as self-proclaimed prophets. Some prophets, who claimed genealogies traced back to founders of principal Islamic orthodox orders, broke away from the main body of the tribe and established separate colonies. Two such splinter groups, led by Gurage Muslim prophets, are described later in Chapter IV where the patterns of fission in Gurage clan organization are dealt with. The first is that of Umar Baksa, a former pagan adventurer from Chaha, who became a Muslim convert and established the autonomous state of

---

[41] The Gurage were allies of the Arussi against Shoan forces led by Ras Dargie. Chief Bačči Šabo of Chaha led the Gurage forces. See Cerulli, op. cit., p. 93. The Arussi Galla *jihad* against Menilek was proclaimed in 1887, organized by Shaikh Nūr Ḥusain. Cerulli, loc. cit.; Trimingham, op. cit., pp. 207–9.

Qabena ($K^w\partial b\partial nna$) from which his followers made religious rebellions against Menilek.[42] More recent is that of Shaikh Sayyid Budella, also known as Abba Ramus, a third generation head of a Muslim cult, the founder of which formerly represented the Gurage Thunder God, *Bozä*.[43] For Baksa, and Shaikh Sayyid Budella, as well as for other Gurage, Chiefs and subjects alike, Islam became a religious asylum, offering a protective political façade behind which many traditional customs and rights were continued.

Conversely, the policy of Menilek and the Church was to uproot the traditional gods and dispossess the Chiefs whom many of these gods supported. To retain their political position, traditional Chiefs were forced to accept and support Christianity, and to encourage their subjects to follow suit, bringing with them tribute in food and labour. Some Chiefs who led their flock in wholesale baptisms received, in addition to the spiritual reward, the political reward of the Ethiopian title, *Balabbat* (lit. 'owner of father'); the economic rewards were large parcels of fertile land which were leased for tenant farming and from which the profits were often considerable. But Muslim Chiefs were permitted to retain their faith as well as their political position. This provision, it seems, was an incentive for many non-Muslim Chiefs and their subjects hastily to join other followers in the protective league of Islam.

The Ethiopian system of rule was dependent upon the labours of the peasant. The excellent description of this system, as it formerly obtained throughout Ethiopia, given by Miss Perham, in the *Government of Ethiopia*, leaves little to be added.[44] Amhara Ethiopians use the term *gäbär* when referring to that system of rule, but Gurage use this word when referring to 'outsiders' and 'aliens'; they pronounce it *gäbbar*. The use of this word in their language probably comes from contact with Amhara Ethiopians; the word used by them, the 'outsiders' to designate the status of the Gurage was reversed in meaning and used by Gurage to designate the 'alien' intruders.

The land of the Gurage, like the land of all conquered territories, was divided into several categories of 'districts', each of which

---

[42] Cecchi, op. cit., pp. 51–52. The autonomous state of Qabena was under the rule of Umar Baksa who made himself Chief with the title of *Imam*. He was succeeded in 1878 by Hasan Injamo, son of one of Umar's companions.
[43] See p. 190 below.   [44] Chapters XIV–XX, *passim*.

supported an institutional hierarchy of military, political, and religious officials. Large parcels of land were divided into smaller parcels, and these divided again into still smaller units; the overall division of land corresponded to the number of strata in each official hierarchy. The system of land use was complex, far too complex to be dealt with in detail here, but the principal categories into which Gurage land was divided are of immediate interest. They are:[45]

(a) Sisso (third) or *Balabbat Meurt* (*Balabbat's choice*). Land decreed by the Emperor, of which the Balabbat had, in principle, the right to choose one-third. Tax levied on *sisso* land varied from one ox, or one castrated goat or bull, or quantities of butter or other goods, for each ten *gashas* of land [one *gasha* = 80–100 acres]. The *Balabbat* was usually an officer in the army; he paid his tithe of the harvest to the Emperor.

(b) *Desseta*. Land belonging to the *Malkanya*; the Governor's Deputy in the district. Tax levied on Desseta land was 100 thalers or a mule. The *Malkanya* retained nine quintals of cereal from the annual tithe payable to the Emperor for upkeep of the animal.

(c) *Gäbbar*. Land of the Peasant. The taxes were: one *goundo*, about 20 litres of honey; one day of work every third day, or instead of labour, three quintals of cereals a year, or both. The *gäbbar* had to grind 25 kilos of cereals and to transport them to the Governerate three to four times a year. During times of war he had to transport 20 kilos of material for the forces. He followed the army but he was not a combatant.

(d) *Metkeya* or *Maderia*. Land given to individuals especially favoured by the Emperor. It was often parcelled out to the soldiery; up to three *gashas* for ordinary soldiers; up to ten *gashas* for higher ranks; up to thirty *gashas* for officers. *Gäbbars* cultivated the land; the soldiery paid an annual tithe to the Emperor.

(e) *Cann Gabb*. Land owned by the Central Government. It was divided into sub-districts, each governed by an appointed *Mislane* [sub-district Governor]. He brought to the District Governor, or the Emperor, bread, flour, and other foodstuffs annually from the area for which he was responsible. He supervised the cultivation of the *houdad*, the other government lands worked by the *gäbbars*;

[45] These data have been compiled mainly from 'The Land System of Ethiopia', a report of the Ministry of Agriculture, *Ethiopia Observer*, Vol. I, 9, October 1957, pp. 283–301; cited later as the Ministry of Agriculture. Cf. also Gebre-Wold-Ingida Worq, 'Ethiopia's Traditional System of Land Tenure and Taxation', (trs. Mengesha Gessesse, 'Ya Ityopya Maretna Gibir Sim') *Ethiopia Observer*, Vol. V, 4, 1962, pp. 302–39.

the produce from these mainly supplied important families of the Central Government, and the food for the annual banquet given by the Emperor, the *Gabar*. The *Mislane* presided over the harvest, collected the taxes, and was under the direct orders of the Minister of the Palace.

(*f*) *Semone.* Land owned by the Church. It was parcelled out amongst the clerical hierarchy and cultivated by *gäbbars*.

In general, a peasant was regarded as a *gäbbar* if he possessed five head of cattle and the value and extent of his cultivatable land was held to be 'sufficient'. He was liable to a tax of four thalers in addition to his obligations of service. If he failed to comply with his obligation to work on two occasions the total of his service was doubled; if he further failed to work an additional tax was levied against him. 'If the chiefs desired they could arrange with the [*gäbbar*] for him to pay three quintals a year in kind in lieu of service in labour, of which he would thus be henceforth entirely free. The payment of three quintals a year was discharged by supplying each month five litres of tief, five of legumes, and fifteen divers sorts of produce, of which ten litres had to be paid over in flour. A faggot of firewood was added to the rest'.[46]

The peasants were alloted as *gäbbar* within the military hierarchy roughly according to the rank of soldiery somewhat as follows:[47]

Governors:	Up to three figures
District Commanders:	From 30 to 80 each
Officers:	From 7 to 10 each
Soldiers:	From 2 to 5 each

In Gurage and the Sidamo provinces, the position of the *gäbbar* was hardly distinguishable from slavery. It was, as Miss Perham has noted, often more profitable for a soldier to be alloted a greater number of *gäbbar* than a greater acreage of land, since he was often given the labour of his *gäbbar*, or some portion of them, for life. Even if he were transferred to another province he could still claim the profit of their labour. The *gäbbar* system was responsible for much of the misery of the inhabitants and their status has generally been described as onerous. Appeal was impossible and resistance useless.

Districts were often carved out of conquered territory to reward Shoan officials who stood in especial favour with the Government.

[46] Ministry of Agriculture, op. cit., p. 288.   [47] Perham, 1947, p. 296.

Fitaurai Habta Giyorgis, under orders from Menilek, finally put down the rebellious Gurage where *Ras* Gobena had failed in several previous attempts. For this victory, *Chaha Woudema*, over two-thirds of the most fertile land of the Chaha tribe, was decreed the private property of the *Fitaurai*.[48] This land was later given to Asfa Wasan, the present Crown Prince of Ethiopia. As Minister of War in Menilek's cabinet, Habta Giyorgis was appointed Governor of Gurageland. To assist in his administration, which in effect meant preventing frequent uprisings of the Gurage, who never accepted 'colonization' as a permanent state, Shoan military colonies were planted in each tribe of the *säbat bet*.

No peace came to the military colony sent to Daquna, a district in the Chaha tribal lands. Chaha Gurage waged war against Shoan soldiery constantly, succeeding in the long run in driving them from the low fertile plains, forcing them to settle in the mountains; later this proved to be militarily advantageous. The heroic fighting of the Chaha at Daquna is remembered today, still being recounted in folk songs chanted during festival times. Professor Leslau has recorded one such song of praise chanted at a wedding of a bridegroom from Daquna. His family and the best men, boasting of the brave men of Daquna, address themselves to the bride:

(O woman), lower (your eyes) and look at the spacious country of the
  Galla!
Raise (your eyes) and look at the mountains of Daquna!
(Brave) boys there were, they were well made.
Like Odja and Agbe and Shorato,
Shafir Fuga and Tidjato,
Like Imam Sidi and Debrato,
Like Oga Abana and Quarato.
All these—where did they go? They are made an end of and have died.
What hand of theirs has one (dared to) give to the ants?
O death! Let what you have killed be enough!
O ants! Let what you have eaten be enough!
What have the mountains of Daquna not seen?
All days the drum, the (?), and the rifle-fire, (it was heard).
What (courageous men) have the mountains of Daquna not hidden?[49]

[48] The annexation of Gurage lands is described in greater detail on pp. 41–2 below. *Ras* Mulugetta succeeded the *Fitaurai* as Chief Representative of the Government in Gurageland; for a brief account of the administration then see Jensen, 1936, p. 276.

[49] Leslau, 1950, p. 114.

It was the policy of Menilek to retain, wherever possible, Chiefs and their functionaries in their traditional positions in the tribal structure, and to allow the hereditary principles of the tribal system to provide continuity of tenure. But Gurage had no institution of Tribal Chieftainship until Menilek created it. The organization and structure of tribal Chieftainship will be dealt with in Chapter V where Gurage political organization is described, thus it is sufficient to state here that efforts to centralize the traditional segmentary authority system met with little success. As in the case of Chaha, appointed Tribal Chiefs were usually outstanding Clan Chiefs within their respective tribes. *Agäz Amärga Oqbato*, Clan Chief of the *Mogämänä*, and 'war leader' of the *säbat bet* at the time of their defeat, was made 'Chief' of Chaha, with the customary Amhara title of *Qänazmač*, and having the principal function of acting as intermediary between his own people and the Ethiopian authorities, and between them and other Chaha Clan Chiefs. These usually retained their titles of *Agäz*, but some of them were awarded honorary titles in addition. The village headman, the *quoro*, came to be known in some districts by the Amhara title for that position, *chiqa-shum*.

I describe the changes made in the territorial division of Gurage-land as a result of Government administration in Chapter II. Tribal lands were split up into districts and sub-districts corresponding to the Ethiopian institutions supported by the land divisions under the *gäbbar* system noted above. These institutions, in sum, formed an elaborate military and political bureaucratic superstructure that was imposed on the indigenous political system. The bureaucratic structure of tribal administration indicated in a simplified form in the diagram on p. 25 was obtaining when the Italian occupation of Ethiopia began in 1935.[50]

Until 1935, the chief source of revenue for the central government was supplied by tribes, like the Gurage, who had the status of *gäbbar*. The Land Act of 1929, a proclamation of Emperor Haile Sellassie I, then Regent, introduced the first measures of reform. Of the several reforms, that making the annual payment of tithe a monetary one is important, for this introduced a new system of land taxation, which for tribes like the Gurage who

[50] The titles shown are Amhara and mostly military for office-holders above the *Balabbat*. The English equivalent of *Dejazmach* is somewhat as 'One who in war camps near the door of the Emperor's tent'. See Walker, 1933, p. 204.

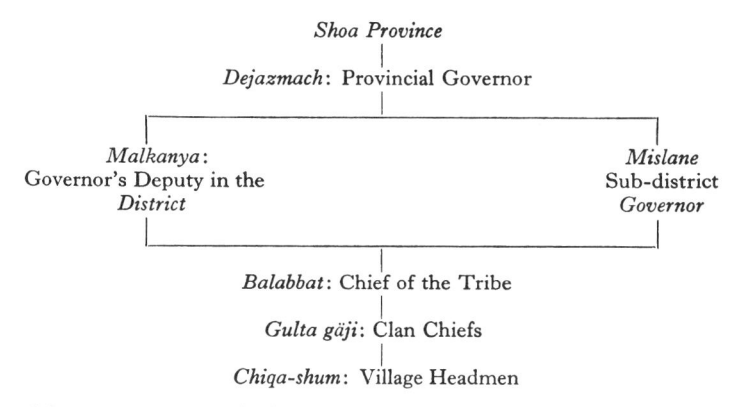

Shoa Province
|
Dejazmach: Provincial Governor
|

Malkanya:
Governor's Deputy in the
District

Mislane
Sub-district
Governor

Balabbat: Chief of the Tribe
|
Gulta gäji: Clan Chiefs
|
Chiqa-shum: Village Headmen

cultivate ensete and lack a cash crop, could be met only through wage labour migration; but other services of the *gäbbar* continued to be paid in food and labour. In some areas land was remeasured and revalued according to the new tax scheme. The tax on fertile land was increased and land formerly considered 'bush' was placed under cultivation to increase government revenue. Yet none of the Gurage tribes was as deeply affected by the measures of reform as those tribes which cultivated grain or kept cattle. The staple food of the Gurage, ensete, has always been unpalatable to the highland peoples, the Amhara and Tigre, who consider it inferior, and at no time were they able to exploit to the utmost the yield of Gurage lands. But human resources were exploited. Ethiopian soldiery from the highlands were often dissatisfied when sent to garrisons in Gurageland; they were never able to adjust themselves to the Gurage diet, and whenever possible remained only for a short time. It is perhaps for these reasons that few permanently settled in Gurageland as they did in other tribal areas. Those that remained in the old military colonies and their descendants of today have assimilated Gurage culture completely, and they think of themselves as Gurage.[51] Gurage consider all of this a good sign; that is, that their land has never been permanently occupied, and this was told to me in many conversations, as an aside, when Gurage spoke about the importance of ensete to them. To the Gurage, the ensete plant is a symbolic monument signifying the role it played in securing their lands.

[51] See Cohen, 1912, p. 48, for a brief description of the Amhara colony in Daquna as it then existed.

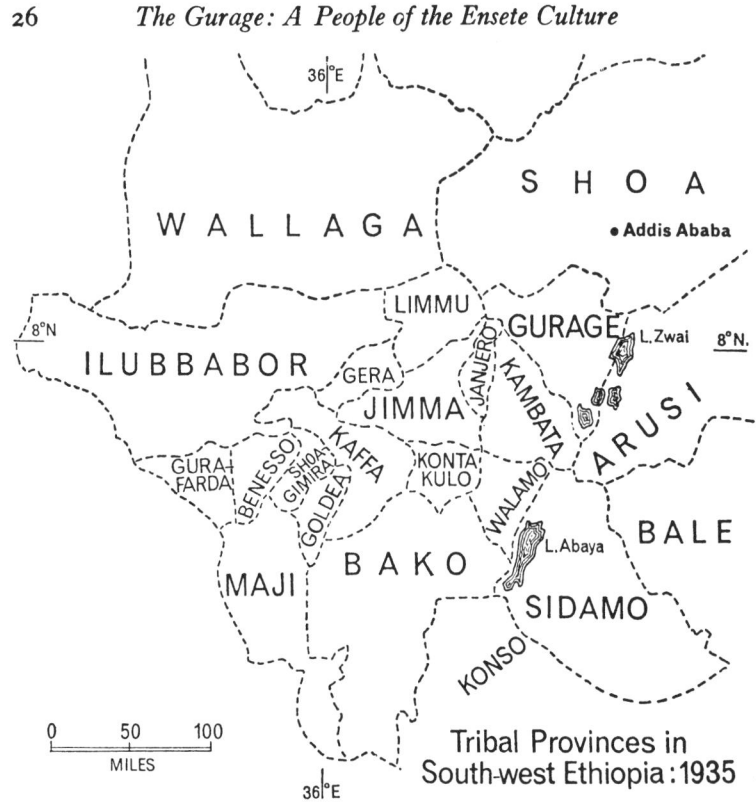

MAP 2. Tribal Provinces in South-West Ethiopia: 1935.

VI

In 1935, the *gäbbar* system in Gurageland and elsewhere in
Ethiopia ended with the coming of the Italians. The Ethiopian
institutions which the system supported collapsed as the Imperial
family and many of the nobility were forced to leave the country.
Those of the nobility and the high clergy in the Church who chose
to remain lost their feudal privileges under the Italian colonial
régime. The Italian policy supported tribalism and religious
separatism. Muslim tribes were especially placated, many new
mosques erected, Islamic centres of learning created, and Muslim
courts instituted. The overall objective of this policy was to widen
still farther the gap between the nobility and the former 'subject'
peoples that had been created by centuries of wars and conquest,

the consequence of which was bitterly relived in subjugation and in the practises of the *gäbbar* system.

The 'liberation' of the Gurage from Ethiopian domination set in motion a short-lived cycle of reorganization of their society along traditional lines. The most important phase of this cycle was land redistribution. 'Native Courts' were established to settle issues that had arisen over the reclamation of land that had been given to former *Malkanya* and *Mislane* officials. The system of land tenure as a whole had been thoroughly disrupted during the *gäbbar* period, disputes over land were inevitable, and many of them remain unsettled today. By and large, the greatest number of Court cases today are those concerning land, dating back to the old system of rule.

Economic innovations were introduced by the Italians throughout Ethiopia but few of them had any noticeable effect on the Gurage way of life. During the occupation period Gurageland was opened-up to the outside world when a dry-season road was built which passed through the interior connecting with the main highway leading to Addis Ababa, the capital of Ethiopia. Now, having fallen into decay, there are few signs that this road once existed; I mention in the next chapter some of the socio-cultural effects of this innovation on the village of Endeber, one of the traditional seats of Gurage tribal polity. This road had other sociological implications also; it provided wage labour for the first time for many Gurage who were employed in its construction; it provided the incentive to those and other Gurage to migrate to Addis Ababa for additional earnings, a motivation which has increased considerably in recent years.[52] Wage labour on a wide scale was an economic innovation introduced by the Italians.

The restoration of Ethiopia in 1941 brought back many of the old forms of provincial administration. Very little trouble was encountered in restoring them, for the Italian system had not had time to affect the customs and attitudes of the people. The restored Central Government redrew provincial boundaries changed by the Italians. Gurage and the Sidamo tribes, which before 1935 were administered as independent provinces, as shown in Map 2 (p. 26), were now combined within new boundaries drawn for the central province of Ethiopia, Shoa. The southeasternmost region of Gurageland was made a district of the Arussi

[52] Gurage labour migration is described in Chapter II, pp. 77–82.

Galla administrative area in Harar province; a portion of the southwestern region of Gurageland was combined with the old kingdoms of Janjero, Kambatta, Jimma, and Limmu, thereby enlarging the province of Kaffa.

The old autonomy of the *Dejazmach*, the Governor, was limited after the restoration. The *Mislane* were restored as officials of each sub-district, which together formed districts and in some instances sub-provinces headed by a District Governor. The control over provincial tribute was removed from the District Governor and the officials were attached to the central government by the payment of their salaries from the central treasury. The new policy of provincial administration aimed at the immediate bureaucratic concentration of the upper layer of administration, linking it with the lower customary strata of tribal groups through the village headmen and elders. Chiefs and their councils were given a modest role in the administration of the tribal province, limited to providing an efficient means of social control. In short, the long term effects of the new provincial administration was, as Miss Perham has stated, 'to sap initiative and responsibility from local institutions and leaders and to provide it mainly from above.'[53]

I have attempted in this chapter to draw together several thinly worn and often knotted threads of ethnographic and historical evidence about the origins of the Gurage people. Their past, as woven together here, is like patchwork; their present, which the following chapters contain resembles this less. The Gurage, in their small, compact, dense settlements, depending upon ensete to provide most of their necessities of life, with most of their face-to-face relations based on kinship, these as with political and economic relations being underpinned by the religious system, are a people living in the twentieth century. But their deeply rooted ways of life and habits of thought remain more a part of the past than the present.

[53] Perham, op. cit., p. 350.

CHAPTER II

Ecology and Communications

THE CENTRAL ETHIOPIAN PLATEAU

THE Central Ethiopian plateau resembles an elongated oval.[1] To the north-west an irregular front of the plateau is formed by the Blue Nile and on the east the plateau has the steep sides of a mountain wall. This is the western edge of the great East African Rift. Topographical features of the northern slopes of the plateau are irregular, consisting of many subordinate plateaux, above which rise several mountains. Situated near the middle of this plateau is Addis Ababa, the capital of the Empire; it is in the central province of the country, known as Shoa. The capital is the centre of all judicial, administrative, and economic activities for the Empire, and from it all main arteries of communication radiate. Highland Ethiopians and Europeans alike consider the geographical position of Addis Ababa most favourable for habitation; the Ethiopians term these uplands 'woina dega', 'highlands of the vine', when referring to plateaux in the range of 5,500 to 7,500–8,200 feet.

The southern fringe of the plateau, lower in altitude, can be approached by vehicle only by one all-season road. This road cuts across numerous settlements, some large, some small, inhabited by the Kambatta, Sidamo, Gurage, and Jimma-Galla peoples. Along this highway, the 'Addis Ababa-Jimma' road, numerous market towns have grown up. The physical appearance of these towns, a monotonous series of unimpressive corrugated iron-roofed huts, grain stores, beer houses, and Arab-owned shops, however, is not worthy of their economic importance. To the untrained observer, the obvious similarities of these market towns immediately suggest a widespread settlement of a culturally homogenous people, whereas, in fact, there are striking internal differences between market town and market town, each distinguishable by the language spoken (other than the *lingua franca*, Amharic). These differences

---

[1] For a description of the geography and social life of the plateau see Buxton, 1949, p. 158.

become more pronounced the farther one moves away from the Capital, since settlements of non-Amharic speakers increase in number and distribution toward the south. The country of the Gurage people is accessible from one such market centre on this route, Wolkite, where numerous time-worn footpaths and trails, shaped by men and pack animals, converge.

The 154 kilometres between Addis Ababa and Wolkite, the junction leading to Gurageland, show a gradual change in the social and cultural features of the plateau. This change falls naturally into two zones; environment, technology and methods of production employed by culturally different groups distinguish these zones, which I call 'A' and 'B', North and South, respectively. Zone A fixes the southernmost extension of the plough-culture economy of the plateau people. In this region the land is mainly rich arable land, the population is sparse, village settlements are widely separated, and grains, cereals, legumes, and root crops are the chief food products. Several varieties of the eucalyptus tree are grown extensively for local use as well as for sale and in addition serve as signposts of village life.

The Gurage country lies within Zone B; here, the natural and cultural features contrast with those of Zone A. Large cultivated fields are rarely seen, most of the plains are covered with low scrub and coarse grasses, and the several specie of acacia tree appear in abundance. From the roadway can be seen bulky round huts constructed on small plots of land overcrowded with vegetation. The eucalyptus tree is rarely seen, village settlement is dense and compact and the hoe is used in cultivation instead of the plough. These natural and cultural features demarcate the upper limit of the 'hoe culture' area, which extends southwards into the East African territories. The altitude of the plateau is lower here, and the air, at 6,000 feet, is not as thin as the air on the higher plains of *woina dega*; the temperature is warmer, with slight variations between day and night. Most of the sedentary tribes on the higher plateau consider the lower plains to be undesirable scrub country, 'wild' and 'uncivilized', like the people who inhabit them. But the people who occupy the lower plateau, such as the Gurage, consider this the most favourable region in which man can live.

NATURAL ENVIRONMENT OF GURAGELAND

In Shoa province, between 38° and 38°30′ E. longitude, where the 8° N. latitude intersects Ethiopia, lies the country inhabited by the Gurage tribes. I call this region Gurageland. Only large scale maps show Gurageland because it is minute in relation to the whole of Ethiopia. Officially Gurageland is termed an *awraja*, a sub-province. An *awraja* is often circumscribed by prominent topographical features and Gurageland can be so identified. Its eastern boundary extends to the near side of Lake Zeway,[2] one of the largest in a chain of crater lakes in the 'Galla depression'. This trough or depression slants diagonally across Ethiopia from north-east to south-west, and is a part of the plateau, or tableland, system of Ethiopia. The long winding course of the Ghibie (Omo) river, flowing southward to Lake Rudolph, separates Gurageland on the west from the old Cushitic kingdom of Janjero and the West Sidamo group who occupy its middle basin.[3] Less clearly defined by features of topography is the northern boundary. Gurageland borders the former 'cattle culture area' that was shaped several centuries ago by Galla migrations, and today is inhabited by sedentary agricultural Mača and Tulama Galla. In the conventional meaning, the northern limit of Gurageland is said to be the Awash river which, flowing in a great sweeping curve towards the Danakil flats, empties into Lake Abhebad. The country of Sidamo lies to the south of the Gurage, but their immediate neighbours are the Kambatta tribes who speak a Sidamo dialect.

At its broadest, Gurageland spans an estimated 150 kilometres of semi-mountainous land. The red soil of its plains has been creased by deep fissures, caused by soil erosions over a period of centuries. Even where heavy rains and the denuding of forest land have not damaged the earth's surface, the natural geological formation of the land makes it generally unsuitable for cultivation. Large expanses of land are barren because volcanic formations of Pliocene and Pleistocene basalts and trachytes have prevented the development of soil, thereby restricting the use of land by men

[2] The inhabitants of Lake Zeway's five islands speak a Gurage dialect differing from that spoken on the mainland. But the shores of the lake are settled by Galla and some of the Watta population. See Hodson, 1922, pp. 65–67.
[3] Ernesta Cerulli, 1956, p. 96.

and animals. Other areas, such as the lowlands, are unhealthy and malaria-ridden. The annual overflowing of tributaries of the Awash and Ghibie rivers has forged marshy uninhabitable tracts of land. The Gurage estimate, in round figures, that only one-third of their tribal land is suitable for habitation and cultivation. Natural factors which restrict land use coincide with settlement patterns. The most valued positions are on high ground in close proximity to streams, and settlements under these conditions are dense. An aerial view of Gurageland gives a consistent and recognizable picture of numerous clustered villages adjacent to subsidiary waterways, but far from the principal geographical boundaries.

Gurageland has never been cut off from the rest of Ethiopia. Historical accounts, dating back to the fifteenth century, record the itineraries of trading expeditions that brought the Gurage into direct contact with commercial linkings to the world beyond.[4] Many of these trade routes are still in use today, and still travelled by foot and mule. There is, in fact, no other way of reaching the interior. Moreover, in the absence of a single semi-improved or dry-season road, this usage, at least for the present, is apparently unchallenged.

Movement within Gurageland is contingent upon the seasons of rainfall. In general, the entire plateau has a single rainy season from about mid-April to mid-September. Within this period the downpour is of varying intensities which the inhabitants term 'big rains' and 'little rains'. There are two seasons in the year, the wet, rainy season—*zär*, beginning in April (*Säräyä*), and the hot, dry season —*abar*, beginning in September (*Yədar*). Fifty to sixty inches of rain fall annually in the wet season, extending over a five-month period.[5] Internal travel is then virtually suspended, and movement between villages is reduced to the minimum as the open grass plains, saturated with water several inches deep, prohibit long-distance travel. Between July and September, when the rainfall reaches its highest level, Gurageland is, to a large extent, isolated from other tribal lands in Ethiopia. The one break in this isolation is the infrequent visit of an itinerant trader. Gurageland is beyond the reach of Ethiopia's post and telegraph system.

The effects of heavy rains on open fields in Gurageland are

---

[4] See Crawford, 1955, for an account of early trade routes in the south-west.
[5] *Economic Handbook* (Ethiopia: Ministry of Commerce and Industry, Dec. 1958), p. 80.

comparable to those in similar conditions described for other areas of Africa.[6] The flooding of the main rivers prevents the already heavily saturated earth from draining. The Awash overflows its banks annually with regularity, and the high waters of the Uabi (Wabi) river seal off the north-west corner of Gurageland from the rest of Ethiopia. During the floods, the vast savannah Plains of Atat, which extend to the deep-sided cliffs of the Uabi basin, give the appearance of a grass-covered swamp. While the rains are at their height, mud is also abundant and the landscape, at times, is depressingly bleak.

By mid-September the plain begins to dry, the grassy stubbles become parched and dusty and the plain itself becomes alive with human activity. The Uabi can now be forded with reasonable safety by trading caravans, migrant workers, and odd travellers; this is the most direct route to the Addis Ababa–Jimma road. As the dry season advances, social relations between villages increase, markets are replenished with their normal complement of personnel and goods, and intertribal exchange is renewed. According to tradition, the cycle from wet to dry is not fully complete until the *mäsqäl* flower (*Coreopsis negriana*) blooms across the plateau. Symbolically, the flowering of the *mäsqäl* marks the end of the rains; it coincides with the beginning of a new year in the Gurage calendar, the first month being *Yᵊdar* (September), and it sets in motion a new cycle of social and economic events.

The Gurage make good use of their environment and they have a simple but efficient economy. *Ensete edulis*, the Gurage name for which is *äsät*, is their chief source of food. It grows well with a minimum of care. Although a long dry spell could have serious consequences, severe rains do not damage it. Its chief enemies are a worm disease known locally as *furtᵊyä*, beetles and insects, and ground hogs, which feed on the roots of *äsät*. Because of *äsät* cultivation, famine and impoverishment are unknown in the history of the Gurage; they have survived the seasons of drought and heavy rain that have occasionally threatened the economic life of many Ethiopian tribes living on the Plateau. For instance, in 1958, the neighbouring agricultural Galla were impoverished by a season of heavy rain, villages were flooded, and the famine which resulted from this compelled many Galla to seek refuge with the Gurage,

[6] For example see the accounts of Gluckman, 1941, and Evans-Pritchard, 1940.

their traditional enemy. A long history of economic survival amidst events of this type has given rise to the general notion of self-sufficiency which Gurage hold. They are not dependent upon Western or Ethiopian goods to maintain their economy, and when the supply of these goods, never great at any time, is interrupted during the big rains, this has no serious effect on their economy or social life. Moreover, the distribution of non-traditional items throughout Gurageland is a convenient index of change in their material culture. This index forms a basis upon which the degree of dependence on other social and economic systems in Ethiopia can be determined. It also suggests that Gurage geographical understanding of the outside world is reckoned, in one way, in terms of time and distance over which goods and services are exchanged.

THE LAND AND THE PEOPLE

The people inhabiting Gurageland call themselves Gurage, and are known by that name to others. The Gurage are a tall people in comparison with other Semitic tribesmen in Ethiopia, hardy and resilient, and not afraid of hard work. They are considered by Ethiopians and Westerners alike to be the most industrious of the Semitic peoples. They have occupied their present territory for over five centuries, and land is their most cherished possession. They have fought amongst themselves and against aggression from without to retain their land as well as their independence. They regard the various Sidamo, Galla, and Amhara, as traditional enemies. Each has attempted at some time in the history of Gurage to wrest away their land and force them into bondage. The Amhara accomplished this in 1889.

There exist no adequate statistics and survey records of the Gurage. The exact number of people classified by Government as Gurage, and the size of the groups who, by reasons of territorial, political, cultural, and linguistic affinities, call themselves Gurage, is also uncertain. The number of Gurage speakers is said to be, in round figures, 350,000, scattered among fourteen tribes or dialect groups.[7] The main linguistic groupings are the Chaha-Muher, Walani, Aymallal, and Selti-Ulbarag. The name Gurage can also

---

[7] No complete census of Ethiopia or of a particular tribe has been undertaken. Only rough estimates have been made, primarily on the basis of reports from travellers, a few government officials, and records from the Italian occupation

be considered a collective term applied to all tribes inhabiting Gurageland, irrespective of the different origins of particular tribes. But to the people, tribal identity is most important; one is a Chaha Gurage, or a Muher Gurage, or a Soddo Gurage, and so forth. These distinctions are used principally by the tribesmen themselves, for the custom among other tribes in Ethiopia is to refer to all Gurage simply as Gurage.

The attitude of other tribes towards the Gurage transcends intertribal joking behaviour. Travel in Gurageland is said to be hazardous, the people truculent, thieving, and completely dishonest; they are even said to have trafficked in the slavery of their own tribesmen. The grain-cultivating Amhara and Tigre Ethiopians, who look down on hoe cultivators and pastoral peoples generally, have an added aversion for the Gurage because their staple diet is said to be the 'roots of trees', which these Ethiopians consider unfit for human consumption. The Gurage have no written form of their language, *Guraginä*, which the Amhara, in particular, ascribe to a lack of *sillətane*, meaning 'civilization'. This term covers a wide range of Amhara customs and observances, many of them religious. To profess Ethiopian Christianity is one criterion of *sillətane* and this rules out many Gurage who practice their traditional rituals and beliefs. Furthermore, the readiness with which Gurage undertake occupations traditionally despised by other Semitic peoples reinforces the stereotyped image of them. Gurage have only two worthy characteristics, according to other tribes: they do not disdain menial tasks, and their women folk are the most beautiful among the Semitic Ethiopians. Both characteristics have been exploited in one or more ways by Ethiopians and Europeans at large.

Gurage chiefly follow their traditional religious calling, but some of them are Muslims and Copts, and there are some 2,000 Roman Catholics.[8] The Sudan Interior Mission, which combines

period. The above figure has been furnished by Tucker and Bryan, op. cit., p. 136. In *The Gurages and Their Social Life*, henceforth cited as *The Gurages*, a population figure of 500,000 is given. This seems extremely high even if it is to include Gurage living outside the tribal area. Cecchi, op. cit., p. 105, estimated in 1886 the Gurage to number 40,000 which seems to be grossly understated. Note that I use 'tribe' and 'dialect group' above and elsewhere in this study as interchangeable terms.

[8] See Azais and Chambard, 1931, p. 187. On the spread of Islam in South-west Ethiopia see Trimingham, loc. cit. Both works have been consulted in compiling the data used in Table I.

religious teaching with education and medical services, is the sole Western Protestant missionary body in Gurageland. The exact number of converts to their doctrine is small, probably no more than one hundred souls.

The Gurage tribes can be divided further along broadly defined cultural lines into two large religious groups. The Eastern or 'Oriental' group, consists of those tribes with a predominant Muslim culture; the Western group, consists of those tribes whose culture is more 'traditional', meaning that it is closely related to the Sidamo culture that was assimilated by early Gurage migrations. When I speak later of the Eastern Gurage and the Western Gurage I shall mean precisely these groups. I have outlined the Eastern–Western grouping of Gurage tribes in Table I.

TABLE I

Dialect and Religious Grouping of Gurage Tribes

	Dialect Group	Primary Religion	Secondary Religion
Eastern	Selti	Muslim	Christian
	Walani	Muslim	Christian
	Ulbarag	Muslim	Christian
	Innekor	Muslim	?
	Zeway[a]	Christian	?
Western	Akilil	Pagan	Christian
	Chaha	Pagan	Muslim, Christian
	Ezha	Pagan	Christian
	Ennemor	Pagan	Muslim, Christian
	Endegen	Pagan	?
	Geyto	Pagan	Christian
	Muher	Christian	Pagan
	Masqan	Christian	Muslim
	Gogot	Muslim	Pagan
Northern	Aymellel[b]	Christian	Pagan

[a] Spoken by fishermen on the islands of Lake Zeway.
[b] Spoken south of Addis Ababa.

The geographical grouping of Gurage tribes is different from their linguistic grouping.[9] A tribal group, or dialect group, in some instances, is a distinct geographical and political unit ex-

[9] Cohen, 1931, pp. 38–52, advances a number of hypotheses for this.

hibiting its own cultural form.[10] The Chaha people are one example of this. On the other hand, a dialect group can be composed of several politically autonomous tribes; the composition of the Selti-Ulbarag group is a case in point. The formation of such politically autonomous, linguistically related, groups suggests that fission within the main language group occurred some time in the dim past; and that regrouping within prescribed geographical limits took place along several autonomous lineage, clan, and tribal divisions. Geographical movements of linguistically related people are taking place today, suggesting that lineage segmentation in the past may have taken this course.

Gurage culture is essentially uniform. Apart from the varied forms of language and religion, there exists a common set of artifacts, a common technology and mode of production, a common design in house building and patterns of settlement, and a common form of economic and social organization. The maintenance of these traditional forms of culture, which distinguish Gurage from other ensete cultivating tribes, is to the Gurage of paramount importance. Culture uniformity has persisted alongside the development of manifold different language groups. The mountainous nature of Gurageland, an essential factor in the development and maintenance of politically autonomous and linguistically different tribes, has had no effect on the form of Gurage culture.

A final geographical grouping is to be distinguished. In the Government system of tribal administration, Gurage *awraja* is partitioned into five districts known as *wereda*; districts are subdivided into *mikital wereda*, or sub-districts.[11] Administrative boundaries, in general, have been arbitrarily defined and there is no rule that *wereda* boundaries correspond with traditional political boundaries of a particular tribe or group of tribes. The Chaha, Ezha, Geyto, Muher, Ennemor, Akilil, and Walani-Woriro, tribes comprise the *säbatbet* Gurage. Three administrative *wereda*—Chaha, Walani, and Selti—divide the grouping externally, but the functions of intertribal affairs overlap administrative divisions. And

---

[10] I mean here, a group sharing a common territorial-political unit, tradition of origin, religious ideas, with the exception of recent religious innovations, kinship system, economy, and technology.

[11] On Government's mapping of Gurage *awraja* five *wereda*-districts are designated; see Map 4, in the Appendix. In *The Gurage*, p. 8, four *wereda* are listed.

because of inefficient communication between districts, the sub-provincial (*awraja*) capital at Buta Jara, in the Soddo *wereda*, is seldom in contact with the more remote areas and with the *säbat bet*. Hence, the sub-district of Chaha, and its capital, the village of Endeber, has increased in importance socially and politically. Clan Chiefs and other political functionaries generally meet in Chaha, retaining in some measure its tradition as one of the seats of politics for the Seven Houses.

As there are no Gurage terms for geographical divisions of tribal territories and as the Government's nomenclature is in-adequate, I indicate here the terminology that will be employed to describe the internal political and territorial divisions of a Gurage tribe. When I use the term 'tribal district', it is to denote a con-tinuous territory occupied by the members of that unit I call a tribe. When I speak of a 'clan' or 'clan district', a unit of territory

TABLE II

Administrative Divisions of Gurageland Awraja[a]

Region	Wereda	Sub-wereda
North	Soddo	Midre-Cabd Atchever Adelle
South	Silte	Dalotcha Ulbarag
East	Masqan	Lanfaro Dabona Shershera
West	*Sabat bet* Gurage	Walani-Muher Ezha-Akilil Chaha Gumer-Gyeto Ennemor-Inor

[a] Data compiled from *The Gurage*, p. 8.

occupied by the clan is implied; it is smaller in size than a tribal district. These terms are sufficient for the present, though they will be modified later to correspond with other forms of territorial groupings that will be discussed.

The Gurage of the Seven Houses, grouped on the basis of a common culture and language, conceive of themselves as forming a Gurage 'nation': a people with a system of ideas about themselves and the surrounding world that is expressed in the form of pan-Gurage. This system of beliefs has not been affected by linguistic diversity, mountainous terrain, semi-isolation, or political autonomy; it has formed an ideological pivot round which the *säbat bet* has become unified against external hostilities. Upon the cessation of intertribal warfare under *pax Aethiopica* pan-Gurage has taken new forms in tribal solidarity. Since my field observations did not cover Eastern Gurageland, I can make only general remarks concerning intertribal unity of the Eastern group. A long historical relation with the larger Muslim world of Ethiopia has obtained, and Islam has been the main unifying factor. Where a common set of social and cultural factors would tend to form a basis for tribal unity among the Eastern group, as it has done in Western Gurageland, such factors have been absorbed by the Islamic movement. There is no evidence that the Eastern Gurage ever united against external forces.

In the remainder of this study, I shall be considering mainly the *säbat bet* Gurage. I now describe how geography has influenced Gurage political groupings.

PHYSICAL AND HUMAN BOUNDARIES

The political and geographical divisions of Gurage tribes are defined mainly by the principal mountains and waterways of Gurageland. Mt. Gurage, which reaches to over 12,000 feet, is the most spectacular mountain in this part of the Ethiopian plateau. Other mountains, lower than Mt. Gurage, define important tribal boundaries. The rivers of Gurageland are shallow and none of them is used for transport or commercial exploitation; their waters are not used in irrigation schemes or horticulture, and thus their economic value is further limited. But rivers have political importance in Gurageland.

To a Gurage, knowledge of his physical geography is one means of reckoning the natural environment in temporal and spatial dimensions. A knowledge of his physical world strengthens that aspect of oral tradition relating to his peoples' origin, migration, and settlement. Historical factors are woven in with social and political events when a Gurage is describing his geography. This is a verbal art of Elders. Young Gurage grow up learning their social geography under the guidance of older men; facts are well grounded, training is precise and accurate, and the maps drawn in the mind have been rechecked countless times when travelling over long distances. Demonstrating one's knowledge of geography is part of the oral tradition, written descriptions cannot faithfully reproduce the style of acting accompanying any narration.

A Chaha Gurage begins a description of Gurageland by pointing north-eastwards to the Muher tribe of Christians. They are bounded on the north by the Uabi River and on the south by the Tirer River. South of them are Ezha people. The Tirer forms the north border of the Ezha, and the Megacha, a large river on the south, separates them from the Chaha. The Megacha also defines the northern limits of the Chaha's settlement. The Wenke, a small tributary of the Megacha River, follows a course across the southern end of Chaha forming a natural and political boundary between them and their traditional enemy, the Ennemor. The East and West frontiers of Gurageland are faced by mountain ranges. The long eastern front formed by Mt. Zebidar cuts right across the Muher-Ezha lands. Behind this mountain lies the country of the Soddo, one of the larger tribes in Eastern Gurageland. At the southernmost point of Mt. Zebidar, the range of Mt. Aster begins, extending in a sweeping curve to divide the Ennemor from the Gyeto tribes.[12]

Political boundaries are not always distinguished by prominent topographical features. Gurage use other features of the natural environment, such as ancient trees and enormous oddly-shaped stones, these stones being legendary symbols of the route believed to have been taken by Mohammed Gran during the wars of the sixteenth century. Even so, political disputes about the exact limits of settlement often occurred in the past. Chaha and Ezha frequently went to war over grievances arising out of the use of the Megacha and Gotam Rivers. The centre of the conflict usually was the land upstream, above the point at which the two rivers converge. These events, firmly implanted in the memories of elders, are now retold as part of their social geography.

[12] For additional descriptions of the principal mountains and rivers of Gurageland see Cecchi, op. cit., p. 105; also consult Map 4 in this study.

Nowadays, more recent problems of considerable political magnitude take precedence over past historic events. A contemporary source of dispute with Gurage is the annexation of *Chaha woudema*. This vast expanse of land that Gurage sometimes call the 'Plains of Atat', extends from the Ghibie River to the Megacha–Gotam tributaries on the east, and northwards to the Uabi River basin. It has been apportioned entirely out of Chaha lands since the defeat of the *säbat bet* in 1889, and its annexation is bitterly remembered by the Chaha. From Government's point of view this was presumably the most favourable section of Gurageland. Its large flat plains were more suitable for plough cultivation, which would be employed by Ethiopian military colonies, than the more mountainous terrain elsewhere; it afforded direct access to Addis Ababa. Its annexation was a penalty levied directly against the Chaha for leading the *säbat bet* to resist Government aggression. But to the Gurage, political subjugation and tribute and land apportionment are separate and distinct issues; the latter creates a deficiency in the amount of available land that becomes more pronounced with each generation. Annexation of land, Gurage argue, should not be made a penalty of defeat in warfare. Hence, in consequence of these issues, *Chaha woudema* is sparsely settled; it contrasts sharply with the densely populated areas elsewhere in Gurageland.

Arable land for habitation and cultivation is scarce. The natural features of soil formation that make it unsuitable for cultivation also limit the range of human settlement. There are also social factors that govern choices and decisions made in the selection of habitable sites. Land must be fertile for cultivating *äsät* and cattle fodder. Water resources must be available, preferably within a distance of one kilometre, at the farthest, two. Settlement must be on land occupied by closely related kinsmen. All of these choices are difficult to combine in the founding of new settlements, and land holdings in older substantially populated areas are jealously guarded. Moreover, corporate ownership of village land is an additional factor preventing immigration, which would further reduce the amount of arable land required for the expansion of the village. The growth of new villages is dependent upon the availability of suitable land for settlement and cultivation. Where friction and conflict have arisen over population pressure, they tend to be released in other areas of Gurage life. The opening-up of *Chaha woudema* for settlement through land sales,[13] emigration to lands outside Gurageland, and temporary labour migration, cumulatively alter the demographic pattern of the country. Seasonal migration is the single principal factor alleviating the problem of over-population.

Gurage are a settled population, at no time are they transhumant, and settlement is fixed in accordance with corporate land rights held by localized descent groups. A Gurage settlement has physical and structural permanence.

VILLAGE SETTLEMENT PATTERNS

Gurage villages are identical in design. They may vary in size and social composition, but not in their density. The closeness of human habitation, as seen in the distances between homesteads, is emphasized by the dense cultivation of *äsät* plants that surround a settlement.[14] The signpost of life is not the homestead, which by Ethiopian standards is an immense structure in itself, but the cluster of towering vegetation. The proud symbol of Gurage technology, as expressed in homestead construction, is often obliterated from view. There would be little to indicate where one unit of habitation ends and another begins except for a single broad main road, *wur ema*, that determines the lateral spacing between the homesteads by its sides. In traditional terminology, this cluster of dwellings is named *ǧäfʷärä*. It may be translated 'village'.

There is no indiscriminate planning of buildings or compounds enclosing them. A Gurage's house is not merely a thatched structure providing minimum shelter for a man and his family; it is an intricately designed work of craftsmanship employing the skills of numerous specialists, chiefly Fuga. The entire structure is supported by the centre mainstay, known as the *äčba*. Apart from its technical function, the *äčba* symbolizes the focus of communal relations involved in its erection. It is a great occasion when the

---

[13] The cost of freehold land in *Chaha woudema* is prohibitive to most Gurage; the current price ranges from $Eth. 3,000 to $15,000 per *gasha*. See Table III, p. 45, for comparative land holdings between Gurage, Galla, and Amhara tribes.

[14] By 'village' I also mean 'settlement': a spatially distinct locality whose inhabitants engage in some social interaction; most of their direct social acts take place within the area. I use these terms interchangeably. Thus a village is a settlement; socially simple and culturally homogeneous.

äčba is raised, demanding the slaughtering of an ox, and all who have participated in the ceremony of 'dragging the log' from which the *äčba* is carved share in the feasting. This is only one aspect of village relations that reinforce the ideal of interdependence between homesteads. No family alone could erect a building; it may take as long as two annual planting seasons to build the house. Houses range in size from 14 feet to 22 feet in diameter. They are circular, with bamboo walls plastered on the inside with a mixture of mud and grass, washed with lime; and the roofs are thatched. There are three sizes of Gurage house varying from large to very large: the *zägar*, the *xärar*, and the *g^weä*, in that order. Men, cattle, and utensils, each have their section in the house. The placing of these in an asymmetrical design breaks the spacious circuitous monotony of the interior.

On the outside, symmetry begins. Land for cultivation lies behind the houses, which form a continuous line. Side by side, facing the *ema* are built the homesteads on plots of not more than one *wädärä*, about 48 yards long.[15] A plot is usually limited to *yä wädärä gəbt*, or one-half *wädärä*, and this length as well is monotonously maintained. A *wur ema* is not to be confused with a narrow footpath. To a Westerner, the *ema*, ranging from 30 to 50 feet in breadth, would be the 'main street'. This is the most conspicuous feature of a village, and the maintenance of the *ema* is a joint responsibility of the settlement.

A *wur ema* is unlike a Western street in so far as village social relations vary concomitantly with the spatial distance between dwellings. In a Gurage village the social distance between widely spaced homesteads may be narrowed by kinship relations. Where no kinship exists, other relationships of equal importance bridge the space between the homes. Economic co-operation during the season of cultivation, sharing of grazing chores by each homestead on successive days, loaning of cattle, grain, and other foodstuffs, rendering services on occasions of birth, mourning at death rituals, participation in village politics; all these are primary forms of social intercourse in which each homestead on the *ema* takes part. Gurage men attach great importance to maintaining this close bond and they congregate nightly in small groups, meeting at each homestead in turn; they are informal gatherings for discussion of

---

[15] Land is measured with the *žər*-pole, about 12 feet in length. One *wädärä* equals 12-*žər*.

contemporary events that usually concern the welfare of the village. In one way, this expresses the Gurage idea of *wänäkä*, 'neighbourhood', in practice.

Gurage have no linguistic expression to differentiate one homestead from another within their idea of neighbourhood. *Yäwänäkä säb* is one's neighbour, and that to a Gurage covers all who live on the *ema*; it maintains separateness, in spatial terms, and closeness of social relations, at one and the same time. This is one aspect of the stress and strain, the juxtaposition of opposites, that is characteristic of Gurage society.

If the *wur ema* is the outstanding feature within a village, earth shrines are the most obvious feature outside the village. These are *zəgba*-trees (*Podocarpus gracilior*), some standing alone, some in large clusters, but all symbolizing one of the many sanctuaries of *Waq*, the Sky-god. An earth shrine is sometimes found within the ring of forest that is cleared from around a village, because, owing to its ritual significance, a sacred tree would not be cut down, as other large trees have been. Heavy forests of ordinary trees are cut down for some distance from the settlement to prevent their falling and damaging homesteads, to provide land for cultivation, to prevent the harbouring of animals and other enemies close to the village. A clearing usually demarcates village-owned grazing land, on the other side of which are the boundaries of another settlement. Thus the settlement of Gurage villages produces a symmetrical pattern: human habitation alternates with tall dense forests, the *dəbər* land, and dense growths of vegetation surround the *wâmb*, lowland, waterways.

In the main, the population is denser in the old settlements than in the new, the large market village of Yəgəzaye, in Ennemor, for example, containing over 100 homesteads. A new settlement, on the border of an older centre, generally contains a smaller number of homesteads and inhabitants. In one such village I found only 41 homesteads, the population numbering 319, or an average of 7·8 persons per homestead. This seems average for new settlements. In both old and new villages, the pattern of settlement ensures a fair distribution of arable land under densely populated conditions. The normative values of the settlement prevent any one individual from exploiting village resources at the expense of others. Similarly, there is a correlation between population density, land fragmentation, and the length of time a settlement has occupied a particular portion of land. And common to all these is the fact that such village resources as grazing and forest land and streams are corporately owned.

A comparison of land-man ratios between the Gurage and the Galla and Amhara, both sedentary tribes on the Plateau, throws into relief more clearly the conditions of population density in Gurageland. I show this in Table III below; figures are standardized on the Ethiopian unit of land measure called the *gasha*, and the average number of families cultivating a *gasha* in each tribe is indicated.[16]

TABLE III

Size of Land Holdings among Three Plateau Tribes

Tribe	Average number of families per *gasha*	Acreage cultivated
Gurage	30	2·6–3·3
Galla	9	8·8–11
Amhara	1	80·0–100

Among Gurage tribes arable land is at a premium; this fact, together with immigration and settlement and the complex social factors already mentioned above, militates against large population settlements and tends to concentrate Gurage on small tracts of land. In the following chapter, the system of *äsät* cultivation is described with reference to the patterns of village settlement. It is sufficient to state here that Gurage patterns of settlement uphold the assumption that an *äsät* planting culture can support a denser population than a seed farming culture. The *Ensete edulis* regions are among the most densely populated in the whole of Ethiopia.[17]

To an outsider, a Gurage village appears as a unit of defence. Its plan, the side by side arrangement of homesteads, makes it easy to defend; and this was so when tribal warfare was rife. Complete enclosure of homesteads by fencing is uncommon and socially disapproved. The normal pattern of interhomestead relations is informal and provides a means by which tension and conflict

[16] The Government's unit of land measure is the *gasha*, the equivalent of 80 to 100 acres. For land uses in other areas of Ethiopia see Perham, op. cit., pp. 277–92, and Nadel, 1946, loc. cit.

[17] Smeds, 1955, p. 34, estimates population density in Sidamo to average 240 persons per sq. mile. See also Shack, 1963a.

between homesteads are reduced. Frequent face-to-face relations, necessitated by congested living, are, in one way, the basis of feelings of security. The threats of danger from warfare and raiding have traditionally made the village the minimal unit of defence. Even today a sound of alarm spreads rapidly, bringing together the villagers from a number of settlements. The social importance of village solidarity and security, a feature of the pattern of settlement, is another expression of *wänäkä*; in conceptual terms, *wänäkä* is those people who are spatially close and socially essential. The homestead is never guarded and the door is never closed. The ideals of village security are epitomized in the Gurage maxim, 'a bull does not bellow outside his village'.[18]

Social and economic requirements presuppose that villages will be within 'neighbourly' distances, which range from twenty minutes' to one hour's walking. As grazing land, *häbər*, is commonly shared by two or more villages, and rules and regulations concerning its use require frequent consultation between those villages, a 'neighbourly distance' extends beyond the boundaries of any one particular settlement. When kinship and lineage factors are introduced, the concept of *wänäkä* links together a number of village units in a network of social and economic relations. Thus the range of distances between villages is socially and spatially narrow and no village is ever remote from other villages.

The spatial arrangement of a Gurage settlement can best be illustrated diagramatically as in Fig. 1. But this illustration is essentially static, for it describes only the local physical features; it does not take into account the social contacts which extend beyond the widest spatial division indicated. Several villages share a common source of water, a common grazing land, a common market, and together compose a wider territorial division. This aggregate of relations, mainly social, is the dynamic aspect of a settlement and does not entirely coincide with any structural divisions. The internal and external relations of villages will be discussed in a later chapter.

In Gurageland, there is no social status differentiation of villages into superior and inferior or royal and common. A village may be referred to by the name of a Chief, although this is not common practice, and if so it has little meaning beyond indicating where the Chief lives. The presence of a Chief in a village does not

[18] Recorded by Leslau, 1950, p. 129.

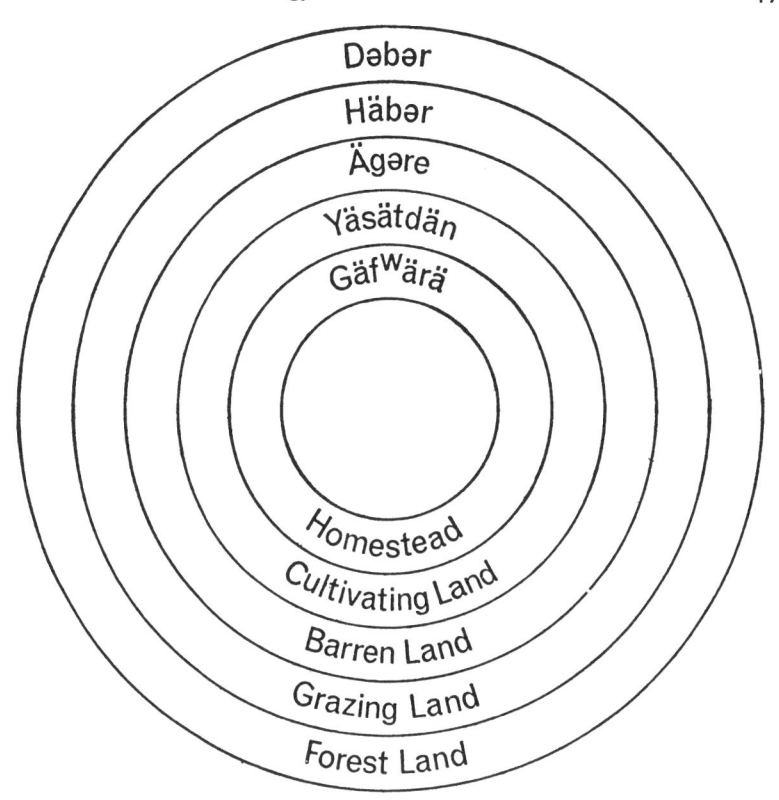

FIG. 1. Spatial Arrangement of a Gurage Settlement.

give status or accord special privileges to the villagers, but considerable status is given to villages where religious dignitaries live. Ritual ceremonies are held there. The sacredness of the area is symbolized by the planting of a forked-stick at both ends of the village *ema* and deference and respect are shown to it. The homesteads of religious or political dignitaries do not alter the pattern of village design, but two features distinguish these dwellings from those of ordinary villagers. An inner and outer circle of fencing encloses the compound, and within there are four or more houses all of the *g^weä* size.[19] In fact, there is a social distinction

[19] Cecchi, op. cit., p. 84, described the compound of one religious dignitary in which there were nine houses within the traditional double-fence enclosure.

between sacred and non-sacred areas, but there is no social distinction between non-religious settlements.

The traditional market centre Endeber is the one village in Gurageland where the accepted social, cultural, and physical form of the village has been radically altered. I have discussed the reason for these changes in the previous chapter; it is chiefly the presence of European-style Government buildings, remnants of the Italian occupation, and the Gurage Catholic Mission. Small clusters of shops and stalls, open daily, supplement the bi-weekly open-air market, selling foodstuffs, cloth, and some tinned goods. These stalls are owned by Gurage, not by Arab merchants as in the rest of Ethiopia; the Arabs have not yet begun to oust the Gurage entrepreneurs from Gurageland trade. There are also huts where locally brewed *sähär* and *ṭälla*, bottled drinks, *äsät*-food and food prepared in the Amhara fashion are available. There are also unattached women, mainly divorced, who in addition to dispensing food and drinks, provide sexual services as well.

In Endeber, there is also a weakening of the traditional social character of the village. Consciousness of the community to maintain the *wur ema*, the cultural esteem of a Gurage village, has given way to random individual action. There is formality in the social atmosphere that surrounds the area; a change in the social climate. Homesteads are invariably closed and less hospitable, and the social ease characteristic of the small settlement is absent from this quasi-urban environment. Endeber is socially and physically a 'town'. There is a social and physical resemblance between this and other market centres seen along any of the principal land arteries in Ethiopia. As with other towns, Endeber is in a marginal position between traditional village life and a more complex urban-like environment. For many a Gurage, especially one living many days walking-distance from Endeber, to journey there is to 'go abroad', the fulfillment of a very limited range of experiences within a lifetime. For other Gurage, the seasonal labour migrants, to go abroad to Endeber is the first stage in becoming urbanized.

I have tried in this chapter to describe the natural and cultural features of Gurageland, and to point to the significant relationship between climate, geography, physical grouping, and communications. The mode of production is seen to be limited by the physical environment, communications, and trade. Gurage economy supports a closely knit form of social grouping and their technology does not extend the area of exploitation beyond the region of habitation. The relationship between these ecological factors is stressed here to give full importance to their role in the social and economic system. They underlie the discussion of Gurage economy in the next chapter.

CHAPTER III

Land, Labour, and Ensete

THE economy of the Gurage is based on the land. Land is at the basis of most of Gurage relationships and, as was pointed out in the previous chapter, availability of land determines the patterns of settlement and modes of production. Logical choices in the allocation of this scarce commodity must be made to provide for the basic Gurage needs. To the lay observer, these choices and alternatives appear limited and narrow in scope because the Gurage have a simple technology. They use the digging stick, the *maräša*, and most of their economic activities centre round the cultivation of a single crop, *äsät*. But the Gurage are skilful in making the most that can be made of the available land.

Soil must be tested for fertility and means found to improve it when it becomes impoverished. Large quantities of manure are needed and, to ensure an adequate supply, a sizeable herd of cattle must be kept. But cattle must be grazed and grazing land is at a premium; too large a herd will overgraze the available land, while too small a herd will not produce the quantity of manure required. The problem is further complicated by the fact that cattle are used to supplement the basic food supply. Still other Gurage methods of land use to be described are of even greater complexity. It is against this background that Gurage economy is to be understood.

The Gurage principally cultivate *äsät*,[1] which provides the staple food of their diet, but they are also mixed cultivators, and they control the bulk of their own food supply by cultivating plants and breeding livestock. *Äsät* is extensively cultivated throughout

---

[1] On the ground of the obvious difference between the inflorescences of the *Ensete edulis* (*äsät*) and the banana (*musa*), these plants are now treated as separate genera. The Linnean Society reports that on the basis of genetical, cytological, and taxonomic grounds, the two genera are distinct. They have redefined *Ensete* with *Ensete edulis* as its type-species, and transferred to the genus a number of species hitherto placed in *musa*. See Scott, 1948–9, p. 131. For additional references on Ensete cultivation in Ethiopia see also Shack, 1963a, Smeds, 1955, p. 25; Murdock, 1960, pp. 521–40; Simmonds, 1958, pp. 302–7; Simoons, 1960, pp. 89–99.

the *säbat bet* except in the colder highlands of Gumer and parts of the Muher tribal lands where cereals and legumes are the principal crops.

Gurage agriculture is zonally determined. The principal crops grown in the lowlands, excluding *äsät*, are *ţef* (*Eragrostos abyssinica*), maize, *dura* (*Sorghum vulgare*), and *noog* (*Guizota abyssinica*). In the colder highlands barley, peas, horse beans, and flax seeds are the chief products. The *woina dega* temperate zone is favourable to the production of coffee, tobacco and *čat*,[2] which are marketable cash crops. In the west, and in the Ghibie and Uabi River basins, cotton is planted as a cash crop. Some vegetables are grown in limited quantities in the *dega* regions, primarily for home consumption, while in the warmer climate of the lowlands several varieties of spice, sugar cane, and some fruits are grown. Cattle, sheep and fowl are the principal domestic animals used as food. The cattle belong to the *bos indious* species (*Zebu*) and have the characteristic hump over the withers. Most of the sheep are of the fat-tail type, and the poultry is small compared with European breeds. In addition to cattle, horses and mules are widely bred in the upland zone, in Eastern Gurageland, and in that portion of the West bordering the Kambatta, Jimma-Galla, and Janjero tribal lands.

The root of the *äsät* plant (*wähta*), the stem of the leaves, and the inner-bark of the pseudostem, provide substance for food. These parts of the plant are decorticated to extract the edible portion which is later ground and kneaded into a flour-paste, and finally baked into a pancake bread called *wusa*; this is described in the next section.[3] On ceremonial occasions, and when important guests arrive, a bread of very refined quality, *ţəquräya*, is served. Meat, vegetable, and lentil hashes (*kətfwä*) prepared from sub-

---

[2] An excellent detailed account of *čat* (*Catha edulis* or *Celastrus edulis*) in an historical and social context is given by Trimingham, op. cit., p. 228. Chewed in small doses *čat* causes a pleasant insomnia, in larger doses a slight intoxication. In flavour it is slightly bitter and astringent. *Čat* is first mentioned in the Ethiopian Chronicles of Amda Syon I. It is widely grown as a cash crop by Muslim Gurage who, as with other Muslim Ethiopians, habitually chew it throughout the day.

[3] *Wusa* and *ţəquräya* are both fermented in the ground; *ţəquraya* is buried beneath *wusa* and remains underground for a longer period. Gurage say that the extended process of fermentation increases the palatableness of *äsät* bread. Leslau, 1950, op. cit., briefly describes the preparation of ensete bread, pp. 77–78. Cf. also the description of ensete in the accounts of Bruce, 1790, Vol. V, 37–39.

sidiary crops are sometimes eaten separately, or used on festive occasions, to augment the supply of food. There are no special foods eaten solely by women or by men; there are no emergency crops, since Gurage have never experienced crop failure. In other parts of Ethiopia *dagusa* (*Eleusine coracana*) is used as an emergency crop, but the Gurage grow this primarily for beer making. Two varieties of grain beers are produced from *dagusa*: *ṭälla*, brewed in Amhara fashion which is flavoured with *gešo* (*Rhamnus prinoides*), and *sähär*, the traditional Gurage beer, without flavouring.

The qualitative differences between *sähär* and *ṭälla* infer status which is often obvious when beer is dispensed at rituals and ceremonials. As a whole, *sähär* is used to bring together different groups or individuals; whenever attempts are made to reconcile hostile groups, *sähär* is offered. At the signing of the marriage contract, the *čäg* feast, the dispensing of beer symbolically represents the sanction of the contract. However, in addition to all its social attributes, such as incentives to labour, hospitality, and tribute of subjects to their chief, *sähär* is always drunk by the *Šägʷora* before performing acts of divination.[4]

THE *ÄSÄT* CULTURE

Since the social and economic life of the Gurage rests on the cultivation of *Ensete edulis*, which satisfies many of their essential needs, and other forms of labour are of secondary importance, we can properly speak of an '*äsät* culture' here.[5]

The Gurage have a vital interest in *äsät*. They depend on it for many of the necessities of life, food being only one of the many needs this plant meets. The uses of *äsät* seem endless and all parts of the plant are consumed in one way or another; this increases considerably the importance of *äsät* in Gurage culture. In house construction, the bark is used as insulating material between layers of thatching; it is also burnt as fuel (*qʷäqʷäsa*). Dried *äsät* leaves, cut into small plates (*ṭäräs*), are used for serving *kätfwä* at all festivals, marriage feasts, circumcisions, and at the time of

---

[4] I note also that *sähär* is used in Gurage burial rites on p. 129 below; its ritual meaning in this context seems to be that of providing the deceased ancestor with beer for the journey into the afterworld.

[5] The parallel I make here is obviously drawn from the distinctive features of the 'cattle culture' complex, among the Nuer described by Evans-Pritchard, 1940, p. 16.

äsät planting. For the wealthy who eat daily from *ṭəräs* at the evening meal, it is a status symbol. During harvesting, *äsät* leaves are used to form a lining in the deep pit in which *ṭəquräya*-bread is buried for fermenting. Leaves of the plant serve generally as a protective wrapping against moisture. A round piece (*čefat*) is constructed from a leaf for carrying heavy 'head-loads', to form the base-stand for pots, and to serve as a seat. Finally, after the stalk of the *äsät* leaf has been scraped to extract the edible substance, the remaining long, coarse fibres, *qanča*, are dried to become a marketable commodity.[6] (See Fig. 2).

Several species of *äsät* are used in Gurage pharmacopeia. According to their beliefs, all forms of illness can be cured with medicines concocted from the roots of *äsät* given the names *Astara*, *Čarkema*, *Orrete*, and *Gwarəya*. On most homesteads *Gwarəya* and *Astara* are grown and given special care because of their believed potency; a special section of the garden is reserved for them (and other 'special' *äsät* as well), and once harvested the root is secretly hidden and carefully guarded, for later use when a personal amulet is needed. Such plants are accorded special deference and Gurage respectfully refer to them as '*yärgus äsät*'. They are the '*äsät* of (the) kings'.

The Gurage have no strong supernaturalistic approach to their environment. The curative attributes of *äsät* have only a minimal diffuse relationship with ritual practices. Gurage technical achievements of planting and harvesting are not associated with ritual acts, nor are they directly related to their idea system. Although their land is believed to be ritually protected, neither it nor any portion of its produce is considered to be sacred. Land is not ceremonially blessed to ensure or increase its yield. There is no association of land with ancestor-worship whereby portions of the crop are set aside in exhortation of spirits to favour productivity. But *äsät* is presented in ritual offerings to *Däm^wam^wit*, the deity concerned with the health and well-being of Gurage. In monthly rituals performed at village earth shrines, women set aside a portion of *äsät*-food to appease evil spirits who otherwise might harm some member of the village. From a Gurage's point of view, land is his personal concern; the success or failure to obtain the maximum yield depends upon his own rational acts within the

---

[6] *Qanča*-fibres are sold in Addis Ababa and used in the manufacture of ropes and paper bags.

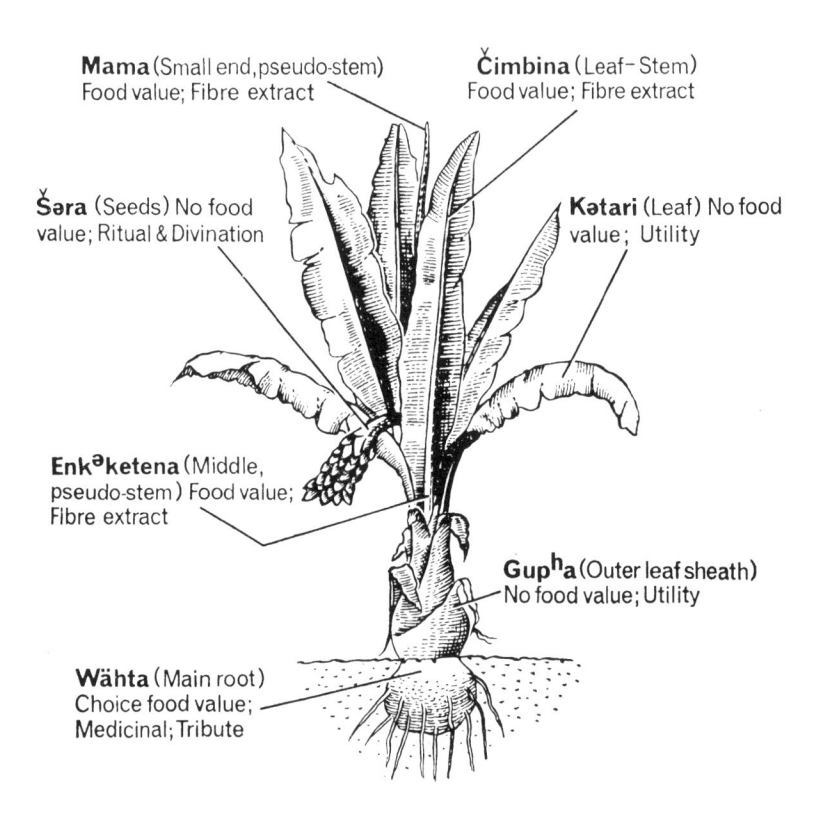

Mama (Small end, pseudo-stem)
Food value; Fibre extract

Čimbina (Leaf–Stem)
Food value; Fibre extract

Šəra (Seeds) No food
value; Ritual & Divination

Kətari (Leaf) No food
value; Utility

Enkᵊketena (Middle,
pseudo-stem) Food value;
Fibre extract

Gupʰa (Outer leaf sheath)
No food value; Utility

Wähta (Main root)
Choice food value;
Medicinal; Tribute

FIG. 2. Gurage Nomenclature of *Äsät*. (After Bruce, op. cit. Vol. V, p. 36.)

limits of his control, even though on occasions a Gurage might utter a prayer to *Waq* as a sign of spiritual gratitude. His land is usually productive, and he relates this to his efficiency and use of rational knowledge and techniques to achieve a logical end. There is no ceremony or ritual to express gratitude to an anthropomorphic or invisible spirit.

A Gurage 'knows the ways of *äsät*'. This expression is commonly used to mean that he can predict the 'behaviour' of *äsät* under a wide range of climatic and soil conditions. A Gurage reasons that gods and spirits are of a different order from man, having no active part in the growing of *äsät* and not being responsible for its origin. He believes, and often says, that *äsät* is older than the first Gurage; whosoever created the world and Gurageland provided *äsät* as a blessing to prevent starvation. No Gurage deity is credited exclusively with the creation of the universe. A Gurage rationalizes the exclusion of women, artisans, Fuga, and slaves from owning land, in the belief that *äsät* was put there for the 'proprietor of the earth'. '*Yafär ab*' is the expression for this phrase, and this is often how he refers to himself and other Gurage men.

The *Gəruyä* feast, celebrated during the rainy season, is a minor ritual expression of the *äsät* culture complex.[7] Then, a two-day period of fasting is observed during which only specially prepared *äsät*-food is eaten, and though songs are chanted in honour of the principal deities, there is no payment of tribute nor are there placation rites of any kind performed. Celebrations are held locally in each village and there are no celebrations of lineages and clans in ritual collaboration headed by a religious dignitary or one of his agents. If *Gəruyä* once had a significance as a feast of rain, or to exhort the gods to improve the yield of crops (and this might have been so), it has lost this meaning in practise and in the memory of the people. Today, *Gəruyä* is essentially a manifestation of the cultural role of *äsät*, which is reinforced by stressing its significance in the social and economic life of the Gurage.

The attitudes of Gurage toward *äsät* are also expressed in their verbal behaviour and in the degree to which *äsät* cultivation dominates all other labour activities. The extensive plant nomenclature, in which all Gurage males, even youths, are well versed, is further indication of the values and interests they associate with growing *äsät*. These interests dominate any conversation Gurage hold about *äsät*. Men have been known to fight over *äsät*, and as well *äsät* is given in compensation to settle such disputes. Ritual tribute to chiefs and other dignitaries is always made with the

---

[7] *Gəruyä* is organized on the basis of membership in the homestead and not that of the village. Owing to lineage grouping, however, several homesteads in a village may feast together. A brief description of *Gəruyä* is given by Leslau, 1950, p. 71.

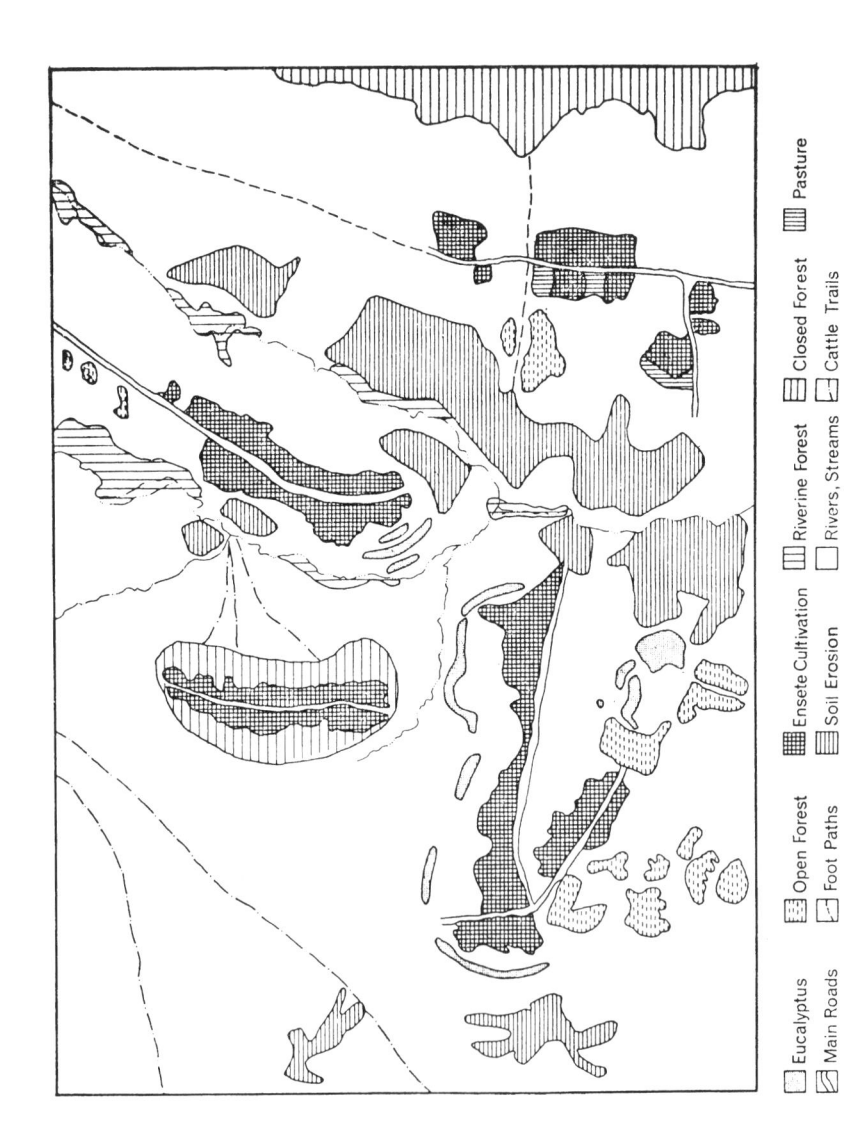

MAP 3. Patterns of Land Use in Gurageland.

best quality *təquräya*, along with other gifts. When the full wrath of ritual punishment strikes a man and he is afflicted with the ritual curse of *Zitänä*,[8] his entire *äsät* holdings are confiscated by the representative of the deity offended. One of the most serious sanctions imposed by the tribal council, *Yä Ǧoka*, is to destroy a man's house and *äsät* field; similarly, it is considered one of the most serious offences that can be committed against another man. Some Gurage grow more *äsät* than others, depending upon the conditions of soil and the size of holdings, but status in this way is assessed largely in terms of the height and girth plants reach. Joking rivalry between homesteads over status so acquired is commonplace. But I heard of no instance where such rivalry turned into serious encounters.

II

The Gurage homestead and field comprise an inseparable unit. There are no irregularities to be seen in the planning or choice of sites for cultivation; there are no alternatives in the selection of a more suitable plot of land; there are no unused tracts by which a system of fallowing or rotation of fields can be employed. Nor do the Gurage, like some other African tribes living in congested settlements, have their fields at great distances from the village.

In the previous chapter, Fig. 1 illustrated the allocation of village land. Grazing land, *häbər*, which is corporately owned by the village can never be used for cultivation; this is also true of *sərage* land upon which the *wur ema* is built. Barren land, *ägəre*, begins where the legal limits of a homestead's field (*yäsätdan*) end. Cultivation does not go beyond these socio-economic boundaries. Moreover, the Gurage firmly believe that soil fertility abruptly ends wherever the limits for land use are set; all land outside this is held to be unsuitable for cultivation. To a great extent, the practice of these beliefs is responsible for the symmetrical character of the village. Thus Gurage fields may vary considerably in size but seldom from the rectangular shape of their unmistakeably overcrowded vegetation. This side-by-side arrangement of fields is important in the system of cultivation. The spatial relationship between homesteads and patterns of land-use in several villages is shown in Map 3.

Gurage practise a system of semi-shifting cultivation marked by

[8] See pp. 166–8 below.

Abar

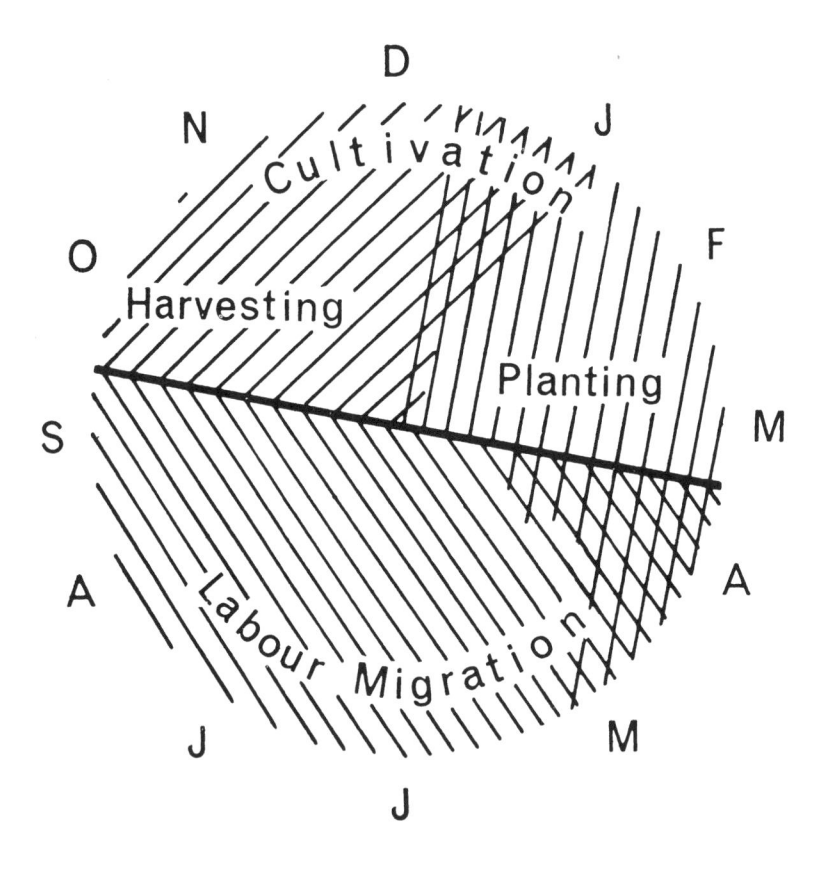

Zär

FIG. 3. Calendar of Agriculture.

an extensive use of manure and crop rotation that enables them to use the same land indefinitely. Harvesting precedes the stages of planting since space required for planting new crops is made available only after matured growths have been harvested. Hence, the agricultural season actually begins at harvest, the beginning of a new year in the Gurage calendar. Preparation of the soil and the setting of *äsät* as well as secondary crops takes place within the dry season which begins in the month of September and extends through March. The calendar of agriculture is based on the scheme illustrated in Fig. 3, which relates *äsät* cultivation with seasonal labour migration, an aspect of Gurage economy discussed in a later section of this chapter.

Äsät fields vary in length and breadth, some large, some small. But the division of fields according to the four stages of *äsät* growth is everywhere the same. Each section of land takes its name from the plant grown there; from the first to the last stage

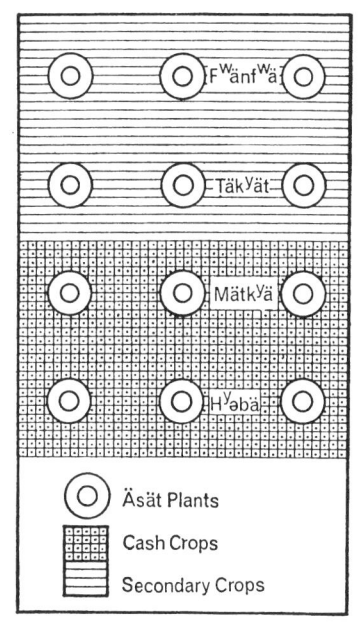

FIG. 4. Primary and Secondary Crop Distribution.

they are named *fʷänfʷä*, *ṭäkʸat*, *mätkʸä*, and *hʸəbä*. Spacing between plants is equally symmetrical. Since all arable land is put under cultivation, the approximately three square metres of land between *äsät* plants is utilized for growing secondary and cash crops. (See Fig. 4.)

In explaining their methods of horticulture, Gurage bring into the description a human element, implying that *äsät* are somewhat like people. For instance, Gurage habitually say that in the early stages of growth *äsät* are like young children, and they must be cared for as though they were the same. This attitude, when put into practice, forms a rationale for their behaviour towards young *äsät*. It is not surprising, then, that Gurage draw a parallel between the birth of children and the reproduction of *äsät*, and refer to it as though they are speaking of men. The propagation of *äsät* by its vegetative parts, rather than by seeds, is a distinctive feature of the *äsät* culture.[9]

To propagate *äsät*, a strong, hardy *ṭäkyät* is preferred. For *ṭäkyät* has reached the second stage of growth when, as Gurage say, a plant is most capable of reproducing, whereas in later stages, nearing the time for harvesting, its capacity for reproduction declines steadily. After a *ṭäkyät* is uprooted, its tall leaves are cut back to the base, these being set aside to be used later as shelter for the young sprouts that will be produced. Then the pseudostem is cored and filled with dry humus, sometimes mixed with soft crushed stones; it is replanted close to the homestead where a manured pit has been specially prepared for this. Within two months as many as 100 or more new sprouts appear. But these young sprouts are not named, and for the same reason that newly-born Gurage are not; that it brings ill fortune if they die young while carrying the name of others. After some weeks, those that survive are called *suma*.

'The war expedition of the hen (goes) as far as the *suma*-plant'[10] is how a Gurage proverb equates *suma* with young children. And *suma* are planted close to the hut. They are never planted in the *äsät*-field along with older, mature plants which, except for occasional weeding in the dry season, are mainly unattended. Because of their size and resilience, older plants can withstand more easily spoilage that straying cattle sometimes cause, and their tall leaves afford them protection from the hot sun and cold night air. Surrounding the small plot set aside for growing *suma* is erected a bier, about six metres in diameter, for which a covering made of *äsät*-leaves, some being from the *ṭäkyät* which produced them, provides additional shelter. Behind this enclosure, *suma*

---

[9] The cultivated variety of ensete plants are seed-sterile or only slightly fertile. Throughout the Ensete Culture Complex variations of a common planting technique are found by which the plant is propagated and spread by suckers. For a description of the general techniques of ensete horticulture, see the review by Simmonds, loc. cit.

[10] Leslau writes: 'this is said of someone who is not very courageous and does not dare to undertake anything far from his village', 1950, p. 135. By extension, this would also be said of children; they also stay close to the house and remain in the village.

appear to grow 'wild' and 'unruly', especially when compared with the evenly spaced field of older *äsät* plants. By the end of one season, *suma* take on the appearance of *äsät*, not in size, but in shape, having then grown relatively tall leaves and a thick outer bark. Then it is transplanted to the field and this sets the *äsät*-cycle in motion.

The pivot on which the *äsät*-cycle revolves is the system of transplanting. The rotation of plants in the *äsät*-cycle (Fig. 5) is

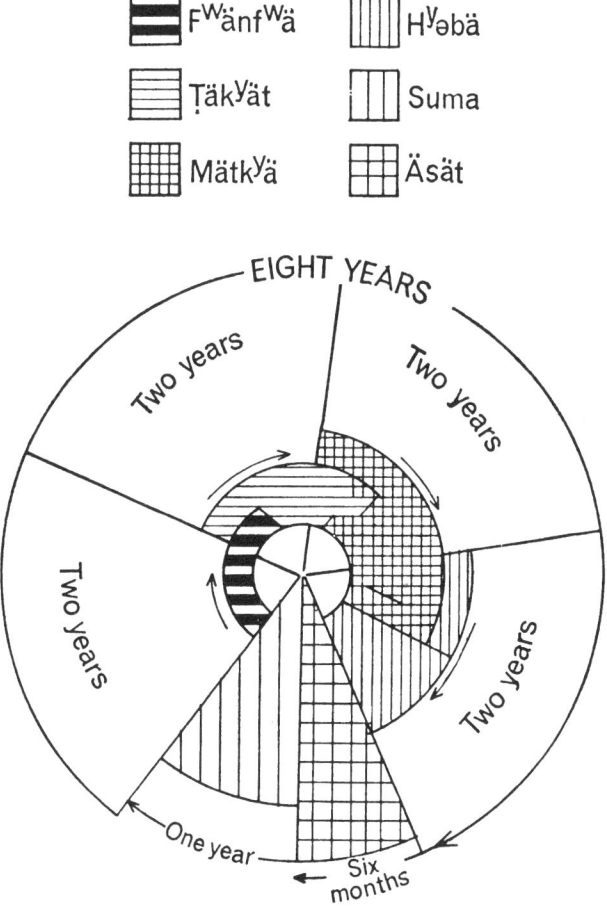

FIG. 5. *Äsät* Cycle of Cultivation.

similar to the rotation of social groups in age-grading systems; but there the similarity ends. All *äsät* that have reached each of four respective stages of maturity within a single season are transplanted. From the planting of *suma* to the harvesting of full grown *äsät* spans a period of eight years; plants rotate to a new 'age-grade' every two years, completing the cycle in four stages. *Suma* planted in the same season move together as a group through each successive stage of rotation, being harvested in the same season, eight years hence. However, sometimes a plant 'becomes sick' (*furṭəyä*), as Gurage explain, and soon dies during an early phase of the cycle; if so, a dead plant is not removed until the group to which it belongs completes the *äsät*-cycle.

As stated above, the *äsät*-cycle is set in motion when *suma* are transplanted. Each *suma* is transplanted to a manured pit from which a *fʷänfʷä*, having grown there for two years, has now been rotated to the second stage, *ṭäkʸät*; the four-year-old *ṭäkʸät* advances to the next grade and is called *mätkʸä*; transplanted it becomes *hʸəbä*. In the second year after transplanting, *hʸəbä* normally bears the 'false banana', *šəra*, the symbol that it is fully matured. Although *šəra* contains no food value, at least Gurage say this, the black seeds from the core are sometimes used in divination. They also say that *hʸəbä* must be harvested in the same season that the 'false banana' appears, for if not, the plant is said to wither and decay, becoming coarse, fibrous and inedible. In Gurage plant nomenclature, the term *äsät* is, strictly speaking, used only when referring to fully ripened plants. Therefore, *äsät* solely is treated with respect, often referred to reverently, and sometimes endowed with supernatural powers.

On most Gurage plots a new *äsät*-cycle is set in motion each planting-season, with two overlapping cycles obtaining at any given time. While this could be increased indefinitely, depending upon the amount of available land, most holdings are already overcrowded and two *äsät*-cycles usually contain a sufficient number of plants to maintain the homestead's food supply above the subsistence level. This optimum level enables the Gurage to utilize more scarce arable land for cash crop production. The number of plants per year required for one adult is estimated variously by Gurage, but the average is about ten *äsät* plants.[11] Food supply

---

[11] Smeds, loc. cit., notes that three *äsät* plants are credited with supplying enough food to feed the average person for one year in Sidamo. I assume the

needs are estimated on the basis of the size of the family unit; taking the family as a unit of consumption, its consumption can be regulated. By planting a definite number of *suma* to provide a concomitant number of matured plants, the harvest is rigorously controlled by the size and composition of the homestead. In this way the dangers of scarcity and glut are practically eliminated; there is in fact little space for stockpiling. The practice of storing food in earth-pits, which are sunk between *äsät* plants, reduces even further the amount of cultivatable land.

Economic factors in themselves do not govern decisions to grow more or less *äsät*; social factors also are important. One index of the status and prestige of a Gurage is the size of his *äsät* holding, and as well the height and girth matured plants reach. If a Gurage can plant more *äsät* than his subsistence needs require, he will do so. Clan and religious dignitaries, headmen, and important elders especially need a surplus of *äsät*-food to distribute among their faithful followers on great occasions. Most families do grow a small surplus, the food from which, kept in earth-storage, may be bartered for other food products, used for payment of services rendered, or used on ceremonial occasions when extra food is required. When extra cash is needed, surpluses of *äsät* may be sold outright on market days. The Gumer Gurage and others who do not cultivate *äsät* extensively, rely upon the surpluses of others in exchange for grain and cattle.

The seasons of harvesting and planting are practically consecutive and there is little time for leisure between them. In each homestead all able adult males and adolescent boys are expected to co-operate in the laborious tasks of transplanting. The division of male labour is organized generally round the age-grades of *äsät*. Young boys, past the age at which herding cattle is their principal chore, normally work in that part of the garden allocated to the *fʷänfʷä* and *ṭäkʸät* growths of *äsät*; their elders take on the transplanting of the *mätkʸä* and *hʸəbä*, and the harvesting of *äsät*. These are the adult stages in the growth of a plant, and moving them requires the strength of adult men. Transplanting

food requirements of Sidamo to be the same as those of the Gurage; from my observations this figure seems extremely small. Two-thirds of a plant are inedible. However, the figures of fifteen to twenty plants often given to me by Gurage seems unusually large. This exaggeration probably stresses the psychological attitude towards the need for more land, but it does not negate the fact that population is dense and arable land is scarce.

towering plants, the pseudostems often scaling more than seven feet in height, is hard and time-consuming work. At least two able-bodied men, sometimes three, are needed. No man can plant and harvest his field single-handed; this fact, in itself, adds to the economic bias of Gurage kinship relations. Hence, all able adult males and adolescent boys of the homestead are expected to labour co-operatively until the agricultural season ends. They do.

Men also make ready the harvested *äsät* for the women to begin decorticating it. Women never handle the special tools men use in their work; contrariwise, the same is true of men. It is their work to cut away the tall leaves, uproot the plant, strip the thick outer bark from the pseudostem, and separate the inner layers; from the latter women extract the edible substance, but first they remove them to a special area where the women work alone.

As soon as the first *äsät* is harvested, women begin to prepare a section of the field in which to work. The area is marked off by knotting several *äsät*-leaves, and attaching them between plants to shape a rectangle; the ground below is covered with loosely spread *äsät*-leaves on which the food substance will collect; later it is ground into flour, *qämä*. On one side, a stout pole is placed horizontally between two plants and secured with *qanča*-rope; this serves as a support for the scraping boards used for separating the edible portions of *äsät* from the fibres. In front of each board a woman sits on a large stone, padded heavily with *äsät*-leaves; one foot propped high on the board holds a strip of *äsät*, thereby freeing both hands to use the bamboo scraping tool (*səbisa*). In large households, where female labour is plentiful, as many as five adult women work at this. But young girls never do; for decorticating *äsät* is strenuous and only older women have acquired the necessary strength for this. Young girls collect the food substance and *qanča*-fibres; the latter they set aside for drying; the former they take to another part of the field where they begin pulverizing it.

Two women usually work together at pulverizing the pseudostem root, the *wähta*, which Gurage claim produces the choicest food. For this, a special wooden implement, *žəbangyəba*, is fashioned. One end is shaped into a blade; the other, round with a serrated edge, is used for chopping. With the *wähta* placed between them, the women make quick chopping strokes whittling it into small diced pieces; only one *wähta* can be pulverized in a work day.

Fuga hunters stalking game

A *Gəžä*, tanner, scraping hair from a cow skin. The tool resembles a
carpenter's plane; the blade is obsidian

A view of a Gurage village

A view of the market at Agänna

Once begun, the tempo of work is steady. Labour among women is especially stimulated by singing or talking, both usually constant. The rhythmic pace is set by an older woman who, somewhat like an 'overseer' on a large plantation, supervises the work of others by seeing to it that each is supplied always with sufficient quantities of *äsät* for scraping. Mainly she cuts away the stem from the leaves, divides sections of the inner bark, making the decorticating of it less difficult, and attends the work of young girls who knead the *qämä*. She sets the length of the work-day and frequently calls for periods of rest, after first having prepared coffee and roasted grains in the sheltered area where women work.

During the planting and harvesting season, Gurage men and women spend most of the day in the field. They retire there soon after the morning meal, after the children too young for work in the field have taken the cattle to graze. With the exception of morning and evening meals all others are taken in the *äsät*-field, mainly small bits of *wusa*, roasted grains, and coffee. Christian Gurage and Muslims in particular often use rest periods to perform their obligatory prayers. Muslim Gurage habitually chew *çat* in large doses, which apparently affords them a mild stimulation and reduces fatigue. But the high values associated with the horticulture of *äsät*, in themselves, provide all the incentive needed to work.

By mid-December harvesting in most homesteads has been completed. Sometimes new earth-storage pits must be dug and women must prepare a new lining for them made of *äsät*-leaves; or the linings of old pits must be renewed. As small batches of *qämä* are made ready, they are wrapped in *äsät*-leaves in preparation for storage; fresh *qämä* is placed at the bottom of the earth-pit, the older fermented *qämä* being removed closer to the opening where it is more accessible for frequent use. When all earth-pits have been filled, covered with layers of *äsät*-leaves and finally with humus, the agricultural cycle for that season is ended.

The cultivation of most subsidiary crops is considered 'man's work' for this, as with *äsät*, requires the use of the digging-stick. Root crops fall mainly into this category, for where 'bush' crops are concerned, such as *çat*, coffee, *gešo*, and peppers, work is divided equally between both sexes. In the main, men make decisions as to the allocation of space for secondary crops and do the planting, while women and young girls are responsible for the harvesting, cleaning, and storage. Women carry out these tasks after *äsät* has been harvested and food from it has been prepared and stored in the earth.

When two or more homesteads are related by close kin ties, and this is more often than not the rule in any village, they commonly assist each other, working as one large, extended family. The factor of common residence in the village presupposes that when a homestead's complement of male labour has been depleted through illness, death, or absenteeism, other homesteads, even those unrelated, will share the more burdensome tasks. But there would be a grudging reluctance to lend aid to a family whose males were absent for no understandable reason, merely to avoid the labours of *äsät* planting. Absence does not seem to occur often, and the few cases that were brought to my notice were always justified. It is expected that all Gurage men working away from home will return to the homestead and take part in the agricultural activities. Most of them do so.

In general, the cultivation of *äsät* is mainly organized round agnatic kin of the homestead. The village or aggregate groups of the village participate as a working unit occasionally, according to demands for labour of an individual homestead. In newly settled villages where virgin soil must be cleared and placed under cultivation, breaking ground, removing trees and wild bush, and preparing the first bed becomes the concern of the entire settlement.

III

The cultivation of cash crops is made possible primarily by making the greatest use of the available land. Gurage achieve this in two ways: by estimating the food consumption of the family, and by using the space between *äsät* plants as land for growing cash crops. Spacing alloted between *äsät* plants seldom exceeds three to four metres and is dependent upon the size of the family which may consume one-third of the total annual crop. Even so, holdings are expansible only within certain limits, and these limits are reduced with each generation as the sons come into possession of their shares of land; the available land for cultivating primary food crops and cash crops decreases in direct proportion to the number of heritable shares. Yet larger land holdings are desirable if crops having a substantial cash value are to be grown. Coffee is the only crop of considerable economic worth and today it is grown extensively, sometimes at the expense of the production of food crops which may be reduced to the minimum level of home consumption.[12] The practice of converting 50 per cent. of a holding into cash crop production is becoming increasingly common.

The basic economic unit is the family and not the wider lineage group of the village. The holdings of neighbouring related homesteads are not grouped together to increase their yield. Homestead land and its yield, unlike corporately owned village grazing and forest lands, are individually owned and the use of the land is the concern of each particular homestead. The distinctive aspects of a corporate peasant community, that is represented in a bounded social system, diminish in a Gurage village where land becomes an issue. Interhomestead co-operation during the season of cultivation commonly takes place, and labour is paid for by labour, not in the sharing of produce. Now that demands for increased holdings to extend cash crop cultivation have been created, the traditional values, attached to land and the sharing of produce, have become more firmly entrenched.

Land factors also affect other aspects of social organization. Nowadays it is becoming increasingly difficult for a man to establish polygynous marriages. Traditionally, each wife should have her own homestead on land preferably in a village apart from that of her co-wife or wives, although levirate practices may be an exception to this.[13] The social and economic status that once accrued from maintaining extensive polygynous households is now difficult to attain; but status acquired in this manner today has a relatively higher value than in the past. Despite the fact that the securing of an additional wife still stands among the traditional values, the frequency with which this ideal is attained has, as Gurage men claim, lessened considerably under present conditions of land shortage.

The cultivation of cash crops has not noticeably affected household chores and recreations, either during the season of farm work or during the rainy season when outdoor work is suspended. The

[12] The amount of *qanča*-fibres extractable from a single plant is small, regardless of its size; it is about 1·5 kg. In 1957–9 the market value was $Eth. 0·10–0·20, about four-pence, per kg. Coffee averaged $Eth. 1·00 per kg.; in 1955 it comprised 55·6 per cent. of the total value of Ethiopia's exports. See Luther, 1958, p. 76; *Economic Handbook*, op. cit., pp. S-11, 12. Cotton, formerly a substantial cash crop in Gurageland, has since been replaced by coffee. The latter requires less work, smaller acreage, and it has increased in cash value according to the rise in coffee exportation by Ethiopia.

[13] This is discussed more fully below on p. 87.

simpler off-season farming tasks of occasional weeding and manuring are performed by women and children according to the division of labour. The boys herd cattle and spend much of their time playing together while their cattle graze. Girls welcome the fetching of water and the collecting of dung as a relief from other more monotonous and confining homestead duties. Women perform the usual household tasks, with the assistance of female domestics, if such are a part of the homestead. Men, if they are not engaged in house construction, clearing fields, weaving, or as in former times warfare, are freed from work confining them to the homestead and village. Older men and women sit and idle time away, occasionally watching over infants, and giving to others the kind of advice that can only be acquired by experience, and to themselves they seem to have lived an uncountable number of years.

For the younger, able, adult men, release from agricultural and domestic activities means that they can go off to other places to earn additional money. Men do not leave full-time agricultural pursuits because these are seasonal and only part-time, as we have shown. The patterns of labour migration will be described later in relation to the adjustments made in the homestead to accommodate the loss of males through migration, and the joint responsibilities taken on by the village when large numbers of their men are absent.[14] Provided that sufficient men remain to work with the women and to represent a token male force guarding the settlement, the subsistence system keeps the village supplied with food and other needs. But it is the movement of men, goods, and services in the market system that we turn to now.

ORGANIZATION AND STRUCTURE OF THE MARKET

I

The market system is one aspect of Gurage economic organization which has to a large extent retained its characteristic structure.

Observations of a Gurage market, written almost a century ago, revealing its ethnic composition of merchants and traders, the variety of goods exchanged, services rendered, and the types of currency used in exchange are characteristic descriptions of a Gurage market today. Among the merchants and traders in the large Muslim market in Qabena, in 1886, were Galla, Janjero,

[14] See pp. 77–81 below.

Sidamo, and some Amhara, who altogether numbered some 400 to 500.[15] Market goods and services broadly coincided with a male-female division of labour. Women, especially Chaha women, came in great numbers bringing tobacco, butter, some fodder, 'ensete paste', ropes, umbrellas, hens, eggs, and 'some few trifles'. Men brought oxen, rams, a very few horses, ivory, coffee, tin, dried skins, and slaves. Ivory was plentiful, with never fewer than 40 to 50 tusks available; some came from Qabena and Gurageland but the majority were brought by the Galla. Most of the iron came from Aymellel, and the Janjero had a near monopoly on woven *šamas*, whereas the Chaha and Ulbarag Gurage were the principal dealers in slaves. There were huts in which fresh meat could be bought, and, when there was sufficient demand and animals were plentiful, upwards of twenty beasts would be slaughtered by the Muslim priest in charge. With every animal slaughtered, a 'custom's duty' of three kilograms of meat was levied by the local *Imam* of the district in which the market was held. This duty was collected by a designated official of the *Imam* who, in addition, policed the market settling disputes that arose between buyers and sellers.

Market items of transaction noted in 1886 are compiled in Table IV; they correspond closely with my observations made in 1957–9 and listed in Table V.[16]

TABLE IV

Items of Market Transactions: 1886[17]

1. *Šamas*	18. 'Ensete-bread'
2. Cotton trousers	19. Butter
3. Umbrellas	20. Hens
4. Dressed skins	21. Eggs
5. Corn	22. Tobacco
6. Barley	23. Knife blades
7. *Tef*	24. Brass and copper
8. Chickpeas	25. Tin
9. Broad beans	26. Beads
10. Peas	27. Salt
11. Horses (draught and saddle)	28. Pottery
12. Donkeys	29. Ivory
13. Cotton cloth	30. Jewellery (horn and brass)
14. Oxen	31. Slaves
15. Cows (non-milking)	32. Fodder
16. Rams	33. Honey
17. Goats	

[15] Cecchi, op. cit., pp. 41–60. [16] See p. 74 below. [17] Cecchi, op. cit., p. 41.

Noted are two important changes that have taken place in the market system. The first is the use of cash currency which has replaced the former media of exchange, salt, brass and copper beads, and occasionally cloth.[18] The second is the trafficking in slaves which, though once an important item of commerce, has now been completely eliminated.

II

Gurage markets are part of interclan and intertribal relations. No market exists solely for the use of members of a single group, but the integral structure of a market is controlled by the group on whose land the market is held.

The market cycle is one aspect of intertribal relations between the *säbat bet*. There are three principal markets, each of which is the central market of a cycle of three markets held weekly. Spatially, the locations of Gurage markets intersect the whole of the tribal lands from northeast to southwest, and the distance between market boundaries is narrowed by the exchange of goods between widely separated tribes. (See Fig. 6.) Temporally, markets are held on alternate days of the week, thereby allowing adequate time for goods and traders to reach each market in the cycle and also preventing a wide dispersal of a limited amount of goods. Markets form focal points of varied services that meet the needs of small groups.

The market cycle begins in the north, on Monday, at the market in Agänna. Although generally regarded as the market of the Ezha tribe, Gurage of other tribes attend it as well as other tribal markets. In the south, Wednesday is 'big market' day for the Ennemor tribe in the district of Yəgəzaye. This is the largest of the principal markets in the cycle and traders from the Kambatta

---

[18] The Maria Theresa dollar ($Eth. 1·50) replaced non-monetary forms of currency throughout most of highland Ethiopia in the nineteenth century, but, as Cecchi noted, it was not an acceptable form of currency in the Quabena market and it is reasonable to assume that it was unacceptable elsewhere in Gurageland. Even today, most Gurage traders are reluctant to accept the new Ethiopian dollar currency in market transactions; market sales are principally made with the 'frank', the Ethiopian ten-cent coin. In other areas of the south-west the 'shilling', bearing an effigy of Emperor Menilek and having a value of $0·50, is the principal market currency. On types of currency in South-West Ethiopia see Montandon, 1913, pp. 197–8; 394; on currency in ancient Ethiopia see Pankhurst, 1961a., ch. 21 and 1962.

and Janjero tribes, and some neighbouring Galla attend it. The Chaha market held on Friday in the village of Endeber completes the cycle. There are also smaller interclan markets held throughout the week in Gurageland, even on days scheduled for big markets. Distances between intertribal markets may be as great as two days'

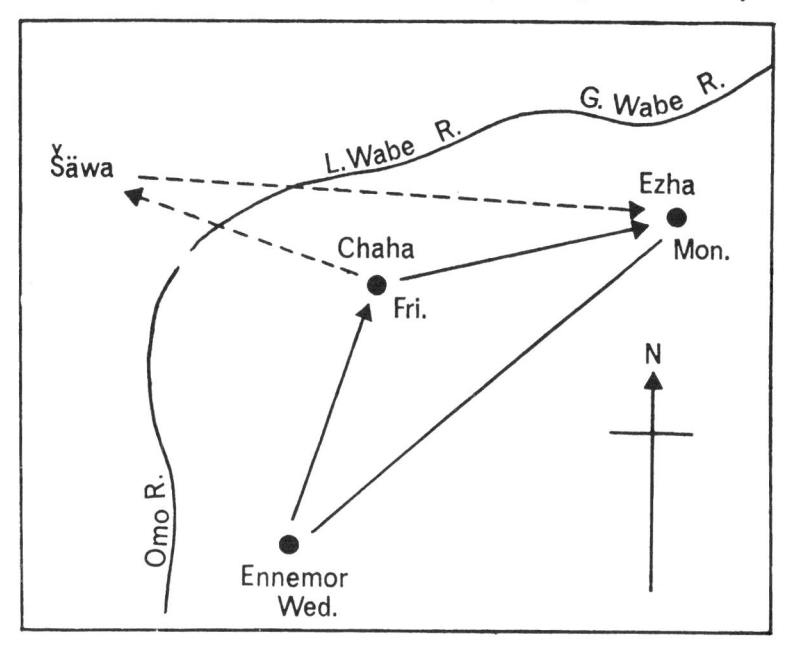

FIG. 6. The Market Cycle in Gurageland.

walking, as between Ezha and Ennemor. Interclan markets are, therefore, useful byposts for assembling and distributing goods first obtained from larger tribal markets. On weekend days small Muslim markets are held which principally trade on an interclan basis. As Coptic Gurage are forbidden to slaughter cattle on the Sabbath, Muslim markets are sometimes frequented by Copts for their supplies of fresh meat.[19]

The Endeber *gäbäyä* (market), like all the other large markets, is held on land belonging to a clan; but it is considered to be a market of the Chaha tribe, and political organization of their market

[19] So also on the days of fast, Wednesday and Friday. In Ethiopian Christianity two Sabbaths are sometimes observed: Sunday and the Jewish Sabbath. Except for some Muher Gurage, the Jewish Sabbath is not closely observed by other Gurage Copts.

is a tribal affair. Clan chiefs who act as 'Market Elders', in their exercise of authority in controlling the market, are supported by the chief of the clan in which the market is held. The chief usually attends every market, and he and the Market Elders and village headmen act as market police and market judges. They uphold the market peace in the market place, on the *wur ema*, as well as on the smaller footpaths leading to the market.

Market pacts between warring tribes are a part of the past; today they exist only in the reminiscences of older Gurage. Formerly, Galla and Sidamo tribes each made treaties with Gurage which prevented hostilities from taking place within the market area, and guaranteed safe conduct for traders en route. Nowadays feuding takes place primarily between Gurage arising out of unsettled brawls between individuals of the same clan or tribe. Disputes can easily occur, in spite of the efficient organization of the market, because of the congestion of people, especially in the big markets. Within a four-hour period, after itinerant and local traders have arrived first, the market reaches its peak attendance, which, for example, Market Elders at Yəgəzaye estimate at 20,000. An overhead view of the market horde shows them as an inseparable mass, while on the ground, within the market site, there is scarcely space to move without stepping into and spoiling a trader's goods. Such a mishap may well end in a brawl.

In the midst of congestion and excitement there is order and organization. There is no indiscriminate mixing of traders and goods. Similar products are grouped together, and in this way they form a distinct market pattern which distinguishes groups of traders according to their goods and services, as the sketch in Fig. 7 shows. In general, the trade of locally produced goods is consistent with the sex-age division of labour. The slaughtering of cattle is men's work; young boys and girls assist in selling the fresh cuts. The major cash crops are sold by men in view of the fact that they control money spent in the homestead. Women are responsible for selling other food products, and, though at times they barter, the profits from cash transactions are dutifully handed over to their spouses.

The large variety of things produced in the area which enter into trade are listed in Table V (p. 74); this table corresponds to the diagram in Fig. 7; Western and Ethiopian trade goods are grouped together in Sections 14 and 15 in both illustrations. Every

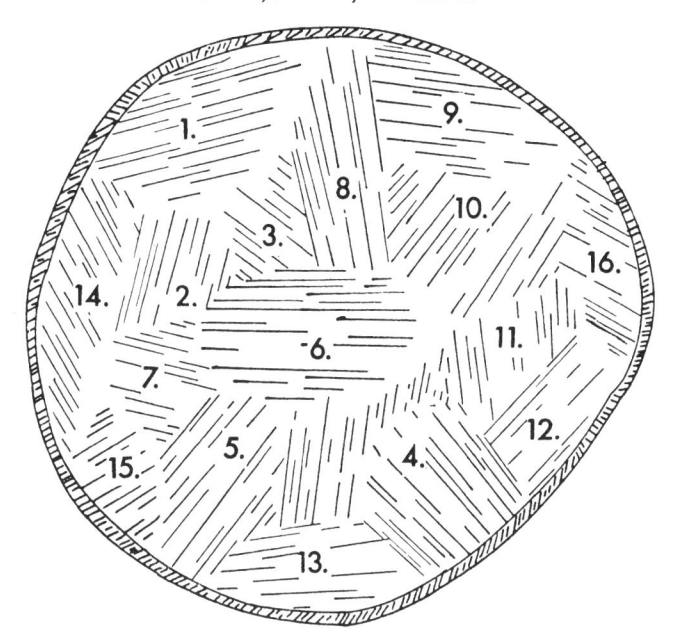

FIG. 7. Sketch Plan of a Gurage Market.

item that came to my attention while I was surveying the principal markets in the cycle is included in this table. Medicines of the diviners and herbalists, though not listed, are still available. But transactions of this kind do not take place on the market site; the goods are bought and sold under the secrecy of the specialists who are to be found in various Gurage villages.

Environmental and technological factors have their effect on the market economy restricting the growth of certain products and favouring the production of others. Some commodities have become 'special' products of a tribe, such as tobacco, *čat* and pottery from Chaha, *ṭef* and barley from Gumer, peppers from Ennemor, bamboo and palm leaves from Ezha; and these all lend a regional character to the market structure. Specialization of goods and services is protected by the market cycle; this can be related to three features of the market system. First, the regular pattern of market days makes for a wider exchange of local produce and provides outlets for a regional aggregate of villages producing similar products. Secondly, the exchange of products between

TABLE V

Items of Market Transactions 1957–9

I

Grains (*tef*, millet, barley)
Roots for beer
Spices of all varieties
Roasting grains
Coffee

II

Qämä-flour
Äsät-bread

III

Butter
Honey

IV

Cattle
Sheep
Chickens

V

Cotton
Čat
Qanča-fibre

VI

Fresh meat

VII

Oil (kerosene)

VIII

Bananas
Sweet-stalked sorghum
Lemons
Potatoes
Onions
Tomatoes
Cabbage, greens
Eggs

IX

Baskets
Withes for basketry
Tables (basket-style)
Reed mats (*Yəwädärä*)
Palm-leaf mats
Horn spoons

X

Pottery
Fireplace stones for griddles

XI

Bamboo poles
Planks
Firewood
Palm leaves

XII

Clay smoking pipes (indoor and
    outdoor types)
Tobacco

XIII

Decorated skins for bed covers and
    pillows
Cattle hides
Pelts (Civet, gazelle)

XIV

Tin griddles
Beer bottles
Tin cans
Safety pins, buttons, etc.
Dyed yarns
Tea kettles
Umbrellas (cloth and palm)
Glass tumblers
Jewellery (pewter, copper)
Salt

XV

Khaki cloth
Khaki jodhpurs, shirts, shorts
Šamas

XVI

Iron tips for digging sticks
Knives
Wooden bowls
Wooden stools
Wooden head-rests
Wooden mortars and pestles
Wooden shafts for digging
    sticks and axes
Axe heads

lowlands and uplands permits intertribal economic competition without seriously affecting the economy of any one particular locale. Finally, specialization compensates for the poorer economic conditions of some regions owing to peculiar ecological factors. The market cycle tends to maintain economic equilibrium throughout Gurageland by linking the economy of the land to the market system.

III

The market is the meeting ground for widely scattered kin. On the big market days, face-to-face meetings take place which are as important as, if not more important than, economic transactions. The genealogical distance between lineage groups that is normally created by the territorial spacing of them is spanned regularly by the recurrent market cycle. The economic values Gurage attach to coming together in market situations surmount their social separation. Correlated with these factors is the element of time reckoning which is co-ordinated by the functioning of the market cycle. Market gatherings are 'points of reference'; they are a projection into the past of actual relationships between groups of kin.[20] Older remote reunions between agnatic and affinal kin are often recalled, kinship ties restrengthened, and new determinations of kin allegiance asserted. In harmony with these revivals of kin folk, beer is freely drunk and raw meat consumed. Social settings of this order can also be the basis of future relationships. Market situations in general can be points of congregation with geographically distant kin with whom renewed social relations depend on the frequency of the exchange cycle, on the one hand, and on changes in economic conditions, on the other.

Some aspects of Gurage political and ritual systems also find expression through market gatherings. Chiefs and other political figures exercise authority here in an informal atmosphere, often using these large tribal gatherings as a convenient time and place for making new pronouncements of tribal policy. The newly

[20] Evans-Pritchard, op. cit., p. 108, remarks that Nuer time-relations are less a means of co-ordinating events than of co-ordinating relationships and are therefore mainly a looking backwards, since relationships must be explained in terms of the past. But I see the 'past' as one element in the structure of time which establishes a basis for 'future' relations. In this sense, 'time' is a continuum of retrospective and prospective relations.

circumcised adolescents annually announce their approach to the status of manhood by ostentatiously parading through the market site. Ritual agents of the deities also take advantage of the market to make pronouncements concerning the taboos and behaviour to be observed prior to important religious ceremonies. And at all times when markets are held persons afflicted with ritual illness circulate throughout them exhibiting some manifestation of the works of the gods. Thus a corollary of the temporal and spatial structure of the market is its element of social control. What has been said about Tiv markets is applicable to Gurage: the market institution operates alongside other features of the social structure to maintain order and unity; it has continuity over time; it furnishes a means of increasing the range of legitimate influence of political and religious figures.[21]

IV

'*Ab emänä*', is the Gurage term for the itinerant trader. Linguistically and in practise he is literally 'master of the road'. The 'travelling merchant', as he is sometimes called, is distinguished from other traders whose activities are generally confined to the smaller interclan markets; the *ab emänä* trades mainly on an intertribal basis with products acquired outside Gurageland by a relatively substantial cash investment. The local market system is linked up with the wider economic system of Ethiopia principally by the exchange of products between the two systems at each of the markets in the cycle. *Ab emänä* is primarily responsible for introducing what few Western and non-Gurage goods there are in Gurage markets; he is the major means of communication between tribal lands and the outside world, especially so during the rainy season.[22] By linking the tribal economy with that of Ethiopia he brings to Gurage goods obtainable only with cash currency; he carries away in larger quantities an accumulation of individually marketed cash crops, and so he extends the range of the flow of currency throughout Gurageland. And on market day, groups of lesser traders and buyers conspicuously congregate around the itinerant trader selling small quantities of their cash crop holdings. This is usually their initial transaction, for money from these petty sales can later be used to purchase other market commodities.

[21] Bohannan, 1958, p. 63.   [22] See p. 32 above.

In Chapter II it was suggested that Gurage conceptualize the outside world, geographically, in terms of time and distance over which goods and knowledge are interchanged.[23] Here, I have attempted to show that one means by which this conception is made real is through the function of the *ab emänä* in the market system. In the first place, he acts as a medium of social and cultural change by introducing into the exchange system a regulated flow of non-traditional goods that eventually find their way into the total socio-economic system. Secondly, he helps to raise an ostensibly low subsistence level economy to a higher monetary standard by combining the aggregate amount of small cash crop holdings of each homestead through the market system. Finally, he influences the rate of cash crop production by the economic value he assigns to these crops in the local market, his interests being determined by the fluctuating demands of Ethiopia at large for Gurage produce.

LABOUR MIGRATION AND THE ECONOMIC CYCLE

Long ago Gurage men began to leave their homes in search of work and money.[24] Even before cash currency became an important issue in the tribal economy, as it is today, they had developed the habit of travelling hundreds of miles on trading ventures. Largely as a result of these experiences, which brought them into contact with other tribes on the Plateau, they earned the reputation for being judicious in their methods of trading and handling money.[25] However, the increasingly expanding number of Gurage who now migrate specifically for wage labour is of relatively recent origin. It is no doubt a consequence of the Land Act of 1929 which made taxation payable in money.[26]

Gurage villages are practically denuded of young adult males when migration is at its peak. In Endeber, for instance, the Headman and Elders say that at least one man from each homestead is

[23] See p. 34 above.

[24] For instance, Isenberg and Krapf, op. cit., pp. 258-9, write: 'The Guraguena merchants go to Sentshiro [a district of the Walamo tribe], and receive Dirgo (maintenance) from the king till they return to their country'. Similar observations were made of Gurage in Gondar by Bruce, op. cit., Vol. IV, pp. 148-9.

[25] So struck was Cecchi by Gurage skills in trading that he suggested 'might they not descend from Jewish immigrations in Ethiopia?'. 'In habits and moral traits they resemble the Jews of the European ghettos too: cunning, shrewd in business, very covetous of money, somewhat miserly . . . etc.'. Op. cit., p. 56.

[26] *Ministry of Agriculture*, loc. cit.

away at all times during the agricultural off-season. They estimate the absentees to number more than 50 per cent. of the total male population.[27] I have no figures of the number of men away from work in Endeber, or in other areas where migration is said by Gurage to be considerable, but the number of migrants from the village I surveyed can be taken as typical of that found in most villages; the figures are listed below.

TABLE VI

Numbers of Men Away from Village
in Labour Migration

Number of Households	Number of men	Home		Away	
		No.	%	No.	%
41	61	33	52·0	28	46·0

The vast majority of men I have known who migrated did so to obtain funds for immediate or long-term needs. There are others who migrate to solve some immediate personal difficulty which makes it advisable for them to leave home for a time. Labour migration on the whole provides a ready means of escaping domestic and tribal control. The death of a parent and the assumption of authority by an unsympathetic guardian, especially a 'step-mother',[28] is also reason to leave home. For the young unmarried men labour migration provides a means to accumulate money, not so much for bride-wealth itself, a small sum largely borne by the family of the wife, but for a man to have a large marriage feast and later to erect a house for his family. Considerable debt is incurred by the family of a man when a marriage feast is held. This festivity lasts several days, the entire village is invited and, even though a family may not be financially able to support this, it is expected of them. The giving of large feasts at marriage and death

[27] Cf. also the Mambwe in Northern Rhodesia where Watson reports a similar high rate of male labour migration without serious consequences to village organization (1958, pp. 53–71). See also Richards, 1939.

[28] The theme of the bad step-mother is popular in Gurage folklore. In general, disagreeable situations in which a man finds himself are compared with the step-mother. Thus, one proverb recorded by Leslau states: 'the cold of today is like the stick of the step-mother'; 1950, p. 129. On the step-mother in Gurage marriage and family, see p. 127 below.

are the few events in which the economic status of the individual can be conspicuously shown and still receive social approval. Accumulated savings of earnings are readily spent on such functions.

The recourse to labour migration as a source of income is, ostensibly, to raise or at least to maintain the standard of living at home. Migration is mainly, but not wholly, the affair of young men; older men have a greater conservatism and they receive gifts in cash and goods from younger wage-earning relatives. A young man usually has a greater need of cash, fewer attachments to the homestead, and at least one trip abroad is an assertion of his independence of kinsmen and a symbol of manhood. Since there are practically no sources of wage labour in Gurageland, those who migrate realize that the only possible way to earn and save money is by leaving the tribal lands. And as far as most men are concerned, leaving their homes to work has no disastrous effect on their families. Labour migration contributes greatly to the general prosperity of Gurageland. Thus men feel, as I will explain below, that their absence is not the sole contributing factor to changes that have occurred in Gurage life.

But, in the main, a migrant learns little from his labour activities that can be of use to him or his family, or the wider community. I have not heard of any instance where new agricultural techniques have been acquired, though some men have increased their land holdings with money earned through migration. The drift away from Gurageland is slow. There is no wholesale abandonment of *äsät* cultivation in favour of wage labour, neither is there a decline in its importance, nor a slackening-off in method of horticulture. It cannot be emphasized too strongly that land within the tribal boundaries is the ultimate of social and economic security, and wage labour is an expedient by which Gurage attempt to achieve this. And though some of them never do, for they never return to the home lands, they feel that they will and make firm asseverations that this will be so.

Men are constantly in touch with tribal affairs since migration tends to be mainly seasonal and the great majority of men return home sooner or later. Not only that, they seem to associate mainly with other Gurage when abroad, and common ties thus formed are sometimes given concrete expression. Organizations for self-help are formed, such as *Iqub* and *Idir*, different from the ritual association of *Gurda*, with recruitments that cut across lineage, clan, and religious bonds; economic benefits from these associations assist unemployed fellow tribesmen.[29] Tribal cohesion does not seem to be weakened as a result of labour migration.

The ordinary short-term absence of the husband-father does not seem to create grave social and economic discomforts for his wife or wives or for his children. However, deserted families do often suffer extreme difficulties, if not actual poverty, from prolonged absences of the father. In one case of family desertion, a wife, having migrated with her husband, was sent home after a short stay in Addis Ababa. During two years of separation, the husband had made only two fleeting visits and homestead responsibilities were assumed by his younger unmarried brother. The wife made no complaints, at least not when I questioned her, but neighbours freely criticized the absent husband for they felt that he had abandoned his family responsibilities. Though the village was not forced to bear additional agricultural labours since the husband's brother attended to these, the villagers responded to the normal social duties arising from inter-homestead relations which have been described above.

The conservatism of some older Gurage militates against the idea of young men leaving home. Elders complain that migration makes young people disrespectful and insubordinate; the influences of *Säwa*[30] cause young men to rebel against traditional forms of discipline. Of the older men, one of the greatest fears which underlies their conservatism is that young men will become 'Amharaized' which implies that they will develop the tendency to look down with disfavour on tribal ways and customs. Elders have what is to them a sound basis for these apprehensions, for some young men do criticize the old ways which have not kept pace with the *sillatane* that gives a distinctive character to Addis Ababa, setting it apart from the rural environment. Some older Gurage strongly assert that they would not permit their daughters to marry a well-seasoned migrant. They regard with apprehension a son-in-law who might leave the homelands for good, making it difficult for their daughter to visit her family or to bring gifts on the

[29] A summary account of self-help institutions in urban Ethiopia is given by Pankhurst and Eshete, 1958.

[30] The Gurage commonly refer to the Government as '*Säwa*', i.e. Shoa Province or Addis Ababa. Henceforth, I follow the Gurage usage of *Säwa* throughout this study.

Transplanting *mätkyä*, the third planting stage of *äsät*

Women decorticating *äsät* at harvest

Young Gurage girls
carrying water

A Gurage woman in typical
head-dress

occasion of the annual feast provided for such a visit. Most important in all these apprehensions, some of the older generation believe that a long career as a labour migrant makes it difficult for a man to settle down with his wife. This belief is not totally unfounded.

Most elders can cite examples of married men who have taken a second 'wife' from amongst the number of detribalized women in Addis Ababa. Seasonal migration is consistent with the marital arrangement of these men, and for some of them it provides a means of maintaining semi-permanent sexual ties without the responsibilities involved in marriage. I have no statistics on the number of matings of this kind, on the marital state of migrants, or as to what extent migration has affected the stability of marriage in general. However, I was repeatedly told that divorce has not increased as a result of migration, and in view of the unstable character of Gurage marriages which normally gives rise to divorce and separation, this claim seems reasonable. Migration may well be a contributing factor and most probably is, but it cannot be easily separated from other more obvious social and cultural causes, nor definitely said to be the only one.

In this chapter I have described various aspects of Gurage economy; the system of cultivation, the allocation of land for cash crop farming, the intertribal relationships in the market system and the pattern of labour migration within the economic cycle. The homestead composed of a group of agnatic kin is the basic economic unit. The village is composed of a group of homesteads, the people of which in living and working together co-operate in a number of economic and social activities. Each village participates in the tribal market system through the action of its members who barter and sell products from their holdings. The holdings from each homestead can be divided roughly into three: one part for home consumption, one part for the local tribal market, and one part for the Ethiopian-wide cash market. Every homestead that cultivates *äsät* has at least one cash crop, the *qanča*-fibres which have a marketable value. The tribal market system links clans and their smaller divisions in economic and social relations.

Labour migration is extensive in Gurageland and each village appears to have many able-bodied men who are away every season earning wages. The traditional obligations of kin relations within the agnatic group work towards a sharing of homestead responsibilities, allowing those members who desire it to have the opportunity to work abroad. There are no local wage markets in any Gurage village and the vast majority migrate to Addis Ababa. Moreover, there has been no noticeable change in material culture, which symbolizes 'progress', as a consequence of increased cash income. Most earnings are invested in cattle, land when it is available, and in meeting marriage and other social obligations; there is no trend towards the purchase of luxury goods. Wage labour to the Gurage is profitable in terms of raising the standard of living and relieving population pressure.

CHAPTER IV

Kinship, Local Organization, Family, and Marriage

T HE Gurage, unlike other Semitic Ethiopian tribes, are a patriline-ally organized people. One line of descent, the male, is emphasized, and the most characteristic social relations are those between agnatic male kindred. Kinship prevails in everyday life, ramifying through the other aspects of social, economic, and even political, organization, and most of the important Gurage institutions are built around consanguineal and affinal relations in homestead and village. This chapter looks at Gurage social structure, and how it actually appears on the ground as it is reflected in a number of small village communities which contain closely related agantic kin. Local agnatic based communities form wider lineage and territorial units; Gurage political organization to be discussed in the chapter that follows is set against this background.

THE KINSHIP STRUCTURE

The basic unit of the Gurage household, *abärus*, is the family and the terms used between its members set the pattern of the kinship system. Husband and wife commonly address each other with personal names and rarely does one hear the terms *məs* and *məšt*, respectively, except in second person usage. *Ab tadot* is the term for parents, but usually they are distinguished according to sex: father is *aba*, and mother is *adot*. Children are seldom distinguished according to sex until after they have been named, the ceremony of which takes place when the mother 'comes out' of confinement; this is two months after a child is born. Since children take the name of their father, it is held to be an ill omen if they die at childbirth or shortly thereafter while bearing his name. Until children are formally named they are simply called *təka*, baby, or child; later, a son is called *ärč* and a daughter

The Gurage: A People of the Ensete Culture

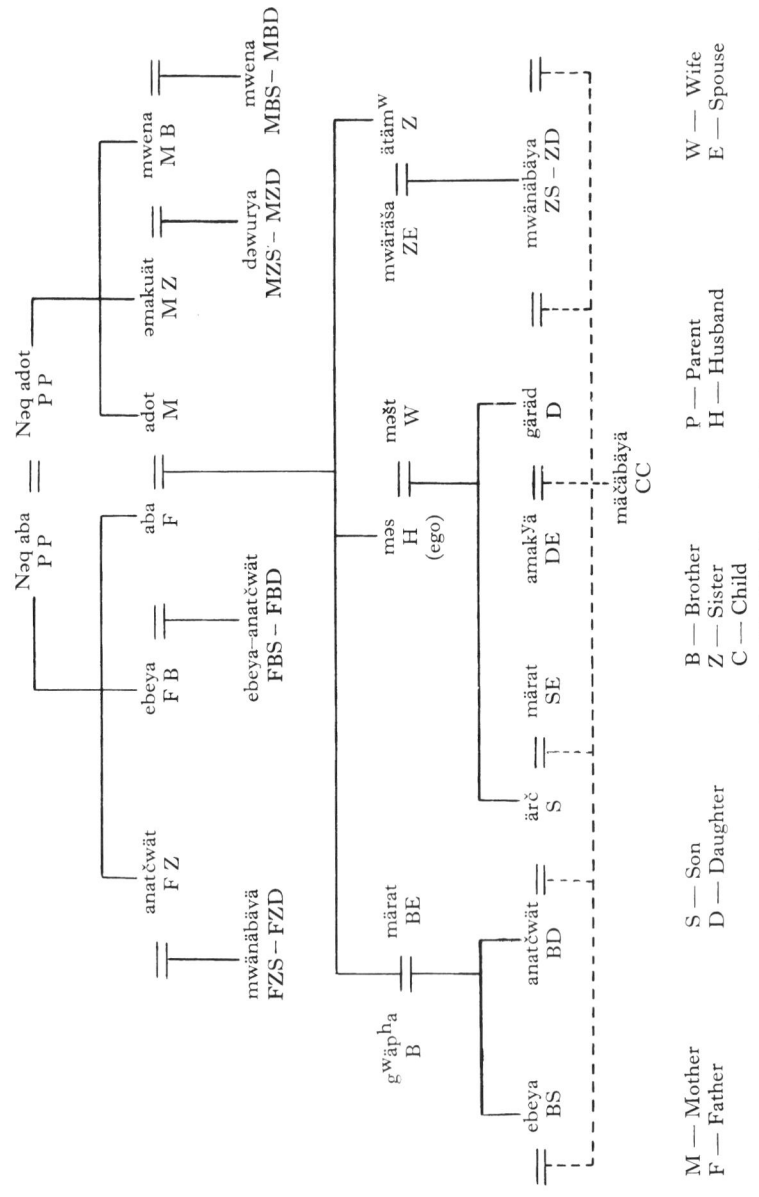

FIG. 8. Gurage Kinship Terminology.

gäräd, the plural of these being *dängya* and *gəred*, respectively. When girls reach the age of marriage they are referred to as *zeä gäräd*.

In the first ascending generation any father's brother is distinguished from the father by the term *ebeya*, the literal meaning of which is something like 'little father'; this term is also extended to all males of the father's clan. Again, there is no terminological distinction based on relative seniority in the female line, any father's sister is *anatčwät*, and females of the clan into which she marries are sometimes so termed; similarly, any mother's sister is *əmakuät*, all mother's brothers and males of the mother's clan are called *mwena*.[1]

In the grandparents' generation the same terms are used on both sides; *nəq aba* and *nəq adot*, 'big father' and 'big mother',

TABLE VII

Gurage Terms of Relationship

Gurage term	English translation
aba	father
adot	mother
ebeya	father's brother, father's brother's son, brother's son
anatčwät	father's sister, father's brother's daughter, brother's daughter
mwänäbäya	father's sister's son and daughter; sister's son and daughter
mwena	mother's brother, mother's brother's son and daughter
əmakuät	mother's sister
dəwurya	mother's sister's son and daughter
nəq aba	grandfather
nəq adot	grandmother
mäčäbäyä	grandchildren
məs	husband
məšt	wife
gwäpha	brother
ätämw	sister
gäräd	daughter
ärč	son
amakyä	male in-laws
mwäräša	sister's husband
märat	female in-laws
amat	mother-in-law

[1] Leslau, 1950, has recorded the term *akäbäya* for mother's brother, but this appears to be the Ennemor Gurage equivalent for *mwena*. Following Murdock's classification of African kinship systems, Gurage kinship is the 'Descriptive Cousin Terminology' type. Murdock, 1959, p. 29.

respectively. The behaviour patterns to the father's father and to the mother's father differ sharply; there is submissive respect on the paternal side against familiarity on the maternal side. Kinship is seldom traced further back than the grandparents, and if so, it is only through the father's father.

In ego's own generation reciprocal terms are used between siblings of the same sex, but no distinctions are made according to age; brothers call each other *gʷäpʰa*, sisters call sisters *ätämʷ*. Those of the opposite sex use these same terms. Younger siblings of both sexes address elder brothers as *abi*, and elder sisters, *awo*. As for parallel and cross-cousins, they are never classed with siblings. Children of the paternal uncle are distinguished according to sex but not age and the two generations are merged; all male descendants are classed with their father and called *ebeya*, females are classed with the father's sister, *anatčwät*. Parallel cousins on the mother's side are all called by the same term *dəwurya*, sex and age distinctions are lacking. Cross-cousins on both sides are distinguished by separate terms, those on the paternal side of both sexes being called *mwänäbäyä*; similarly, on the maternal side they are called *mwena*; again sex and age distinctions are not made. But in the next descending generation children of paternal parallel cousins are classed with children of male siblings, whereas children of paternal cross-cousins are called the same as female siblings' children.

In general, the husband calls all male affines, including his wife's father, *amakʸä*, except his sister's husband who is called *mwäräša*. He calls all female affines of his and the next descending generation *märat*, which means literally 'girls of the same age', but for specific purposes they are referred to by name. His wife's mother is called *amat*.

Kinship affects sexual relations, it determines the behaviour patterns of persons formally recognized in the system of terminology, but does not prescribe preferential mating in Gurage society. Gurage have no institutional form of preferential mating. As we shall see, marriage is customarily arranged between exogamous kin groups by the parents of the prospective bride and groom; seldom does the woman know her future husband and usually her first meeting with him takes place at the marriage feast. But though a man does not obtain a wife through the rules of kinship, there are still numerous prohibitions on marriage between close and distant kin, and putative kin. Marriage and cohabitation is prohibited between all agnatic relatives, all women to whom a man is related in the direct line of descent, all half-sisters, their daughters, and half-sisters of either parent. A man cannot take a wife from his mother's minimal or minor lineage, and it would be equally unthinkable for him to marry into his mother's clan; the practice among the Amhara and Tigre tribes which permits a man to marry into his mother's or father's line as long as seven generations separates the spouses, is incestuous to the Gurage. The same attitude is held toward a man who marries or cohabits with his mother-in-law or his step-daughter, regardless of their clan affiliation.

Some Gurage tribes show a definite preference for maintaining ties through intermarriage. In the past, more so than today, such marriages served to strengthen military and economic positions. On the other hand, wives of ritual chiefs are taken only from the maximal lineage of the clan that traditionally fulfilled this function, and that lineage has rights vested in the ritual office. As in the case of the ritual office of 'the Lord of *Wågäpháča*', representative of *Waq*, the deity of Gurage men, power and wealth associated with the office tend to be strengthened through interclan 'ritual' marriages.[2]

While the levirate and sororate forms of 'secondary unions' are practised, they are not prescribed by rules of kinship nor enforced by institutional sanctions.[3] In such cases the person replacing the original party to the marriage is regarded as a bodily substitute, and not as an independent spouse. A man is not obligated to marry the wife of his deceased brother; the lineage of a wife is not compelled to replace her when she dies, or if she is barren, with her sister. But for a man, there are social and economic advantages accruing from heading a dual family and this is made possible through leviratic practices. By such means a man gains control over additional land which increases his status and prestige, and his nephews give him additional protection in the homestead which in the past was an asset. For a woman, there are no economic advantages entailed in sororate unions though they do afford a means for some women to obtain a first marriage and for others,

[2] See pp. 181–4 below.

[3] The position of secondary unions here is the same as that obtaining among the Southern Bantu; namely an extension of an existing marriage. See Schapera, 1950, p. 149.

a second marriage. As it is often said, a Gurage woman would prefer to be the step-mother of her sister's children than to be among the few, never married, 'worthless' women.

In short, Gurage kinship terminology places an emphasis on the roles of individuals within the structure of kin relations, rather than on the classification of kin *per se*.[4] The immediate and future roles of agnatic kin are defined and given especial stress. It is more important that the role of a man in the system of relations should be defined; he is a potential father, that is, a 'little father'; it is less important that he should be considered, as it were, the 'father's brother'. Role definition lies at the core of the system upon which the agnatic line is built. The pivot of the system is the father who, as we noted above, is called *aba*. The father's brother, his son, and his son's son all derive their term of relationship, *ebeya*, that is, their role in the system, from the root *aba*. On the contrary, women do not hold permanent membership in the agnatic group, they are taken out of the system upon marriage, and the terminology indicates that they are not regarded as permanent members. For this reason the mother's and father's sisters are given separate terms from those of their children. The behaviour pattern of familiarity toward the mother's brother and his children is basically the same, which might explain their being called by the same term. The term *mwänäbäyä*, which appears on both the maternal and paternal sides, translates literally as 'child of a woman of the agnatic line'. But I cannot account for the term *dəwurya*, mother's sister's children; a term that does not appear elsewhere in the terminology for kin. It has been suggested that both of these variations may indicate that the system is shifting from a bilateral to a patrilineal direction in keeping with the agnatic lineage structure; the term *dəwurya* might have been recently introduced.[5]

Gurage kinship system employs descriptive cousin terminology which is characteristic of Semitic Ethiopian tribes, but Gurage reckon descent patrilineally as do most other tribes in the Ensete Culture Complex.[6] But unlike the Semitic Amhara and Tigre, the Gurage have no institutional relationships established along cognatic lines whereby property, status, and titles are distributed. The agnatic kindred are the most important in Gurage society;

---

[4] I am grateful to Professor Firth for helpful comments and suggestions in summarizing these features of the kinship system.

[5] As suggested by Professor Fred Eggan.   [6] See Shack, 1963a.

they form the corporate group in the homestead and the community which is exclusive of members traced through women. A Gurage never denies kinship with any close kin, maternal or paternal; such an omission would be considered wrong. But the duties of maternal kin to a man are of little consequence relative to those of his paternal kin. The kin of the mother are not obligated to defend a man, to perform morturary rites for him, or to support his heirs, and if they perform any of these it is not as a consequence of institutional norms of kinship behaviour. The mother's brother is just as much kin as the father's brother, but the maternal uncle cannot in any circumstances be 'little father' to his sister's sons. Gurage have no term such as *mar*, as used by the Nuer, to bring into the system anyone to whom a man can trace relationship.[7]

The extensive distribution of prohibitions against marriage and cohabitation with women traced through the mother as well as female affines, and the lack of a firmly rooted institution of the sororate, all tend to emphasize the exclusiveness of the agnatic group and the autonomy of the political segments formed by agnatic kin relationships. An overall view of Gurage society suggests that the structural opposition of groups in its widest sense begins, at one point, on the principles of the corporate agnatic group.

It is worthwhile noting at this point some structural features of Gurage kinship in terms of bridewealth and marriage patterns. Marriage transfers a woman's fertility absolutely to the agnatic kin group of her husband, and an essential element in the contract is that she have children. For reasons prefaced to the beginning of this study, I lack enough statistical details of the frequency of divorce in Gurage marriage, but it is said to be high. The marriage ceremonial is complicated and chiefly expressed by the hostility and conciliation of the two lineages concerned in 'ritual vituperation'.[8] Bridewealth hardly exists, the possibility of divorce hangs

----

[7] Evans-Pritchard, 1951. I note, however, that the Gurage term for defining the agnatic kin of the household, *däbwa*, is sometimes used to refer to paternal and maternal 'relatives' generally, though the extension of the term beyond the aggregate of household kin does not define institutionalized social, economic, and political relationships. In this sense its linguistic usage appears to be chiefly that of defining a category of members related by consanguineal and affinal ties. Further description is given on p. 95 below.

[8] A term used by Monica Wilson, to describe a similar feature of Nyakyusa marriage ceremonial. See Wilson, 1957, p. 223. Described for the Gurage on p. 123 below.

over every marriage, men divorce their wives easily and at personal will yet Gurage women are not, in Gluckman's terms, 'straining to be released'. The extreme endurance of the rights of a Gurage husband are passed on his death to his agnatic heirs. The rights of inheritance are vested in children exclusively from the agnatic lineage of their father. Only unredeemed illegitimate children have rights in their mother's family; I am not certain how they rank with other members of her agnatic lineage under such conditions.

Gurage data provide little support to the thesis that marriage payments fall with the decreasing dominance of patrilineal descent.[9] It is tempting to suggest the opposite, but distributional studies have proved this to be unsound. The consequences of marriage, the affiliation of children, the transmittal of property, all reflect on the attributes of the marriage payment. But other less tangible factors in the structure of the kinship system, such as the morals and laws which sanction the stability of Gurage marriages, and the relations between affines which affect this stability, override the functional purpose of bridewealth, in goods or services.[10] Later in this chapter I show that the moral and ritual systems tend to act as a counterpoise to stabilize marital unions. Even so, bridewealth has a bearing on affinal relationships and the character of the agnatic group and these are important among the Gurage.

Gurage cognatic ties are not strengthened through the payment of bridewealth which is neither a substantial amount nor is it distributed amongst kin on both sides. Indeed, such ties would work in opposition to the authority of the agnatic principle which is present in all other aspects of Gurage social, political, and ritual life. In point of fact, no Gurage would put up with the sharing of his land or its produce with his mother's brother or with his wife's male kin; he is often unwilling to share his land and its produce with members of his own agnatic group. There may be a danger of overstating the case for a lack of strong institutional ties existing outside the agnatic group. Yet I am not suggesting that Gurage have manipulated their structure of kin relations to conform with such economic conditions as land shortage. Environ-

[9] Gluckman, 1950, p. 200. Cf. also Fallers, 1957.

[10] See DeLuchon, 1945. The author presents the thesis that marriage is unstable in Gurage because the man's family makes no substantial bridewealth payment. But DeLuchon fails to consider other features of Gurage social structure that can be related to marriage instability.

mental factors are not solely responsible for the cleavage and opposition between cognatic and affinal kin, nor for fission within the agnatic group itself. But they are important. The factors that hinge on the quest for land and its consequences in Gurage society cannot be underestimated in the analysis of Gurage kinship.

On the other hand, without doubt, Gurage kinship has been influenced by the patrilineal Sidamo, but the extent to which this has obtained can only be determined by the comparative method, if then, and such data are at present lacking. It is conceivable that the balanced bilateral features characteristic of Semitic Ethiopian kinship, such as in naming and inheritance, and as witnessed in Gurage terminology, have given way as much to Sidamo influences as to adaptation to the ecological setting of South-West Ethiopia, where land shortage and population pressure are crucial. These and other features of Gurage kinship have even greater meaning in the setting of lineage and territorial organization to which we now turn.

TERRITORIAL ORGANIZATION: THE VILLAGE

The Gurage village is the smallest territorial and political unit. It occupies a defined area of land, the ownership rights over which belong to members of the local community, and its boundaries are recognized by groups living outside it. The political unit is formed by the community and the community is a local aggregate of related patrilineal homesteads, the heads of which exercise authority over internal village matters.[11] Village heads act in conjunction with other village heads in a system of alliances to form the basis of intervillage politics. These and all other relations grow out of the core of the village which I call the *minor lineage*, composed of an indeterminate number of homesteads related by actual or fictional kin ties. The permanent existence of the minor lineage is ensured so long as a single descendant of the lineage founder remains alive. Gurage include in the minor lineage not only living members but also their ancestors; the dead, those people who are now a part of the past, form symbolic reference points linking them to the present members of the community.

[11] Although members of different clans are sometimes found in the same village, this is not the norm. But in such cases all homestead heads participate equally in local affairs; if marriage takes place within the village clan exogamy is observed. See also p. 92 below.

Ideally all inhabitants of a Gurage village should be related. Older Gurage affirm this by pointing out that village composition in the past was always based on kinship. It is difficult to know if this was the norm throughout Gurageland in bygone days, but at present, in what I have termed 'older' areas of settlement, there is a preponderance of kin-related homesteads. In villages of relatively more recent origin, however, all the inhabitants may not be related through the same ancestors, but their descendants will in time all adopt a single line of descent. Village exogamy is practised even where two local families have no known genealogical or fictional relation. The exogamous character of the minor lineage demands that men seek their wives from the outside, making the village less self-sufficient in this respect.

The village may be spoken of as a corporate group[12] which controls the rights of ownership and use of its residential and arable land. It may own grazing land and streams independently, or these may be shared with neighbouring settlements. Village heads, as representatives of the minor lineage, uphold the rights in village land as a corporate body; no homestead can dispose of its land to an 'outsider', that is, one from another clan, without approval from minor lineage heads. The control of land by the corporate group is a means of restricting the expansion of the community through immigration. Thus a person may change his residence by moving to another village, becoming attached to or adopted by a homestead there, but full membership in the community can be obtained only through the ownership of land. Land ownership implies lineage affiliation and all its ramifications in the organization and structure of community affairs. A 'stranger' has no place in a Gurage village since his presence would be in contradiction to the ideology of the village as expressed in *wänäkä*.

The headman and elders of the village meet often to make economic and political decisions. Economic assemblies are frequently called to discuss the formation of work parties, the distribution of market goods, or the sale of cash crops. Political assemblies are called less frequently than economic ones, and they may be called by any adult male of the village or by the village headman. Inter-

[12] I am using 'corporate group' in the sense that Radcliffe-Brown has defined it. A group may be considered corporate if its members, or its adult members, or a considerable proportion of them, come together occasionally to carry out some collective action; if it has representatives who act for the group as a whole; if it possesses or controls property. Radcliffe-Brown and Forde, 1950, p. 41.

woven through both types of assembly is the thread of *yäwänäkä säb*, which reinforces the principles of village life. The daily pattern of intravillage behaviour favours visiting so that people often see each other and frequently stop to chat and drink coffee or *ṭälla*-beer, and eat *äsät*-bread or roasted grains, as they pass each other's homes. All of this reduces, in one way or another, the formal character of village behaviour.

Village men form the core of local politics. They participate in discussions and they make decisions, but Elders actually administer the decisions taken in assembly. Elders come together more often than young men and in a variety of circumstances: to reiterate old political pronouncements merely for the satisfaction derived from having relived, for the moment, an occasion when a decision vital to the welfare of the community was reached; to argue some important judicial matter which will be settled sometime in the indefinite future, although some past historical event has given precedent on which judgement will be based. A favourite pastime of adult Gurage men is debating both actual and unreal situations merely for the sake of discussion. In this way, some men develop skill in the art of litigation, on which tribal-wide status and reputation are built.

On the contrary, women have fewer occasions to meet together apart from work chores in the *äsät* field; usually they meet as a body only when they gather with their husbands or male kin. Religious ceremonials restricted to women, such as the *Näqʷa* and *Dämʷamʷit* festivals,[13] are the chief events at which they meet as a sex.

The village political and judicial system is the primary source of social control at the local level. It is recognized by *Šäwa* which has not interferred to any marked degree with its traditional form and function; it retains the village headman at the pivot of village political life. In Chapter V I deal with some recent modifications to the role of the headman.

Although villages are largely economically self-sufficient, they maintain relations with neighbouring villages. The extent of social relations varies more or less concomitantly with the spatial distances between them. The geographical distance between settlements is directly proportional to the structural distance between minor lineages. People in neighbouring kin-related villages

---

[13] See Chapter VI below, p. 175; p. 185 *passim*.

normally have a higher frequency of intervillage relations than those farther removed in spatial and genealogical distances. Reciprocity as a principle of intervillage relations varies in the same way. The sanctions governing behaviour of individuals towards members of a village are most strongly exerted when the village is far removed in lineage and physical space. The breakdown of intervillage relations culminating in quarrels and fights occurs oftener between widely separated lineages of the same clan or even of different clans, than between closely related lineages of the same clan.

The ideal composition of a Gurage village, as stated above, is that all men living there are members of the same minor lineage. Elder Gurage usually give an explanation of this ideal by constructing a genealogical model based on a living male in the community. They can demonstrate with this model, whenever they take the time and effort to do so, that any male member of the minor lineage can be traced to the founder of the clan. Gurage are not faced with the problem that often confronts other Semitic tribes in Ethiopia, of tracing their ancestors' relationship to the area of settlement beyond three or four generations.

A Gurage knows he is a Gurage and he can prove it whenever the occasion calls for it. As he would say, he knows his '*zär*', a word which is translated as his 'origin'.[14] In beginning to trace his *zär*, or that of another, in the lineage tree, a Gurage tends to take as a point of departure a married man who has already procreated a family, rather than a young single man. Gurage give several reasons for this, one being the uncontrollable factor of life expectancy. Children often die young. Thus, a branch of a lineage tree may never reach full maturity through them. Another reason is that nowadays young unmarried men often leave the tribal land for good without establishing a household, which means in fact that they do not perpetuate the lineage. Young Gurage, and especially those who annually migrate, are thought of by older men as being a part of the expansible nature of the lineage rather than a part of the stabilizing element of the lineage. Thus Elders often exclude young 'unstable' men from the household and village census.

---

[14] The term *zär* above is not to be confused with '*zär*', which also means 'rainy season' (p. 32 above); or with the Amharic '*zar*', which refers to the possessive spirit of that name.

The depth of a lineage is also expansible, depending upon the number of generations included and the point of departure for counting ascendants. A lineage may begin with ego, his father, or ego's grandfather or great-grandfather. However, an adult male usually includes about three generations in his lineage; a young boy might name four, but in either instance, from their point of view, this is the lowest level of the lineage. This is what I term a *minimal lineage*. It is the domestic group of a homestead consisting of a man, his wife, married sons and their wives, and unmarried sons and daughters. The Gurage word to describe this aggregate of agnatic kin is *däbwa*, a term that has most analytical value when defining a category in which the relationship between persons is by virtue of membership in the group. It has little use in descriptive terminology; *däbwa* does not define individual relations within the homestead as they are described by the terms of kinship, as shown above. In common everyday usage the term *bet säb* is employed to designate individual agnates; this means 'man of the household'.

However, apart from the linguistic distinctions between *abärus*, 'household', and *däbwa*, agnatic kin of the household, also of importance are the sociological distinctions. *Abärus* is used to designate an aggregate of individuals in a household, or the combined number of households in a homestead, a compound, without specific reference to the genealogical composition of the group. This is not true of *däbwa*. A household may vary considerably in its composition; a single elementary family, or an extended family headed by the father, father's brother, or grandfather, and attached to the household may be adopted kin and individuals with non-kin status. In lineage terminology, *abärus* has only a minimal value, its use is best restricted to kinship *per se*. On the other hand, *däbwa* does not include the cognatic category of kindred, for which group, in fact, I have recorded no specific term.

The Gurage term for lineage is *ṭəb*. Gurage make no terminological distinctions of descent groups regardless of their genealogical depth. As they explain it figuratively, a person enters the *ṭəb* at birth passing through the *ənfoča*, the 'entrance' or 'doorway', thereby gaining membership in the lineage and rights of citizenship in the community. Each Gurage village is a part of a *ṭəb*; a number of villages compose a group of *ṭəb* which, in turn, form a larger *ṭəb* structure. Therefore the totality of *ṭəb*-related villages, dispersed throughout a number of *ṭəb*-related districts, comprises the entire *ṭǝb* or clan territory. A clan is merely one large *ṭǝb*. A village is a small *ṭǝb*. In sociological terms, the geographical distribution of villages within the clan's territory, corresponds directly with their structural relationship, in genealogical terms, in the *ṭǝb* lineage or clan.

But Gurage do not think in terms of differential segments of lineages, as I have expressed them above. As far as Gurage are concerned, every male tracing descent to the mythical clan founder is a 'relative', more specifically, a 'brother', and this relationship is sometimes expressed with even greater intimacy by extension of the kinship term *ebeya*; rightfully he is a member of the *ṭǝb*. Any segment of a clan may be simultaneously expressed under the term *ṭǝb*, or each segment may be singled out when necessary. But the corresponding use of *ṭǝb* must be separated, since a village community presupposes habitation of a common territory, while a lineage, a *ṭǝb*, is a group determined by agnatic descent from a common ancestor. The composition of village and *ṭǝb* groups is not the same. For one reason, women are brought into the village from other clans. For another, there are often persons attached to homesteads in non-kin relationships, such as domestic servants and friends who extend their visit indefinitely. The lineage and the village are not the same. But the lineage structures the Gurage village, for the village is organized about the core of the patri-lineage and the lineage gives the village its principle of continuity.[15] Lineage groups have different functions in relations to one another and as a part of the lineage system as a whole. This we shall see later, but these functions can be best understood in the light of some preliminary form of classification.

In a word, in every Gurage village, two features of lineage organization are commonly found: a significant number of adult males are related through the minor lineage, and the principles of clan organization determine membership in the village.

I turn now to the *major lineage*. This is what I term a cluster of closely located and related villages. An older cluster of villages is known by a name which applies to all of the related villages as a group. Thus if a man says that he is *Siqora* or *Jegär*, the meaning implied is twofold: it is the name of his major lineage and it is the

---

[15] The structural similarity between Bwamba and Gurage villages has permitted me to draw upon the analysis made for a Bwamba village by Winter, 1956, p. 88.

name of his 'sub-district' as well. For instance, *Jegär* would not be the name of his village; a village may or may not have an ancestral name, whereas a sub-district is invariably named after the founder of the major lineage. A Gurage would consider himself as a *Siqora*, the major lineage to which his village is related, and not as an 'Astepo', which could be the name of his village. However, relative to the levels of segmentation above and below it, the major lineage has slight function in the wider system of Gurage political, economic, and ritual relations. It is primarily a division in time and space which seems to have sociological meaning chiefly in terms of the geographical distribution of segmented social groups, for in all other ways the *maximal lineage* is of greater importance to the Gurage.

THE DISTRICT

A territorial division occupied by a number of related major *ṭəb* is what I call a 'district' and what a Gurage refers to as his *gän* ('country'). A district is built up on the minimal, minor, and major lineages, the territorial expansion of which depends, more or less, on the number of lineage groups, and their density of population. As with some other Gurage terms, *gän* also lacks sociological clarity; it may be used to refer to a village, district, or tribal area, but *gän* is most frequently used to designate a district. Similarly, when asked the name of his *gän* a man usually gives a name such as *Amya* or *Gura* which denotes a region having the sociological form which I have described for a district; he does not as a rule give the name of his village or some wider territorial area.

Historical as well as sociological meaning is associated with the linguistic usage of *gän*; it signifies a point of reference in geographical time and space. To a Gurage, *gän* is also his genealogical reference point where the maximal *ṭəb* values, in historical or present social and political contexts, are given their fullest expression. Beyond this point of ascent, in genealogical reckoning, the values and idioms associated with the clan and tribe are difficult to realize, and are only occasionally manifest in periodic ceremonial and ritual situations. Not only that, the difficulty of establishing ancestors becomes greater the farther back the search is pressed. Young men seldom know them. Young men are more versed in the commonly related myths and folktales that rarely include remote ancestors, and older persons frequently disagree on the number and order of remote ancestors in the line of descent. When disputes arise between Gurage during the discussion of their genealogies, disagreements always seem to cluster round the more distant points in lineage time. Only certain Elders possessing specialized knowledge of tribal history can settle these disputes, not always to the satisfaction of all those concerned. Young boys are commonly instructed in the names of their immediate ancestors, while remote forefathers merely form part of the oral tradition. Gurage oral tradition has relative historical value but it lacks genealogical accuracy; it is often more fancy than fact.

On the other hand, descent traced between minimal and minor, or minimal and major, or maximal, lineages, can generally be expressed with exactness and precision. Moreover, a significant number of concrete political and ritual relations between these lineage groups, involving Elders, headmen, and clan and religious chiefs, takes place at the district level. The district is that part of the lineage structure in which several major *ţəb* form an apex within the total system of descent. This apex forms what I term a *maximal lineage*; it is built up on the aggregate of major lineages converging at a point in genealogical distance.

Let me illustrate this. The three largest groups of the Mogä-mänä clan of Chaha live in the districts of Amya, Yädäbe, and Gura. Spread unevenly throughout these districts are a number of major lineages; they form in varying groupings the maximal lineages *Gwetagänzya, Abicзwä*, and *Addamädäwa*. The apex of each maximal lineage is linked to form a single line with a descendant of the clan founder; at the lowest level of descent, the village, are the youngest living descendants of the clan founder. A skeleton diagram of this arrangement of lineages is given in Fig. 9. In a structural sense each maximal lineage is in total opposition to every other maximal lineage, but on the ground, in actual situations, opposition between maximal lineage groups diminishes relatively according to the kinds of situations involving lineage interaction. In the past, the highest degree of opposition which could develop into open conflict, existed in political relations between maximal *ţəb*, as a consequence of efforts at territorial expansion. As each district is territorially and politically autonomous, it seeks to retain its independence while at the same time combining with other districts to form a common body for the clan.

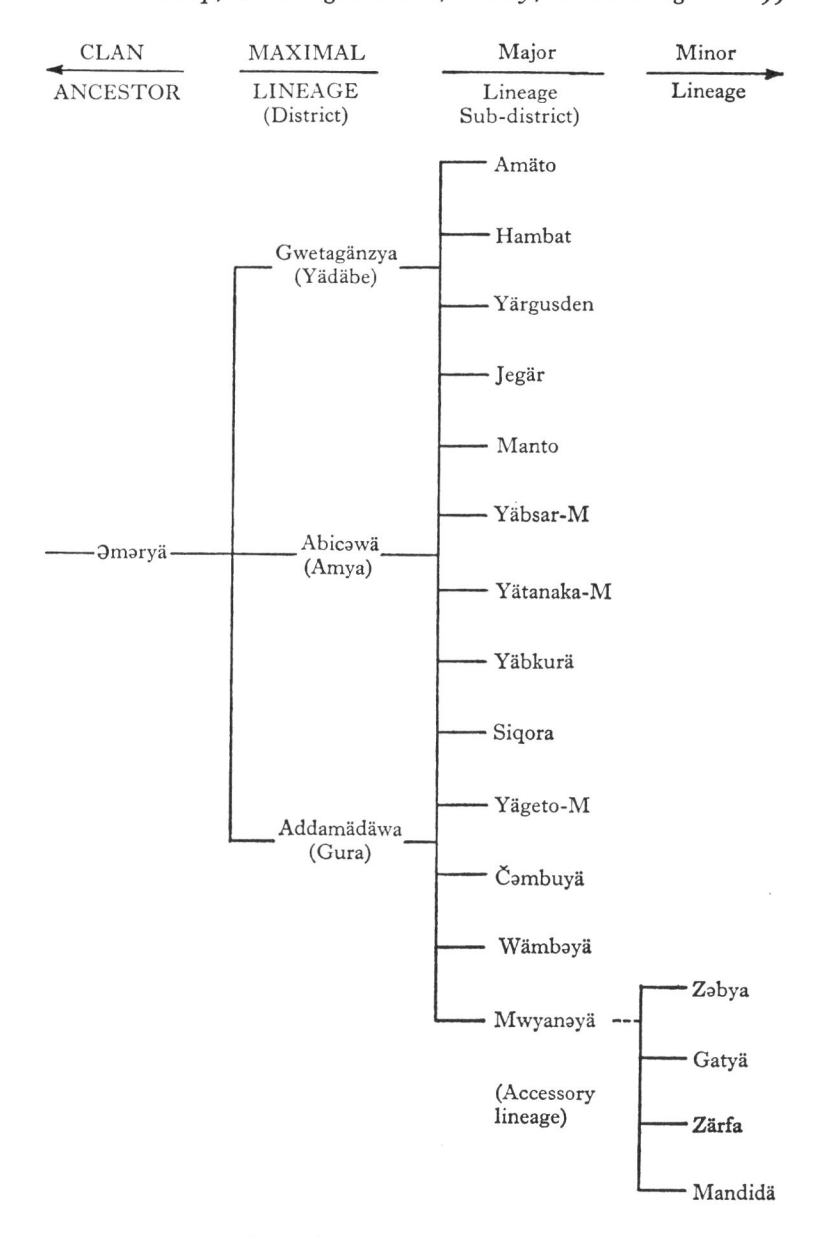

FIG. 9. The Interrelationship of Component Lineages of
the Mogämänä Clan.

In economic relations, stress and strain between structurally opposing districts is reduced considerably through market exchange, although competition to corner a portion of the market for cash crops may often result in a temporary increase in economic conflict. But it is in the arena of ritual relations that maximal lineage opposition is chiefly tempered.

The relationship of lineages illustrated can be taken one step further, to the village level of lineage organization. Astepo, a village, is one of a cluster of villages related through an eponymous founder of the sub-district named Siqora. Woldä is a man of the village Astepo. Beginning with his father, Woldä traces his genealogy back five generations to the lineage ancestor Siqora, who forms the apex of Woldä's major lineage. There is a depth then of five steps between Woldä's minimal and major *ʈəb* in present day reckoning, but his lineage is potentially expansible through his children to the Nth generation. Siqora is an example of an older sub-district in the Chaha tribe which in rough calculations has an origin dating back to more than 125 years.

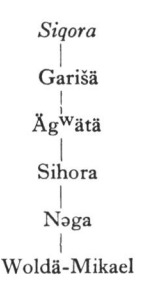

Siqora

Garišä

Äg^wätä

Sihora

Nəga

Woldä-Mikael

LARGER TRIBAL DIVISIONS: THE CLAN

All Gurage claim descent from a founder of a clan. The non-totemic exogamous patrilineal clan is the largest genealogical structural unit of the tribe. It is characterized by its derivation from the nucleus of original ancestors from whom smaller groups have continually proliferated and fused over the generations. The system of lineages upon which the clan is built is highly dynamic, breaking away and merging at various times and in various places. Before Menilek's conquest of the Gurage, it seems that some clans did in fact break up while others merged to form new ones. Nowadays clan boundaries are no longer expansible as they

were in former times, for then expansibility was largely determined by the character of warfare which often led to the overrunning
and absorbing of the territory of a less powerful neighbouring
clan.

Some Gurage tribes contain only a few clans while others, like
the Chaha, contain many. Most certainly during an early period of
Gurage history developments such as the expansion of larger clans
under the leadership of powerful war leaders, and the creation of
permanent alliances between smaller lineage groups against the
real or potential threat of other groups, took place. These mainly
account for the disproportion in numbers, size and importance
of some clans and their related tribes in comparison with other
clans and tribes. Such factors are also significant where the origins
of certain clans are obscure, and they underlie the problems involved in the attempts of Gurage to trace their genealogy with
accuracy above the level of the maximal lineage. A closer study of
the myths and clan traditions usually reveals, though not without
some conjecture, that 'adoption' of what I call 'accessory lineages',
as shown in Fig. 9, took place in the distant past of the history of
the clan. The clan composition of a few tribes illustrates this and
offers some explanation. The largest Gurage tribe is the Chaha
which was also, according to their oral traditions and from accounts
given in Ethiopian Chronicles, politically the most important as it
still is today. I have recorded fifteen clans for the Chaha, for the
Ezha tribe four, for the Gyeto tribe three.[16]

The importance of some clans in political and ritual matters for
the tribe as a whole has led to a great deal of confusion in what
few writings exist on the Gurage. What are in fact tribes have
been called clans or sub-clans, and some clans have been called
tribes, while maximal lineages, as I have defined them, are said by
some writers to be clans, 'sub-tribes', or even tribes.[17] To avoid
further confusion I define a Gurage clan as a system of exogamous lineages within which exact genealogical relationships are
not traced although the clan is usually believed to have a single
founding ancestor.[18]

[16] See Table VIII, Chp. V. I can only speak with some accuracy for the
Chaha and even this listing of clans may be incomplete. Others may find later
that some clans have been omitted or appear under different names.

[17] An example of this confusion in terminology can be seen in Basset, 1897,
pp. 222–4.

[18] See Middleton and Tait, 1958, p. 4.

A tribe is based on clans, it is the largest unit of common values, and there is within it a strong sense of tribal loyalty. But in the oral traditions of tribes there are no hero-ancestors belonging to the real or spirit world that founded tribes, as there are in clans; all tribal myths have clan origins; no genealogical principles relate clans to tribal ancestors. The origins of tribes are obscure and Gurage attempt to explain these in the myths of hero-ancestors of clans. Tribal names appear not to have a personal origin; there were no ancestors named Chaha, or Muher, or Ezha, and so on. Nor do Gurage give an explanation, mythical or otherwise, as to how clans became incorporated into tribes. Most Gurage resort to circumlocution when pressed on this aspect of their tribal history. Whatever be the truth as to its origins, a tribe is today a territorial unit based on autonomous clans. At one time these clans might have been small linguistically related 'chiefdoms' that were forced more and more into interdependent relations because of threatening hostilities that always lay beyond the boundaries of the combined chiefdoms. This must have given rise to the strong sense of common values, a factor that is important to Gurage of each tribe. Tribes based on clans are the largest units that have political significance, but a tribe is politically significant only because of the functioning of its territorially related clans. Chapter V is devoted to a full discussion of this which we call the field of clanship relations, but the traditions of some clans that I recorded are worth noting here. They give us a clue as to how the larger unit, the tribe, might have been formed.

In Chaha oral traditions Mogämänä and Yənäk^{w}amt are claimed to be the founders of the two principal clans which bear their names. The *zär* of these brothers is obscure and this often leads to the recounting of different versions of the myth relating to their settlement and subsequent founding of the clans. Some say that they are of Sidamo origin and that their father came from Alaba, a district in Hadiya,[19] and settled in Yäbqura, a *woina dega* region between Chaha and Gomare. After the father's death, a feud took place between the brothers born of their father's servant, and their half-siblings, the sons of the father's wife, over the

---

[19] This ancient Muslim trading state, in what is now South-west Shoa province, was overthrown by Amda Syon I. See Perruchon, 1889, p. 334; Trimingham, 1947, pp. 70–71. 'Alaba' is presently considered as forming a 'dialect cluster' in the Sidamo Language Group; see fn. 11, p. 6 above.

inheritance of his land.[20] With the help of followers, Mogämänä and YənäkᵂWamt waged a full-scale war, defeated the forces led by their half-brothers, decimated the population of Yäbqura, and then divided between them a large part of Chaha land. YənäkᵂWamt took possession of the eastern part of Chaha, where his clan descendants are found today, in the highlands of Gumer; Mogämänä settled in the lowlands of the western region, which consists of the districts of Amya, Gura, and Yädäbe. This myth gains some support from Ethiopian Chronicles. For it is not improbable that the fall of the petty Muslim and pagan Sidamo kingdoms under the incursions led by Amda Syon I,[21] and their later feudatory status under Zara Yacob and his successors, gave cause for many former Sidamo Chiefs and other dignitaries to flee to neighbouring territories, and seek to re-establish their rule over new lands and people. Mogämänä and other Gurage clans might well have this historical origin. Illustrated below is a partial genealogy of the Mogämänä beginning with the mythical clan founder.[22]

Another Chaha myth relates that the territory was originally settled by the Säga, one of two groups that migrated during the reign of the Ethiopian King Zara Yacob (1434–68). The second

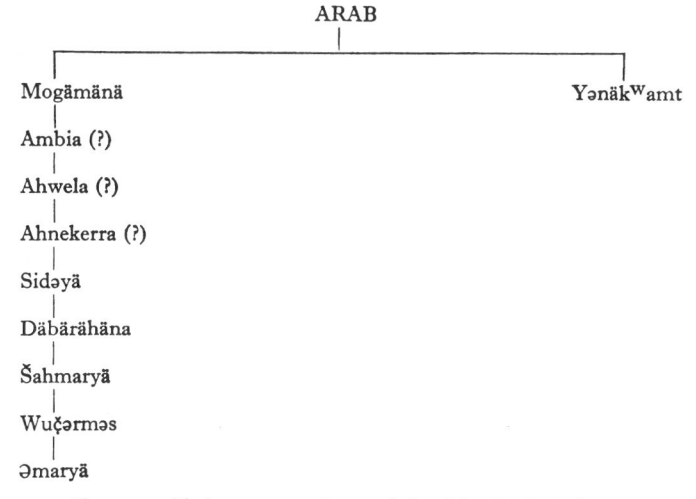

FIG. 10. Skeleton genealogy of the Mogämänä clan.

[20] Cf. the above version with that recorded by Leslau, 1950, p. 34.
[21] See pp. 16–17 above.
[22] The YənäkᵂWamt clan genealogy is illustrated in Appendix II, p. 207.

group, the Kawana, is said to have moved farther south and occupied a region in Walani, now one of the tribes of the *säbat bet*. The story claims that the Säga 'king' was defeated at the hands of Mogämänä, who is then said to have seized the murdered king's *gʷândär*, the silver arm-band which symbolizes the rights to 'kingship', and proclaimed himself 'king'. Although the Säga are said to have been a powerful group and at one time the 'rulers' of Chaha, they are today practically extinct, presumably having been absorbed by stronger migrating groups after the defeat of the Säga king.

The evidence for the origin of other clans is even slighter. The Janjero tribe was described to me as the ancestral home of the Yädəbər Žära clan of the Ennemor Gurage; another Ennemor clan, the Yätəwa Gäzära, say that they 'came from the sea'. Among the Geyto Gurage the most important clan seems to be the Bäräsəya, so-named after its founder, whose descendants claim that he was of Galla origin.

Even though the facts of Gurage clan origins are random and often slight, it is apparent that the process of immigration of small, perhaps war-like, groups into Gurageland gave rise to numerous clans, the founding ancestors of many of them being obscure in the oral traditions of the present-day descendants. The reverse of this process is equally significant. The breaking up of groups, and perhaps even the breaking away of individuals, was still occurring in the late 1880's before the conquest of Gurage. Some Gurage seem to have emigrated because of the force of external pressures, but others apparently fled in an attempt to escape the exigencies of tribal authority. For instance, Cecchi[23] observed in 1886 that a number of *'Ciaha Gurage'*, mostly deserters, warriors, adventurers, and brigands, sought refuge under the Muslim Chief Hasan Injamo in his colony at Qabena. Injamo encouraged runaway Gurage to settle permanently, through inducements of gifts of land and cattle. Strengthening the alliance further, these Gurage adopted Islam, and engaged in periodic raids on pagan and Christian Gurage settlements as part of Injamo's army; the principal booty was cattle and slaves, and many of these slaves were sold in the Qabena market.

---

[23] See p. 19 above. Huntingford, 1955, p. 20, writes that the old Sidamo state, Guma, was ruled about 1770 by a man called Adam, 'the hunter', who is said to have come from a Tigrean colony in Gurage.

The following remarks are worth restating summarily on the origin and composition of Gurage clans. The variation in genealogical structure and composition of clans is the result of an extended period of growth, fission, and movement of populations. This process is often expressed in clan mythologies. That some clans have political seniority over other clans in tribal affairs seems to be accounted for on the basis of the heroic deeds of their ancestors, although these same clans may have only shallow genealogical depth relative to other clans of the tribe. Finally, the dispersal of Gurage clans is to a considerable extent attributable to both ecological and social factors.

II

In every Gurage tribe there is a definite relation between the political structure and the clan system. There is also in each tribe a clan, or the maximal lineage of a clan which occupies a dominant position over other clans in political and ritual matters. The importance of interclan political relations will be considered in the following chapter. Here follows a preliminary account of how clans and lineages are associated with other such units in the context of clan status.

It has been seen that one of the status-determining characteristics of a clan is defined in the political and historical events of clan mythology. A clan is important, moreover, because of the relative social and political status of its leader in relation to other clans and their leaders. Thus, if the maximal lineage of Clan *A* takes a dominant position of leadership in political affairs for the tribe as a whole, in this phase of tribal life 'major' Clan *A* has a dominant position over related 'minor' Clans *B, C, D*, and so on. Leadership assumed by a 'major' clan is legitimated by heads of 'minor' clans. The scope of authority of a 'major' clan leader over 'minor' clan leaders is generally restricted, his authority seldom exceeds the political boundaries of his own constituency. 'Minor' clan leaders must still be relied upon to implement fully important political decisions that involve the tribe as a whole.

The term status as I have used it to define dominant-subordinate positions of clans in political affairs, is best used with qualifications. Status in interclan relations is manifest primarily in the context of clan politics, such as when clan leaders assemble at *Yä Goka* council meetings; status is not a useful term to apply to the relations between clan members. Gurage would strongly object to the use of status criteria as a means of ranking men into higher or lower categories merely by virtue of their membership in a particular clan. Members of a 'major' clan have not, merely by rights of citizenship in that clan, important status positions outside that clan's territory, even though its leaders may have such status.

However, Gurage do make other kinds of distinctions between 'important' men and 'ordinary' men. War leaders, known as *Agäz*, and large land-owners who are sometimes called *G^weta*, or 'nobles', have important status.[24] Men of important status add prestige to their lineage as well as to their clan and tribe, and after death they may be immortalized in poetry and song. During the lifetime of a noble he is usually recognized by others, even outside his own tribal land, by the elaborate trappings of his horse or mule, by the number of servant 'boys' following afoot, or by other easily identifiable accoutrements of status; his dress, ivory-handled cane, and fly-switch. Women always turn their backs to a noble, and take cover in the nearby bush when he passes; young children kiss his hand; older men bow in respect. An *Agäz* or noble is received in any homestead within his own or stranger village without prior notice of arrival. But as an outsider in that village he cannot, by reason of his privileged position, interfere in the political affairs of that community. In his own *gän* a noble may use his status position to influence political decisions, to exact favours for his minimal lineage, and to add prestige to the wider lineage group in general.

Gurage have no 'aristocratic' clans giving their members status in their own clan territory or elsewhere as some tribes do. The absence of institutional forms of clan status allows for social and political equilibrium between close as well as distant genealogically related segments of the clan system to be maintained. In general, there are few symbols of clan status and these are primarily politico-ritual; socio-economic status is of secondary importance. Religious functionaries are the intermediaries between man and the supernatural world, and they are not a part of the same status framework by which ordinary men are sometimes ranked. As far as Gurage are concerned, no man, not even a political leader, has,

[24] Note also that the religious dignitary who represents the Thunder God, *Božä*, is termed *G^wetak^wäyä*; however, I have not been able to unravel the suffix meaning of '*k^wäya*'.

by virtue of his specialized rank, a superior position which allows him to exercise power over all others. Even a wealthy Gurage cannot disregard the rights of an individual, though his status position may stem from that individual's indebtedness.

In anticipation of the discussion later of clan and tribe inter-relationships, I state now that each tribe is corporate and each clan within a tribe can be corporate depending upon the particular situation in which the clan or tribe is involved. A tribe could unite for war against another tribe, and theoretically so could clans of these tribes be in conflict without involving other clans of their respective tribes. Clans of the same tribe could engage in war or feud without involving independent clans of the tribe; *Yä säbat bet* Gurage could unite in defence against a common enemy. This field of Gurage clanship will be taken up again. Now I turn to the structure of interfamilial relations in the homestead and Gurage patterns of mating and marriage.

So far we have seen that the core of a Gurage village is formed by the cluster of lineally related agnatic groups. The pattern of relationships between members in the homestead reflects the dominance of the patrilineal line. This is clearly shown in the father–son, sibling, and husband–wife relations. The pattern of authority established by the kinship system spreads out from the homestead and male seniority is again seen to be the dominant factor in village, clan, and tribal politics. Apart from the daily contacts members of the family have with one another, and with other members of the village, aggregate groups of the community, at some time or another, join other groups in activities organized outside formal kinship associations. Few of these activities are wholly secular in nature. The family and the local community are linked up with the wider society principally through religious observances, for even lineage and clan political ties are inter-twined by religion. Most of the important complexes of Gurage life are composed of ritual mechanisms.

STRUCTURE OF THE HOMESTEAD

The husband and father of the extended family group is the head of a Gurage homestead, *abärus*, fundamentally a domestic group, consisting of the agnatic group of kin. Authority is vested in the father and all persons in the *abärus*, related or unrelated, permanent or temporary residents, are under his jurisdiction. When a son takes a wife and sets up patrilocal residence, he might, if money and land are available, erect his own family hut, but even then he remains in a subordinate position as long as his father is alive. A son cannot assume position as head of an *abärus* until he comes into possession of land. When he acquires land a son gains such status symbols as wealth, a greater degree of participation in the jural politics of the community, and within his own sphere of influence he can, through various social and ritual acts, add prestige to his lineage. A senior male of the agnatic group is always at the head of the authority structure. Even though variations might occur in the organization of authority in the homestead owing to the death or absence of the father, there is no change in the structural form of this authority. A woman can never become head of her husband's or her patrilateral household.

The settlement pattern as well as the rules of residence reinforce the Gurage concept of male superiority. This is borne out by the daily relations between men and women. In the first place older kin of the father's generation, especially the father's brother, living in the same compound, maintain close watch over the wife and mother in the absence of her husband, and thereby restrict as far as possible any freedom she might otherwise gain. This has already been noticed in the previous chapter as one of the features of family organization that facilitates labour migration. In the second place, the Elders of the village, acting jointly, administer the property of a deceased man and undertake the disciplining of his sons whenever there is no adult son or elder of the minimal lineage of the deceased to take his place. Boys are considered adult and ready for marriage at about the age of eighteen, and some of them do marry then, but many must wait longer before obtaining a wife; they must then wait even longer before becoming head of a homestead.

It is difficult to make broad generalizations about the variations that are most likely to occur in the structure and composition of Gurage homesteads. However, from observations based primarily upon the two villages to which my field work was confined, it can be said that the structure of authority in the homestead as described above is the norm to be found in every Gurage village.

Moreover, under normal conditions of village life this pattern does not vary and homesteads do not break up because of marriage, divorce, or death, though other circumstances may arise which may temporarily alter the composition of the homestead. Feuding, which often results in the loss of lives and the fleeing of some members from the homestead, changes its composition. Other changes might be brought about by the destruction of a homestead by fire, or by a supernatural act such as lightning, which Gurage consider to be a manifestation of the powers of the Thunder God *Bozä*.[25] Distantly related kinsmen who extend a visit to an unexpected stay of long duration; a woman who returns to her family after a short career at marriage; or an elderly parent who comes to reside with a son in their old age; all of these give new character to the *abärus*. Agnatic kinsmen who commonly occupy the *abärus*, widows of the former head, his father, or real or putative brothers, may properly join the homestead. On the other hand, members of the wife's lineage never join the *abärus* either temporarily or for an extended stay; they are expected to live with their own patrilineal relatives.

There are no hard and fast rules or institutional norms preventing the presence in the homestead of totally unrelated persons as long as they are not members of despised groups such as the Fuga and persons afflicted with an incurable ritual illness. Individuals of low status such as domestic servants (and formerly slaves), commonly used to assist with household chores, are considered the personal property of the *abärus* to which they are attached. A Fuga has a different relationship to the *abärus* from that of domestics; he is not attached to any single homestead of the village, and his services are considered the corporate property of the village. Even though a wealthy Gurage might set aside a small plot of land for a Fuga to cultivate and on which to build himself a hut, he has only priority rights over that Fuga's services to the village.

The relationships between heads of homesteads and their kin, as well as with persons outside the kin group, will appear later in this chapter when forms of social grouping other than those based on kinship will be considered. It is sufficient to note here that the primary relationships in the homestead centre upon the head of the agnatic group and that subsidiary relationships consist mainly of those obtaining between lineal kinsmen of the domestic group.

[25] Ritual control of fire through agents of the Thunder God's representative is discussed on pp. 176 and 191 below.

HUSBAND AND WIFE

The ideal pattern of relations between a husband and his wife is that of male domination and a separation of the sexes. This pattern is commonplace and variations of it are so seldom found that Gurage find it difficult to cite examples of a woman being treated by her husband in a manner other than 'normal'. A man treats his wife with reserve, and with very little show of affection, as a rule. She in turn respects his position as the family head who makes all major decisions which he considers necessary for the welfare of the group. These decisions, when put into practice, reinforce the ideal pattern of their relations. An outsider might consider the husband-wife relations as cold, formal, and perhaps sometimes even antagonistic. If couples are affectionate and intimate in their private lives, and they must be sometimes, these affectionate feelings are never shown in public. Not only would behaviour of this kind be contrary to the institutional expectations of male superiority, it would be openly criticized by men of the village; no Gurage man would jeopardize his standing in the community by offending other men in this way.

Social and economic activities in the homestead are primarily regulated by the division of labour by sex. The care of the children and the cleanliness of the homestead are the responsibility of the wife who is usually relieved of some of the burden of these tasks by assistance from her unmarried daughters and older female affines. A wife is also expected always to have ready large quantities of beer and coffee for her husband and his guests. A man controls the actual production of food supply for his family, but his wife is expected to regulate with considerable caution the consumption of food which is taken periodically from earth storage.[26]

One variation from the normal pattern in the sex division of homestead chores deserves mention. All domestic activities within the homestead of *G^{w}etak^{w}əyä*, the representative of *Božä*, are performed by unmarried girls or young girls who have not yet reached puberty, or by men. Even the preparation of *äsät* food, which is normally the work of women, is done there by men. Similar restrictions are placed on the presence of women in the homestead of *Yäwäy dämam* who represents the deity *Däm^{w}am^{w}it*.

[26] See Chapter III, pp. 65–66 above.

The ritual notions of female impurity and the common interdictions making for a separation of the sexes are so plainly indicated
here that no more need be said about them at this time.

The earning of money is mainly the work of men. This is especially true where wage labour is concerned, but the marketing of
cash crops, which involves the handling of money is, as I have noted
above, also undertaken by women. I cannot say with certainty
whether or not money received from the sale of crops is left entirely
in the hands of men. Gurage men always say that the head of the
homestead controls the resources and dispenses them in accordance
with his own views. Wives do not dispute this; but wives are not
supposed to contradict their husbands and especially not on such
matters in the presence of an outsider. Moreover, since contradictory views expressed by a wife might be overheard, she would
seldom make statements contrary to those of her husband even if
he were out of hearing. Coupled with this is the fact that Gurage
men and women are unwilling to discuss their household expenditures, the family budget, the earned income, or any matter
concerning finance that they assume might be used for the purpose
of levying additional taxes.[27] On the control of money in general,
all that can be said is that the regulation of family income is a
prerogative of the husband and the degree to which this prerogative is exercised is largely dependent upon the strength of a husband as head of his family. Wherever the structure of authority is
weakening and a break-up of the agnatic group is occurring as a
result of the social and economic factors we have noted, control
over family income by the husband decreases.

Several causes contribute to this. One is the breaking up of the
family as an economic unit which results in the combined earning
power of the group being decreased. Another is the exercise of
more rigid controls over the earnings of younger men which often
has the effect of driving them away from parental authority; and
this is coupled with the economic independence young men gain
through labour migration.

Most Gurage men I questioned, who practised polygyny, claim
that the relationship between their co-wives is tenuous. One of the
reasons for this is a consequence of the settlement pattern of
polygynous households; co-wives are practically strangers because

---

[27] The Gurage are not alone among Ethiopian tribes in being suspicious of
inquiries concerning income and expenditures.

they live in separate villages and seldom meet each other. In sororal polygynous unions, with both wives coming from the same lineage, co-wife relationship is said to be more harmonious. The same is true in levirate unions, for here co-wives have had longer associations with each other, living as part of the extended family. But in all the above forms of marriage sex rivalry, economic jealousy, and conflicts over prestige and status within the family group as well as in the wider community add periodically to the exacerbation of a man in plural marriages, and most probably of a woman too.

Polygynous marriages also extend the terms of reference in the kinship system. When a man takes a second wife she is called by a temporary term of address, *wågiyät*, the closest translation of which seems to be 'elder woman who is taken as a wife'. This term is used mainly by the villagers to explain the arrival of a new woman in the community; it is not a reciprocal term of address between co-wives. Villagers are said to refer to a woman as *wågiyät* for one week to a 'short while'. After a short while she is referred to by name by the villagers; co-wives very often use the term *g^wåbsa*, meaning 'one wife in relation to another', when addressing each other.

There are many causes of strained relations between polygynous households, but there is seldom conflict over the inheritance of land. Each household, as a separate lineage, inherits its own land separately. Thus, no problem arises because of preference being given to the senior son of the first wife, over the senior son of the second wife, and so on, in the inheritance of land. As said above, co-wives live in separate villages on land owned by the husband, and his sons by each wife inherit land only in their respective village. Spatial distance between collateral lineages and the system of inheriting property conceivably reduces the latent tension and hostility between male half-siblings. But within the single lineage, strained relations between brothers, and especially half-brothers, over the inheritance of scarce land may and often does develop into a feud.

One way in which a woman can put into practice the ideals of the 'good wife' is always 'to know her place'. A wife should always show proper deference to her husband, especially when he has guests, and when the couple are in public. A common sight today is a woman walking a few paces behind her husband. Most husbands and wives go about separately, and though this trend is changing in some areas, it is still unusual to see them together, even marketing. At mealtime, a wife is expected to serve her husband first, then she takes her meal later with her daughters and young sons, and sometimes they eat apart from the men. If young children or servants are not available to wash nightly the feet of the husband, father and head of the *abärus*, then the wife is expected to do this for her husband; she should also wash the feet of his guests who stay overnight. When her husband retires, a wife must sleep on the floor alongside his bed.

There seems to be little variation in this pattern of husband-wife behaviour even when long years of marriage have bound a couple together. Most certainly there is a mellowing of relationship between man and wife over a period of years; intimacy and respect have grown, and perhaps in general these are taken for granted. It is doubtful if any new forms of connubial control have emerged by the time middle-age is reached. Then the roles of husband and wife have formed strong institutional patterns, and the ideology of male domination has crystallized to form the social and psychological framework for marital relations. If any old marriage were stripped of its withered age it would show unchanged the structure of male superiority on which it was originally based.

Gurage men have their own ideal model of the 'good husband'. Obviously this model is based on the inequalities of the accepted husband-wife relations. A Gurage man tries to extend the principles of male superiority outside his own homestead. He not only keeps his own woman in subjection but expects all women, including the wives of his close as well as distant kinsmen, to acknowledge his superiority. When he passes women on a path, especially if he is a $G^{w}eta$, they are expected to step into the nearby bush and turn their backs to him, although hiding themselves completely from his sight would be better still. This kind of deference demonstrates to a Gurage man that not only his wife but all women in the community recognize his position. Only on the basis of this recognition does a Gurage feel he can fulfil his conceptual role of the 'ideal husband'. This is but one facet of many of the behaviour patterns that are eulogized in the good life, which in itself is an integral part of the Gurage system of religious ideas. To a great extent the moral and ritual systems influence the institutional norms in male–female relations.

PARENT–CHILD

The nucleus of the Gurage ideology of male dominance and the separation of sexes is formed by the father–son relationship. From birth a boy is expected to follow in his father's footsteps, to become the pivot of authority within his homestead, and to represent his lineage in the wider jural community. Father-son relationships change as the boy grows up and reaches maturity and the cyclical pattern of these changes is the exact antithesis of that of the mother–son relationships. During the period of breast feeding, which lasts for about four years, a father has little to do with his son and their relationship can be described as 'distant'. At the end of this period and until the boy reaches manhood he and his father maintain 'close' relations. Finally when a son marries and assumes the responsibilities of a husband his relationship with his father becomes 'distant'. Notwithstanding this cyclical pattern, the respect a son has for his father, and his subordination to him, continually cut across the formal pattern. By openly and boldly showing his firm respect for his father and his filial subordination, the boy approaches the more closely to the image of the 'ideal' son.

As said before, one way in which a woman can show that she is an ideal wife is by maintaining the formal respect relationship between her husband and herself. Another way in which a woman can realize the ideal concept of a wife is to bear a son. The birth of a son is the most important event in the domestic group. To a noble the birth of a son is one of the occasions on which he can display his position and wealth by giving a feast to the whole village. His minimal lineage is enhanced by the birth of a son and the prestige associated with this event is shared by related major and maximal lineages who also participate in the festivities.

A man relies a great deal upon his sons. They are expected to extend his concept of the good life into the spirit world through prescribed ritual practices; they are duty bound to bury their father in the lineage plot located in the *äsät* field, provided that he is ritually clean; and above all they must perpetuate the lineage. They are responsible for carrying out a father's wishes, because his daughters, losing their connexions with their natal lineage when they marry, have no obligations of this kind. There are also other reasons why a man wishes to have a son, one of the more important being that a man wants to have protection in his old age. He cannot rely upon his daughters for protection and his brothers frequently fail to provide him with security. These anxieties of a father are reduced considerably when his son takes a wife, since the latent hostility between two unrelated lineages is reduced when they are linked through marriage. Only in extreme circumstances do relationships between affinally related lineages break down and feuding supervene. Therefore, having a son is vital to a man. Having at this time neither a wife nor a son, I was more than once ridiculed by Gurage males when this subject was discussed.

At the time when relationships between father and son are distant, a woman has full responsibility for training her son. Between mother and child there appears to be an intimate relationship at all times. Mothers carry their small children while doing most of the household chores, minor work in the *äsät* garden, and when marketing. Children never go hungry when they are under the care of their mothers and they are seldom heard crying, for the treatment to solve both of these annoyances is for a mother to give her child the breast. This she does frequently, and usually the practice extends for a period of four years.

But this period of close, intimate relationship between mother and son is brought to an abrupt end. With no transitional period, a boy begins training under the tutelage of his father, or in his absence, the father's brother, in the steps toward manhood. He learns to herd cattle and to accept responsibility for their care, and in former days he learned to use the bow and arrow and to carry his father's spear. A son grows up fully alive to the values of lineage solidarity by his work alongside other boys in the village in such communal activities as herding, cutting grass, collecting dung, and keeping clean the *wur ema*. After circumcision he begins learning the work of *äsät* cultivation, the tasks being gradually increased with age, until at full maturity he can alone, if called upon, supervise the labour of the *abärus*. Today a few boys attend district schools and some even go away to provincial boarding schools, but on their periodic visits to the village they usually take part again in the common activities of work and play. In still another way, seasonal organization of competitive games for youths on a village-wide basis probably helps to promote lineage solidarity.

Apart from talking to his daughters, occasionally giving them advice, and at times administering mild forms of punishment, a father has little to do with their training. The mother, her husband's sisters, or the grandparents teach young girls the work of a woman in the household and in the *äsät* fields. But young girls normally begin early in their training and preparation for marriage and the duties of a wife and, in this informal education, a father takes little part.

When children reach puberty they 'belong', as Gurage say, to their father. This means that the father assumes complete jurisdiction over his offspring and their membership in the patrilineage is fully recognized. If a woman is divorced after her children have reached puberty, they remain with their father's lineage; if they are younger at the time of her divorce, a mother cares for them until they reach puberty when they join the paternal group. A boy establishes permanent ties with his lineage during the time that his relationship with his father is close and, at least in theory, the exact antithesis of his relationship with his mother.

When a man marries, the pattern of behaviour between himself and his father changes, and the final cycle of their relationship opens. In contrast with the close pre-puberty phase of their relationship, there are marked differences in father–son behaviour during this final cycle and their relations are often strained and distant. 'Young men are impatient' is what older Gurage say about this, but young men put forward different reasons for their attitude, and claim to be sufficiently mature to be independent of parental control. Many young men involved in such conflicts are well-seasoned migrants who have accumulated considerable earnings by the end of a successful season abroad and they consider that their earnings and savings entitle them to independence. Older men tend to be more authoritarian, resisting the aggressiveness of young men, and ordering their sons about as though they were adolescents. Even young married sons object to this. In a few cases, sons make attempts to secure their independence by going to live in new villages, provided that land is available, thereby avoiding the more rigid disciplines associated with living as part of their father's extended family. The thought of the personal rewards that accrue from being at the pivotal position of the authoritarian structure in the homestead most likely governs the decision of many young men who make this choice.

The crucial factor underlying the strained relations between father and son, as well as between siblings themselves, is the inheritance of land. The eldest son expects to inherit the major portion of his father's land, but he only comes into possession of this inheritance if in the opinion of his father he has been an 'ideal' son. In short, a boy must not attempt to override the authority of his father. And a father is able to retain authority over his sons as long as he, the father, lives, because he controls the inheritance of land. This strained relationship is further weakened when a son is economically independent, but is unable to purchase his own land because of its scarcity. Both factors tend to reduce lineage fission, but at the same time to increase substantially internal conflict. Similarly, conflict often arises between siblings; younger brothers hope to receive a larger share of land when their elder brother is withdrawn from the inheritance because he has failed to live up to the ideals expected of a son. Moreover, the eldest son cannot expect to receive his share of land solely by reason of his seniority even upon the death of his father. The father's brothers or Elders of the minor lineage, administer the inheritance, and they can override the rights of primogeniture, and distribute the heritable shares of land to younger more 'ideal' sons. When an elder son feels that he has been thwarted from receiving his share of the inheritance by a younger sibling, the conflict that arises between them often involves other members of the village and larger descent groups. Men have been known to undertake ritual safeguards, such as *gurda* to protect their rights to inheritance.[28]

For obvious reasons, parent–child conflicts over the inheritance of land, seldom involve the mother. During the time that a son's relationship with his father is distant and formal, his relationship with his mother is close and informal. This is especially so when a young married man lives in the homestead of his father, and he has close contact daily with his mother. She often attends to his children, assists his wife, and is usually sympathetic to his problems. Though the mother's brother is not a part of the household, he visits frequently, and he is treated in the same way as the mother. In contrast, the father's brother's behaviour towards his nieces and nephews is stern, rather like that of their father. As expressed in the kinship terminology he is *ebeya*, 'little father', and characteristic of patrilineal societies the father's brother often has full or part responsibility for the raising of his brother's children. In

---

[28] Sibling rivalry as a factor promoting *gurda* is further discussed in the next chapter, p. 166 *passim*.

Gurage society, with the frequent absence of the father from the homestead in quest for wages, the father's brother's role as a key figure in the structure of authority is becoming increasingly important.

Before next describing relationships between siblings we must mention briefly a child's behaviour toward the woman who assists at his birth. When a child is born, the *yanfuna adot*, the 'nose mother', shapes the nose of the infant, annoints him with butter, and assists with the delivery of the after-birth, the *aräfa*. She is the specialist in midwifery for the village and sometimes several villages. In later years a child treats his nose-mother, to use an English equivalent, as a 'god-mother'. She is always treated with respect and, as a man would not marry his own sisters or near kin, he would not marry the daughters of his *yanfuna adot*.

SIBLINGS

'A close and intimate bond should always exist between siblings of the same sex' is characteristic of what Gurage say especially about male sibling relationships. The hostility that so often disturbs the relationships between brothers is not a factor of socialization, and is not fixed during childhood; sibling rivalry becomes pronounced as men reach maturity.

The pattern of behaviour between older and younger brothers changes between childhood and maturity from that of a junior respecting his senior to that of equality. When brothers are young they share what they have with each other, but when they reach manhood possessions become more personal. A man is no more willing to share his land with his brother than he would be to share his wife with him, although his brother might come into possession of both of these upon the death of the other. These attitudes are epitomized in the Gurage proverb: 'if I fail to find bread, may I (rather) fail to find my brother'.[29] In adulthood, brother to brother relationship is characterized by mutual help and assistance rather than by warmth of affection.

Sisters usually maintain the close relationship of childhood throughout their later years. An older sister watches over her younger sister, chaperones her in public, at festivities, at the river

[29] Recorded by Leslau, 1950, p. 134. The meaning Leslau writes, is that bread and food are more important than one's own brother.

when drawing water and washing; and she attempts to protect her sister against the advances made by young village males. All of this is intended to protect the virgin status of a young girl; the loss of virginity would not prevent her from getting married absolutely but it would make marriage more difficult to arrange and it would bring shame and a lowering of prestige to her family. Brothers also help to protect their sisters in this way, since the stigma associated with having an unmarried non-virgin sister affects the entire minimal lineage. When sisters marry and leave home their relationship with their brothers becomes one of respect; their behaviour towards them closely resembles that of an affinal relative.

Obviously, since Gurage women do not inherit land and other property, it is no surprise that there is not so much enmity among female siblings. Even so, it is too easy to dramatize the conflicts inherent in male sibling relations at the expense of amicable female sibling relations. Yet male sibling rivalry in Gurage society cannot be underestimated. It is rife. The myths of the Mogämänä clan, which tell of the rivalry between brothers over the inheritance of land, are an epitome of actual situations. In everyday life, a man often resorts to ritual practices seeking supernatural protection against the real or potential threat of his brother's hostility. Among the Gurage, as in other societies, sibling rivalry is perhaps a consequence of the patrilineal system, because of the stern pattern of domination of father over son, and because the unity of siblings as a whole is based upon authority and not upon affection.[30] Coupled with these factors of kinship and lineage are the ecological and social conditions which we have seen working in opposition to the fundamental principles of lineage segmentation underlying the structure of Gurage society. When the function of Gurage ritual bond-friendship, *gurda*, is discussed in the next chapter it will be possible to complete the picture of sibling rivalry that has been partially drawn here; we shall also see how *gurda* is one means of resolving these conflicts.

MATING AND MARRIAGE

Marriage is the most important social event involving two unrelated homesteads that can occur in Gurageland. This is a most

---

[30] Cf. the patterned hostility between male siblings among the Soga as described by Fallers, 1956, pp. 82–83.

significant occasion in the life cycle of every man and woman, for marriage is not only the starting point of the family, it is also the starting point of the kinship ties which link together the genealogically independent segments of two clans.

By Gurage standards something is wrong with men and women who never marry. It is inconceivable to the Gurage that anyone of their own volition should refrain from marriage throughout life. Every man tries to find a mate and he usually does find one; no man wants to be ridiculed for having never married. For this reason there are few people in any village who fall into the category of 'never married' and these are usually the mentally or physically defective. Even the blind and the lame, if they are otherwise ablebodied, are often successful in finding a mate. Both the old and the 'ugly' men, especially if they are wealthy, are also able to obtain a woman though in most cases, as with the blind and the lame, this will be the second marriage for the woman.

Sooner or later a man must have a wife, and a woman a husband, to lead a normal, socially acceptable way of life. Most unmarried men talk a good deal about marriage, all the more so as the desire for sexual experiences increases. For many men, especially those who have not yet been abroad to experience the sexual freedom made available by the urban *sillətane* of *Šäwa*, or the few sexual outlets made present by unattached women in beer houses in Endeber, premarital sex relations occur relatively late in life. In contrast, a girl's life is entirely directed toward marriage from puberty on, and the strict surveillance under which she is kept before betrothal is an additional factor limiting the premarital sexual experience of young men.

By obtaining a wife, especially one who bears him a son, a man puts into practice in still another way the ideals of a good son. An elder will seldom include a son in the inheritance who has not yet taken a wife; this would be an added incentive for a young man to marry, if an added incentive were needed. A woman, therefore, is a medium through which the potential inheritance of land is made more certain.

Social, economic, religious, and ethnic factors govern the decision a father makes in selecting a wife for his son. Social and economic differences between families may not in every instance rule out an eventual union. Families of different religions occasionally intermarry, but those of different ethnic backgrounds never

M^{w}ᵊyät Chiefs leading the girls in ceremonial dancing. Some M^{w}ᵊyät
are carrying the *lumẹ̈ä*-stick

A Gurage bride astride her husband's mule being led by the *mᵊze*. The
dress and umbrella are the main items of bridewealth

120]

Yä Goka council meeting being presided over by *Šehotč* seated under the sacred *zǝgba*-tree. Seated second on the right, Chief Täsämä Amärga

The sacred forest and ritual shrine of the deity *Däm^{w}am^{w}it*

do.[31] A Gurage will never marry a member of a despised class. For that matter, parents go to great length to give genealogical proof as evidence that there is no trace of 'non-Gurage blood' in their family history. They make even stronger asseverations that they have never intermarried with slaves or Fuga, and that no member of their family has ever been afflicted with a ritual illness. This last assurance is most important, for it is held that illness incurred supernaturally can be passed on to the offspring of the couple and succeeding generations.

In traditional times, marriages were arranged entirely by parents, and children had no choice in their selection of a mate. This is true to a great extent today even though many young men choose their own brides while allowing their parents and village elders the satisfaction of symbolically conducting the customary prenuptial arrangements.

The lineage of a man takes an active part in assisting a father in the selection of a wife for his son, and Elders of the village acting as 'go-betweens' for the two families give final approval in sanctioning the choice of the father. Elders examine the bride attesting to her physical fitness, her colour and features, which should be 'light' and not 'Negroid'; they should not be *ṭäqʷärä-m*, that is, a woman should not 'be black'. Any peculiar body marks that might later be attributed to wife-beating, if a woman is sent back home during the early stages of marriage, are also noted. Though a man does not undergo similar examination he is warned by the Elders that if his wife is sent home after a short career of marriage she should not show signs of recent beatings. On the day of the *čäg* feast, signifying that marriage has been agreed upon, the parents of the bride provide *äsät*-food, meat and beer for her new in-laws and the Elders. At this feast the amount of the bridewealth which usually consists of a small sum of money, about $Eth. 10, is settled. Also provided are some clothing for the bride, including a veil for hiding her face from her in-laws, and a mule for the best man, the *məze*, and his friends, on which to lead the bride, the *məšra*, away from her parents.

The act of marriage is expressed linguistically as *agäpʰa-m*, 'to

[31] Of course I do not mean Gurage marriages which take place outside Gurageland. Many Gurage men in *Šäwa* take wives from other tribes; likewise, Gurage women have always been favoured as wives by men from other tribes. See p. 35 above.

marry', derived from the word *gäp^ha-m*, which may be translated as 'come in' or 'enter'. A man and woman 'come in' to the state of marriage some months following the payment of bridewealth. Christian Gurage usually marry during the month of *Yədar*, after the rains end, or in *Wäto*, the month preceeding the lenten fast, whereas marriages of Muslim and other Gurage usually take place during the off-seasons of cultivation.

A man may also enter into marital unions which are normally subsequent or additional to his first marriage. These are widow inheritance and concubinage. Another commonplace variation of a first marriage is for two men, often brothers, to marry two sisters. This relationship is distinguished by the term *sandərəs*, which is also a term of address used between husbands. Widow inheritance is a traditional mode of marital union expressly countenanced by Islamic custom, but it is no less widely practised by Gurage of other faiths. I was told that although concubinage is still permitted it is not largely practised. This is at least true within the tribal lands, but many migrant Gurage practise concubinage, with the second wife and her household being domiciled in *Šäwa*.

Although subsequent or additional marital unions may take place, the first marriage of a man is the most outstanding event of his life, where his lineage is concerned. For it is then that the duties and obligations of his lineage, to provide the proper setting in which the prescribed customs of marriage can take place, are performed. His lineage also has obligations to the lineage of his wife, and to try to evade these can bring about a lasting enmity. His own family is responsible for the principal marriage feast, but in this they are supported by closely related kin in the village and elsewhere. They make preparations for the feast several weeks in advance. Extra *äsät*-food is removed from earth-storage, the best quality *ṭəquräya*-bread is prepared, cattle and sheep are set aside for slaughter, and large quantities of *ṭälla*-beer are brewed and stored in both villages. On the day that the bride is taken from her village to be presented to the groom, her family gives the first feast; the second, *Yəft zpwärä*, as described below, is held some time after the marriage takes place.

A few days before the marriage feast takes place celebrations are carried on nightly in households of near-kin of the bride and groom in their respective villages. Girls of the same age-group as the bride (*merät*) entertain her nightly, in singing, dancing, and drumming. Some of these girls, the closest friends of the bride, are chosen to be 'bride's maids', the *mäsetäna*, and on the night preceding the marriage they symbolically challenge the husband for the rights to claim his spouse. In opposition to the *mäsetäna* are the 'best men', the *məze*, who feast the groom; later they attempt to seize the bride who is being guarded by the *mäsetäna*.

The ritual of vituperation, the song-duel between the *məze* and the *mäsetäna*, consists of an enumeration of the deeds of valour and renown of their respective clans.[32] Narrations are made in rhyme and song, some of which are well known in the oral traditions of the clan, but many new verses are made impromptu during the performance. If, by relating a more extensive record of the heroics of their clan, the *mäsetäna* endure the song-duel longer than their opponents and so emerge victorious, they reject the advances of the *məze* for several hours by refusing to release the bride to them.[33] Contrarily, if the *məze* succeed, there is no opposition from the *mäsetäna*, and the *məze* triumphantly bring the bride astride her husband's mule, to his village and to the marriage feast.

Contesting a man's right to obtain marital and sexual privileges over his prospective wife is one of the ways in which a lineage ritually prolongs its hold over its women.[34] Symbolically, it expresses the structural opposition between clans and, at the same time, the unity of smaller groups in the clan. This mechanism of the social structure tends to offset the tensions that might arise when a lineage is about to lose one of its women. Interclan relations are stabilized by channelling the real or potential friction between them into the symbolically hostile institution of the 'song-

[32] An example of one such song is recorded on p. 23 above; see also Leslau, 1950, pp. 112–125.

[33] Azais *et* Chambard, 1931, noted that when the *məze* are victorious they retain the bride throughout the night until 'the cock crows', then she is given to the groom. (p. 194). I did not observe this variation in the pre-marriage ceremony. The *məze* of the Gurage differs significantly from a similar institutional practice among the Amhara known as *mize*. One function of the later is to assist the groom in deflowering the bride on the wedding night. The group of *mize* hold the bride who resists the husband's attempt to penetrate her, or failing this, one from among the *mize* group is chosen to make the penetration for the groom.

[34] Cf. Zulu marriage celebrations; opposition between Sib groups is expressed by a song-duel between the bride's and the groom's parties, and by the symbolic refusal of the bride's family to accept *lobola* (cattle payment). See Hoernle, 1925.

duel' which juxtaposes one clan in opposition to the other. This hostility and opposition between clans is seen in action again before a marriage is finally consumated.

Before two lineages are finally linked through marriage their relationship is tense. Once the *čäg* feast is held a marriage is seldom called off, but open quarrelling between the two lineages can take place before the lineage of a wife gives up its claims to her and she is formally recognized as a member of her husband's lineage. Both the husband and wife must remain out of sight of their respective affinal lineages until the customary time arrives for them to be seen. The avoidance of one's prospective in-laws must be observed up to the day of the feast or a lineage will be offended and the 'go-betweens' from each lineage will have to be called in to attempt a reconciliation. At the marriage feast the bride and her female companions are kept secluded behind a curtain in the small hut of her in-laws, and remain out of sight of the wedding guests, who are mainly people of her husband's lineage, as long as the feast is held; this may easily be for several days. After the feast, another, more rigid period of seclusion begins. Formerly the bride was prohibited from leaving the hut for a full year, living there hidden from the kinsmen of her husband, being attended daily by her *mäsetäna*, but today she often leaves the small house after only six months of seclusion. During these months of marriage the wife rejects the sex advances of the husband which he makes nightly in an attempt to enter the marriage hut. Customarily a wife should not submit sexually to her husband until the period of seclusion has ended.

On the other hand, a man should avoid coming into contact with his in-laws during the time his wife is resisting his advances. Gurage characterize this avoidance behaviour by saying they should not 'see his face'. However, after a woman comes out of seclusion, her family invites the man to 'show us your face', and a ceremony named *Yəft zpwärä* is held to mark this occasion. After a visit of three days to his in-laws the husband returns to his village. He leaves his wife with her parents for about two or three months, but after she rejoins her husband she cannot leave her husband's homestead, even for short visits to them, without his permission. When she rejoins her husband in his homestead he sleeps with her for the first time. The marriage is then consumated and the rights of the husband over his wife are firmly established.

There is no absolute guarantee that a proper wife chosen for a son, and his fulfillment of all premarital obligations, will ensure the stability of the marriage. The sexual bond is of vital importance in any marital relationship, but the real foundation of a lasting marriage is built upon the mutual adjustment of the roles of the marriage partners, the transference of reciprocal rights and obligations, and the pursuit of common interests.

But the reciprocity of roles and interests is often submerged in practical situations by the overwhelming stress placed upon patrilineality. A man has more prerogatives at his disposal in marital relations than his wife because of custom, and jural and ritual sanctions. He may strike her at the least provocation; he may neglect her in favour of a co-wife; he may send her home to her parents and yet jealously hold her to her marital fidelity; he may exercise all these prerogatives without fear of reprisal from his wife's family or the wider affinal descent group. Retaliatory action on their part would only lead to the feud, and the tensions created when affinally related families clash often proliferate and involve other groups of the tribe in conflict.

Of the many prerogatives a man has, no man in his right senses would take the wife of another man, for even when a wife has been sent home, she is not free to consort until her husband formally renounces his claim on her. If a woman is sent home because of barrenness or laziness, her chances of obtaining a second husband are remote. She may eventually resort to drifting from husband to husband, or take to making and selling beer as a means of livelihood, or leave the tribal land for good. If she does not emigrate, a woman taking any other course is likely to be singled out by other women of the village by the term *m^wanwät*, 'a worthless woman', meaning, in this context, a woman who is unable to secure a husband. A *m^wanwät* is always vulnerable to easy accusations of adultery, *yänkit*. But most cases of infidelity seem to involve married women. In Gurage customary law, which still obtains in *Yä Ǧoka* council, the lover can be fined up to fifty head of cattle or $Eth. 500, and she can be ritually cursed by her husband to prevent subsequent marriages. Any offspring from second unions may also be cursed, even though the husband has been compensated for his injury. Contrariwise, a woman can neither accuse her husband of adultery nor can she instigate action for divorce.

Ideally, children are the principal factor giving stability to

Gurage marriages, since a woman cannot formally be sent back to her parents if she has borne her husband eight children. If a woman is sent home for infertility she brings shame to her family and to herself, making a second marriage difficult, and she must resort to performing special rituals and sacrifice to her deity in hopes of renewing her fertility. But when a woman gives birth to eight children a feast called *samər*, taken from the word *səmut* or eight, is held in which the entire village partakes. The celebration of *samər* is important for a woman, for it makes public the fact that her marriage is legally tied, and although divorce can still take place after *samər*, it is rare. *Samər* also makes a marriage ritually binding since the ceremony is legitimated by *Däm^wam^wit*, and no man would chance the ritual sanctions that are handed down for offending the deity, by deserting his wife or attempting to send her home to her parents. But if a woman is returned before *samər*, young children remain with her until they reach puberty, when they join the lineage of their father.

Some indication of the relations between family size and the factor of *samər* is revealed in Table VIII below. In my village, the mean of 6·80 children was distributed among 39·0 per cent. of the homesteads. Of the 41 homesteads, 17·0 per cent., or 7·0, of them had celebrated the *samər* feast.[35]

TABLE VIII

Distribution of Children per Homestead and the Relationship to Marriage Stability

Frequency of children per homestead	Homesteads		Children	
	No.	%	No.	%
12–14	1	2·4	13	6·0
9–11	4	9·8	40	18·4
6–8	16	39·0	109	50·0
3–5	11	26·8	45	21·0
0–2	9	22·0	10	4·6
Total	41	100·0	217	100·0

[35] It is clear that these figures would have greater meaning in determining Gurage marriage stability if such variables as age, years of marriage, and first or second marriages could be correlated.

These religio-legal features of marriage emphasize the stress Gurage place on patrilinealtiy. They also underline two aspects of the institutional norm of male dominance that are characteristic of marriage instability in Gurage society. Firstly, a man is able to procreate a large family, which is a status ideal most men strive for, either through polygynous marriages or through a number of second marriages, since his children remain members of his lineage. Secondly, this ideal is attainable without being legally and ritually bound to one wife because she has borne him eight children. Moreover, within this pattern of marriage, a man can both be a father and have relative sexual freedom without creating inter-lineage tensions.

The unstable character of Gurage marriages is also reflected in the widespread complex of folktales and proverbs concerning the 'step-mother'. This complex suggests that children are commonly put under the domination of their father's second wife ($g^w\mathring{a}bsa$), and that step-mothers are a common feature of homestead life. 'The cold of today is like the stick of the step-mother' and 'the disgust of the present day is like the bread of the step-mother' are two commonly repeated proverbs.[36] Another reflection of the insecurity of a wife in the homestead is in the linguistic taboos she observes in not revealing the name of her husband to other women. For instance, if the name of her husband is 'Gabre', his new wife will refer to him as 'Gabaya', the word for 'market', when in the presence of other women, which presupposes a fear of losing him, or of misfortune befalling him, should she give away his real name.[37]

A great deal of the insecurity in marriage that a woman feels, as well as undergoes, is merely a consequence of the patrilineal system. A woman is always subject to the social and psychological strains of her own patrilateral group although some relief from this tension is found in the early stage of marriage prior to its consummation. The repeated rejection by the wife of her husband's sexual advances is one way by which the conflicts arising out of the antagonisms between the sexes is relieved. In yet another way, the long period of time, during which this process of rejection takes

[36] From the selection of proverbs recorded by Leslau, 1950, pp. 134–5. In some Gurage tales the step-mother is seen sacrificing her children to save her life or to retain her husband.

[37] Leslau, 1959, pp. 105–6.

place, symbolically prolongs the control a lineage can exercise over one of its female members.

Other features of Gurage social life, such as the annual festivities at which affinal relatives are placated with gifts, work toward reducing tensions between lineages linked by marriage. The annual *Antrošt* feast, the 'mother's festival', is the occasion for a man and his wife to present gifts to their respective mothers-in-law; fathers-in-law are given gifts during the *Mäsqär* festival, celebrated in the month of *Yədar*, September. In daily life and in non-ceremonial situations, formal respect-relationships between an individual and his or her relatives-in-law are perhaps the most important factors resolving tensions between affinal relatives.

We have discussed the patterns of mating and marriage without reference to individual practices of religion. All that need be said is that people of different faiths seldom marry, and when they do the woman usually changes her religion for that of the man. Perhaps for that reason I heard of no instance of religious dispute between husband and wife. There have been no significant changes in the form of marriage, residence, or authority patterns in the homestead as a consequence of Gurage adopting new forms of worship.[38]

THE CORPORATE GROUP

If acting together to attain a common end is the basis of the corporate group, the kinship system is the core round which corporate group social relations crystallize. We have dealt above with the more important aspects of Gurage kinship and marriage, and to some extent with the part played by individuals outside the homestead and lineage. Apart from the wife, no other members of her patrilateral group have rights of membership in the corporate lineage group of her husband. Unity and solidarity of the corporate group are expressed in two ways: the degree to which its members are mobilized in action and the extent to which sanctions governing the participation of its members in lineage activities are applied.

Gurage corporate group action takes place at rituals of death, as at rituals of marriage. The lineage of the deceased have rights and

---

[38] The only variation from traditional Gurage marriages that I observed was the 'blessing' of the union in instances of Coptic Christian, Catholic, and Muslim marriage ceremonies.

duties associated with the death ritual that vary according to the lineal distance between the deceased and the living kin. Age, sex, status, character, and reputation of the deceased all determine the range and degree of participation in the rituals of death. Traditionally a Gurage is buried near his house, in his *äsät* garden, and male kin farthest removed from him in lineal distance symbolically assist in digging the grave by removing a few spades of earth, but the major construction of the burial vault with its inner chamber is undertaken by Fuga. The lamentations of the members of the family most closely related to the deceased are expected to be, and are, the loudest. And all close kin, male and female, of the minimal and minor lineages perform the funeral dance. The ritual dance is to 'go on the sides' as Gurage call it, $m^w ar\ddot{a}\ w\ddot{a}r\ddot{a}m$. In expressions of grief women fall down or strike their breasts and men strike their hips with their elbows or scratch their faces with thorns. The more remote kin of the deceased mourn respectfully, occasionally emitting loud lamentations, and every year, together with the family of the deceased they pour *sähär* beer on the grave.[39] Muslim and Christian Gurage have separate burial grounds, near the mosque or church, and are seldom interred in the *äsät* field. But otherwise there are no differences in the obligations of the living kin from those described for Gurage who follow their traditional religious calling.

The marriage or death of a Clan Chief or other political or ritual dignitary, or the birth of a son to one of them, are events which concern every segment of the clan. Clan members are obliged to extend respect individually or through their representative who is usually the village headman, respect being signified by gifts of *äsät*-food, *ṭälla*-beer, honey for making hydromel, or cattle. When an important Chief or other dignitary dies, obligations of respect extend beyond the clan and tribe to include the entire *säbat bet*. Such honour was extended in 1958 at the death of the late Chief of Chaha, Amärga Oqbato, when all other tribal dignitaries joined his clan to mourn the customary thirty-day com-

---

[39] I have no clear explanation for the pouring of libations on graves since ancestor worship is not an aspect of the Gurage belief system. The use of beer to propitiate ancestral spirits is common enough among African peoples, and D'Almeida writing about 1620 describes the Agau (Agao) custom of placing beer and cups near the head of the corpse in the burial chamber. See Weld Blundell, 1922, pp. 513–14. This ritual might represent one of the many pre-Christian survivals in Gurage religion. See also p. 52 above.

memoration period, *täzkar*.[40] Although other clans pay their respect, it is the direct obligation of every member of the minimal and maximal lineages, inclusively of the clan of a deceased ritual or political official to perform the mourning rituals.

Feuding also involves the corporate group to which a man belongs, for he depends upon his minimal lineage for protection and the members are obliged to come to his defence. It is usually the close agnatic kin of both factions that are immediately involved in disputes of this kind, but the results of their action are often widespread and sooner or later distantly related lineages are affected. A man who has been injured by a fellow tribesman, or by an outsider, by reason of adultery, theft, or fighting, has the right to seek the support of his lineage in either exacting compensation or in seeking vengeance. When all attempts at mediation carried out between village elders and headmen have failed and social relations have broken down, the groups in dispute may take to fighting. Active hostility leads to loss of life and it is usually avoided at all costs. But it does occur when formal mediation, conciliation, and persuasion have been unsuccessful; when the ritual sanctions of the tribal council, *Yä Goka*, no longer exert moral suasion and restraint over an individual; when ritual affliction of an incurable illness is no longer feared as a consequence of recalcitrant behaviour.

The mechanisms of sanctions, such as those outlined above, are primarily ritual in nature, they protect the community as a whole, and they are, in their application, governed by authorities outside the corporate group. In the terminology of Radcliffe-Brown, these may be called 'primary sanctions' of social control.[41] But the corporate group has sanctions at its own disposal which we may term 'secondary sanctions', and the application of them governs to a large extent the actions of individual members. An example of secondary sanctions of social control can be illustrated by the following case, which was brought to my notice during my stay in Gurageland. In this case a minimal lineage took the life of one of its members who, after refusing to accept the judgement of the tribal council, had fled from the village and had set about exacting blood-price from his sworn enemies. According to my informants, the lineage took this action to prevent the further loss of lives on both sides. I was told of another case in which a Gurage

---

[40] See p. 152 below.   [41] Radcliffe-Brown, 1952, pp. 205–11

had been taken into custody in *Šäwa*, and imprisoned for being unable to pay the fine levied by the Court. He later returned to his village and took revenge against his minimal lineage by burning several of their huts, thus exacting vengeance for their having failed to fulfill their obligations to him.

Even on this slight evidence, two characteristics of the corporate function of the minimal lineage in maintaining clan and tribal solidarity can be seen in the above examples. The lineage tries to maintain an equilibrium between unrelated groups by the application of primary sanctions originating from external bodies of authority, such as *Yä Ǧoka*, the tribal council. The lineage also regulates the behaviour of its members through the imposition of sanctions independent of clan and tribal councils, thereby maintaining lineage stability. The overall effectiveness of the corporate group in maintaining social control depends on time and space: the farther removed the lineages of dispute are in geographical and kin distances the more strained the relationship and the greater the difficulty in reaching a settlement.

In the important political and ritual aspects of Gurage lite, such as jural action above the village level and at the principle religious festivals, to which we refer in the following chapters, corporate actions takes place at the level of clanship. Even so, smaller lineage groups form the nucleus round which clan and tribal political and religious assemblies take place.

SEX AND AGE GROUPS

Gurage have no tribal-wide organizations established for males solely on the basis of age. As we have seen, within any household the hierarchy of age is important, and the first step a family takes formally to initiate a boy into this hierarchy is through the circumcision ceremony, the *ṭebär*. Circumcision is performed on boys and clitordectomy on girls between the ages of eight and ten; several children in the *abärus* make the *rite de passage* into 'adolescence'[42] at the same ceremony, after which they are separated and

---

[42] I use 'adolescence' here loosely to mean a social rather than a psychological stage in a child's life which precedes marriage; thus it coincides with 'adulthood' in Gurage thought and behaviour patterns. There is no 'adolescent' stage in a Western-European understanding of the term.

secluded in different parts of the homestead. Sometimes in homesteads of wealthy Gurage special huts are erected for the ceremony.
But the *ṭebär* is always performed by a Fuga acting as a ritual
specialist, one of his many roles.

The ritual separation of young initiates according to sex at
ṭebär formally symbolizes for them a pattern of behaviour that will
determine their attitudes toward the oppposite sex in later life.
A period of confinement in the homestead, lasting from three to
six months, follows the *ṭebär*, during which time initiates are kept
under the tutelage of elder kin of their respective sexes. Boys learn
from their elders the duties and responsibilities of manhood, which
entail taking on a greater share of work in *äsät* cultivation, knowledge of their clan genealogy and the traditions of their clan and
its heroes; they are also introduced to *gurda* and the binding moral
obligations involved in making a ritual covenant. *Ṭebär* marks the
close of childhood, the age of irresponsibility.

Following confinement, the *ṭebäränä*, the 'one who is circumcised', and others in his group are introduced to the village by
being publicly paraded through the market place. Each *ṭebäränä*
wears, as a symbol of honour, the skin of the lamb that was
slaughtered for the occasion by his respective kin group. The most
important phase of this *rite de passage* culminates in competitive
games between individual *ṭebäränä*. The game most frequently
played is that of 'bird trapping'. In former times the bow and
arrow were used, and to wing a bird in flight demonstrated the
greatest skill and earned the highest honours. Nowadays boys use
bird snares and sometimes birds are felled by stones thrown by
sling or by hand. But regardless of how the game is played, the
most ingenious competitor is given the symbolic status of 'warrior'
as his reward. *Agäz* was the highest title a warrior could receive
when warfare was a common feature of Gurage life and only those
Gurage who had killed 'a hundred of the enemy' could win it; but
even today when the *ṭebäränä* who, having trapped the greatest
number of birds, is rewarded in mock ceremony with the title of
Agäz, the social values traditionally associated with this title
apparently remain important.

The passage of girls into adolescence is signalled by initiation
into an age group called *mʷəyät*. The *merät*, as they are called, a
term which may be translated as 'girls of the same age', remain
members of the same *mʷəyät*-group until they marry, but even then

they often come together conducting their social and ritual functions as a group. The initiation ceremony which, expressed in Gurage linguistic idiom, is to 'throw the $m^w\partial y\ddot{a}t$ girls', is conducted yearly in each maximal lineage district by the Fuga 'Chief $M^w\partial y\ddot{a}t$'. Once the chief has 'thrown' the girls, they remain under his ritual authority, and together with his Fuga assistants they attend the ritual needs of women.

$M^w\partial y\ddot{a}t$ initiation rites begin with a symbolic ritual 'abduction'. On the first night a band of older $m^w\partial y\ddot{a}t$ girls led by the Fuga Chief $M^w\partial y\ddot{a}t$ 'sieze' the young girl from her homestead, while her parents stay hidden in the rear of the hut in symbolic awe, fearful of the Fuga's malediction. After each initiate in the village has been abducted, the entire group is taken into the 'bush' and secluded for about one month, being kept under the tutleage of the Chief $M^w\partial y\ddot{a}t$ and his assistants. Here they are taught 'secrets' and most important the ritual 'language' called *Fedwät* which only Gurage women and Fuga ritual assistants are said to speak, and which is kept carefully guarded from Gurage men and strangers.[43] *Fedwät* is used principally at religious festivals when girls and married women chant and sing songs in the ritual argot.

Between initiation into $m^w\partial y\ddot{a}t$, when a girl is 'young', about seven to nine years of age, until she is 'old' and married at about fifteen, most of her social life is confined to $m^w\partial y\ddot{a}t$ activities, over which the Chief $M^w\partial y\ddot{a}t$ rules. The first of these occurs when a girl comes out of the 'bush' and, along with other initiates, is presented to the village. Then the Chief $M^w\partial y\ddot{a}t$ leads all his charges through the market, singing songs in *Fedwät* as they go about jokingly disturbing the traders and buyers and jostling their elders, men and women alike. In this *plaisanterie* the $m^w\partial y\ddot{a}t$ speak only in *Fedwät*; if a bystander tries to make conversation in Guraginä they feign ignorance of it and respond in the argot. The Chief is responsible for disciplining a $m^w\partial y\ddot{a}t$ until she is married

---

[43] Gurage term *Fedwät* a 'language' but this usage is perhaps incorrect. Most probably *Fedwät* is an argot composed partly of Gurage words inverted in meaning and perhaps partly of survivals of a Fuga dialect. The latter is admittedly purely conjecture since a study of Fuga 'language', if it exists at all, is yet to be carried out, and this is so for *Fedwät* as well. The problem is compounded further by the fact that *Fedwät* is a 'secret' argot. See Leslau, 1950, pp. 57–58. A parallel here might be drawn with the argot spoken in Amhara Zar cult rituals. Cf. Leslau, 1949.

and her family has little to say in this matter. While the ties with *mʷəyät* are never completely broken for a woman, even after marriage, they are lessened when she takes on the role of a wife. In later life older *mʷəyät* meet as a group only on special occasions, such as to mourn the death of an associate by keeping strict silence or speaking only in *Fedwät*, or at the annual *Näqʷä* and *Dämʷamʷit* festivals. But individually women call upon the Chief *Mʷəyät* throughout the year to perform special sacrifices whenever a spiritual uplift is needed.

The *mʷəyät* grouping forms the central point round which the social and ritual life of Gurage women is organized. Socially, *mʷəyät* initiation symbolizes the transition into 'adult' life; Gurage make no distinction on the basis of age for adolescent girls, they are simply 'young' before marriage and 'old' afterwards. Becoming a *mʷəyät* also incorporates a girl into the female sector of Gurage religious life. During the pre-marital period when a girl is under the ritual authority of the Chief *Mʷəyät* social ties with her family and lineage are gradually lessened; marriage and incorporation into her husband's lineage severs them completely. In yet another way, ritually 'giving up' a girl to *mʷəyät* before her betrothal tends to reduce the hostility often seen when a lineage is about to lose a female member through marriage. Apart from its use in religious ceremonials, *Fedwät*, the knowledge of which can be acquired only through *mʷəyät* initiation, provides a woman with a ritual safeguard for crises that arise during her marital career. When serious marital disputes arise, which if prolonged might threaten the stability of the marriage, women often go into a trance, speaking only in *Fedwät* which is incomprehensible to their husbands, and which testifies a state of ritual possession; no man would interfere with this. On the other hand, *mʷəyät* association enables a woman to strengthen her marriage by performing fertility rites and being repossessed periodically. In both rituals incantations are made in *Fedwät*.

Among the Chaha and Muher Gurage, where respectively Catholic and Coptic Christian influence is considerable, initiation into *mʷəyät* has virtually ceased to exist. The *ṭebär* is still performed on boys and girls, being countenanced by both religions. In areas where the traditional religion is dominant, and even in those areas where Islam is extensively practised, *mʷəyät* group rituals are still the primary form of social groupings for girls and unmarried women outside the homestead.[44] Groupings on the basis of sex rather than age form naturally on all occasions, and sex differentiation plays its part throughout the whole social system.

STATUS, RANK, AND SOCIAL DIFFERENTIATIONS

I

Social classes were not traditionally institutional forms of ranking among the Gurage. Hereditary rank was mainly confined to political and ritual functionaries. Clan Chiefs were in most instances titled warriors. Relatives of a leader shared to some extent in the prestige of his exalted position, but his title was not the corporate property of the lineage and therefore could not be inherited by his sons. Village headmen and their close kin also enjoyed considerable prestige and a range of social privileges within their own village and clan territory, but these decrease the farther one is removed from his own district.

Many symbols of status by which ordinary men and women were formerly ranked are not important today and often are seldom seen in practice. An important mark of status in former times was the wearing of cloth which was exclusively a male prerogative; the quality of the cloth a man used in his *šama*,[45] and the extent to which he was clothed, indicated his rank. Complete attire signified some degree of nobility and the man would be addressed as *Gʷeta*; lesser amounts of clothing, decreasing to nakedness, identified serfs and slaves. A woman was forbidden to wear cloth

[44] Gurage women in Addis Ababa periodically perform *mʷəyät* rituals, now surreptitiously, but a decade ago the ceremonies were held publicly. Since they have been banned, some women return to Gurageland to partake in these and the annual *Dämʷamʷit* cult festival.

[45] The *šama* is the toga-like white cotton rectangular shawl worn both by men and women. Today men wear with it cotton trousers or jodhpurs, while women wear skirt-like dresses woven from *šama*-cloth. Unlike the Amhara women's *šama*, that worn by Gurage women is wrapped around the body and tied at the waist; the upper portion of the *šama* can either hang loosely as a tunic leaving the breasts bare, or the tunic can be used as a shawl for carrying a child or even goods on a woman's back. For the Amhara-style dress, see the description given by Ullendorff, 1960, p. 177. On traditional Gurage symbols of status refer to Cecchi, 1886, p. 60. Signifying status according to the amount of clothing worn is probably a survival of an older Amhara-Ethiopian custom. Men of low status and women were naked except for a waist belt, while kings, priests, and other dignitaries were fully clothed. The king was always concealed behind draperies when holding court. See Alvarez, 1881, pp. 154–217.

regardless of the status of her husband; she wore instead a skirt sewn from skin and her breasts were bare.[46]

Status as well as age was also implied by the manner in which a man wore his hair. There was roughly a three-fold scheme of social rank: 'poor men' had completely shaven heads; 'common' or ordinary men wore small plaits knotted at the back or hanging at both sides from a centre plait; elderly 'rich men' wore a full growth of hair, and that of ritual dignitaries was said to be even longer. Such status criteria are gradually disappearing but even today 'coolie' migrant labourers can still be singled out from other more prosperous Gurage by their shaven heads which, in *Šäwa*, have nearly become a characteristic sign of their occupation.

Many other traditional symbols of status remain intact today. Social differentiation is still to be seen in the rituals of death. If the deceased is a common man, lamentations at his homestead are carried on for two days; and in the death of an *Agäz* or other hero, the dirge is one day longer and the funeral dance is also performed for him; his family also observes a five-day fasting period, taking only small quantities of beer. As described above, Gurage express this form of status by saying 'they go for him on the sides', which means that a member of the family of the deceased, or a close friend, runs throughout the gathering of mourners uttering chants about the hero that relate the deeds he performed during his lifetime. Formerly, if the hero had killed many of the enemy, or large game, lions, elephants or leopards, the narrator carries about skins and other trophies of the deceased in performing the dance. In spite of these changes, Chiefs, heroes and other important men are still today eulogized in songs depicting heroic events in their lives which eventually become permanent records in the oral history of the tribe. Common men, reputed for some particular skill, litigation or knowledge of tribal history are notable attributes, will often be honoured at burial, thus setting them apart from other ordinary men.

The most important social distinctions have always been based on tribal origin. From the Gurage's point of view anyone who is not a member of a lineage is an alien and is referred to as *gäbbar*, an 'outsider'. Apart from slaves and Fuga, there are no other culturally and ethnically alien groups in Gurageland. Nor are there

[46] Among the Ensete cultivators, the Sidamo and Kambatta women still dress in skin skirts, whereas the Darasa women now often wear Amhara-style clothing.

any districts or smaller territorial divisions composed of 'strangers' adopted into clan or lineage groups. In pre-Menilek times, the vast majority of slaves were captured in war or bought, the chief sources coming from the Negro tribes in the West Nile region and the Sidamo and Galla tribes, each considered inferior to people belonging to Gurage stock. Gurage captured in war were seldom employed by other Gurage as household slaves because they were a lucrative source of income, particularly in the first half of the nineteenth century when slavery was rampant throughout the whole of Ethiopia. Although slaves generally occupied an inferior position, there is no evidence to suggest that they constituted a social class. Most families, it seems, kept domestic slaves, the numbers attached to each homestead varying according to the status of its head and his demands for additional labour, especially in *äsät* cultivation. Since no ritual stigma was associated with slaves, they could assist in agricultural chores, whereas Fuga could not. Slaves were never adopted into the household's lineage through which the inheritance of land and, concomitant with it, jural rights in the community are made possible; the few of their descendants that are found today have attached themselves as domestics in Gurage households.

On previous pages, the variety of economic and ritual occupational roles performed by Fuga specialists has been described. That there are status differences between Gurage and Fuga, and among Fuga themselves, has also been made clear. In the ritual sector, male and female Fuga, the chief ritual experts, rank above other Fuga assistants, because of their specialized knowledge of ritual traditions and their ability to manipulate supernatural phenomena through sorcery and magic. When we turn to Gurage religious organization, it will be seen that Fuga Chiefs take the role of ceremonial leaders at the annual *Čəšt* and *Däm^wam^wit* cult festivals, over which the dignitaries representing the deities preside. Fuga Chiefs are engaged in full-time ritual work; most others depend for their livelihood on their skills as craftsmen.

Social distinctions made in Gurage linguistic idioms have ritual implications as well. A man is said to be either *žära*, which implies that he is ritually clean, having not committed a ritual transgression, or he is *fesä*, which implies that he is ritually unclean and despised, the consequence of serious ritual misdeeds. The ritual curse, *Zitänä*, wherein a person is ostracized from his lineage and village, illustrates the social distinctions between *fesä* and *žära*. More is said about *Zitänä* in the context of *gurda* ritual covenants.

There were several ways by which a man could acquire status and prestige in former times. When tribal warfare was a conspicuous feature of life in Gurageland, bravery and skill in encountering the enemy were perhaps the most important means by which men could acquire individual prestige and influence. Status, obviously a concomitant of wealth, was measured in terms of the size of a man's *äsät* holding, and this was dependent upon land and cattle. Both of these were prizes of success in warfare. The command of a large following of kin and unrelated persons were amenities that accrued from achieving the title *Agäz*. But there were other ways in which men of lowly birth could command a certain amount of respect from their fellow tribesmen. Specialized knowledge in particular aspects of tribal law gained for some men, mostly elders, the title of *Danä*, judge; *Yänkit danä*, judge of adultery; *Yäheche danä*, judge of land, and so forth. Men with outstanding ability to debate, to practise medicine,[47] and to compose and recite religious poetry relating the powers of *Waq* (*Bädriyä*), or heroic poetry (*Wäyäg*), are still as important in tribal life today as in former times. Influence and respect tend to be commanded even today by wealthy men who are able to exert their power beyond the village to the wider clan unit, through the lending of cattle (*wäkᵞa*) or money. Although the amount of influence a poor man can exert is of little consequence, he would be reluctant to admit to any inherent difference between his status and that of a wealthy man.

Nowadays a few men have been able to enjoy greatly increased prestige because of persistent efforts of *Šäwa* to form a bureaucracy out of the traditional political system. Formal education together with a reasonable knowledge of tribal laws are prerequisites a man should possess when seeking government employment. The unfavourable opinion with which some older and more conservative Gurage regard such occupations, however, often outweigh the prestige and influence that might be gained in this way. Despite this, younger educated men find that this is the only

---

[47] The Gurage distinguish two kinds of practioners: those administering cures through non-ritual means, as above, and those resorting to ritual and magical cures.

gainful occupation suited to their newly acquired learning.[48] Elders who are slow in recognizing the voices of younger educated Gurage are often in conflict with them as they attempt to influence village affairs. Young educated Gurage, as well as others with specialized knowledge, are recognized only for possessing special authority within their respective fields; they do not represent a group possessing distinctive influence and authority.

Apart from the few Gurage teachers, religious dignitaries, and Fuga specialists on the one hand, and the caste of artisans on the other, there exists nothing in the nature of what may be termed a 'professional' class in Gurageland. There are perhaps less than a score of Government clerks, and other than this, no new forms of occupation have been created since the coming of Ethiopian rule. Administration of tribal affairs is conducted almost entirely through the traditional authority system. From the point of view of Government, the village headman is the most important authority figure. In tribal matters even a 'backward' headman commands far more authority than an 'educated' man, unless the latter is himself a man of high rank. For the most part then, almost every Gurage remains primarily a cultivator; the specialist skills he puts to use continue to be supplementary to his *äsät* activities. Moreover, with educated young men constantly being drained off by the lure of *Šäwa*, it seems hardly likely that an enlightened group large enough to challenge the old way of life will emerge.

II

In Chapter III I said that land and cattle, the principal determinants of wealth, are corporate holdings of the minimal lineage. Individual accumulation of extensive holdings to the exclusion of close relatives was, at least in former times, highly improbable. The few Gurage who have recently acquired some considerable wealth from cash-crop farming, trading ventures, wage labour, and small business enterprises in the towns indicate a slight trend toward the development of a new class. Thus if a 'wealthy' class does emerge it will be a direct result of these new economic undertakings in *Šäwa*, rather than a consequence of the indigenous social and economic organization. It is to this matter that I devote attention in the remainder of this chapter.

The accumulation of small sums of wealth, traditionally and

[48] This problem is discussed in Shack, 1959.

now, is a prerogative of the offices of ritual and political leaders and village headmen. A political chief receives no direct tribute because of his office, but he can accumulate cattle, money or both from time to time from the payment of fines levied in his court, and when he takes up office it is still customary for every responsible head of a family to make gifts to him. There are no overt social or ritual sanctions to reinforce these gifts but public opinion is sufficient to exert moral suasion on most family heads who feel it is their duty to pay a Chief tribute. Ritual chiefs, on the other hand, receive annual tribute in specially prepared *äsät*-bread, cattle, honey, ivory ornaments, and often gold and silver jewellery from their followers. Moreover, their following is under the burden of ritual obligations to support religious leaders who, in consequence, enjoy a relatively high economic standing. The fear of supernatural sanctions which could be brought to bear for failing to uphold ritual obligations helps to maintain the economic position of religious leaders. Apart from the annual tribute, religious leaders occasionally receive placating gifts from members of their flock who expect some spiritual benefit in return. The assistants of religious chiefs, the Chief $M^w \partial y \ddot{a}t$ and the *Maga*, ritual agents of the Thunder God's representative, receive their share of payment by virtue of their various trusts. They collect tribute in their respective districts on behalf of their chiefs and distribute sacred amulets, and other paraphernalia, for which payment is given both in cash and goods.

Ritual agents have at their disposal at least potential control over considerable wealth, and are better able to accumulate riches than ritual chiefs themselves. The assistants meet the people daily and can refuse them ritual services unless they are well paid for their good offices. Religious chiefs are dependent upon their assistants. Apart from the annual tribute, it is principally through the loyalty of $M^w \partial y \ddot{a}t$ and *Maga* assistants that their Chiefs receive periodic subsistence. Reciprocity on the part of religious chiefs, in ritually and economically supporting their assistants, maintains the patron-client relationship, which is necessary if the system of tribute is to endure.

Before *Šäwa* took direct control over the office of village headmanship, administering it through the District Governor, a village headman received little or no payment for his work. The office of village headman was traditionally considered to confer political prestige, rather than wealth. A village headman in good favour with his villagers as well as with his Clan Chief was occasionally rewarded by both. Now the village headman receives a salary commensurate with the tax revenue appropriated from his district. This has added to his office a small measure of economic status, which formerly did not exist. The dilemma that confronts the village headman of today is partly due to this. His aggressiveness in attempting to accumulate wealth which was virtually non-existent in traditional times is stimulated by the changes in the function of his office. On the other hand, his anxiety is often increased by the rebellious nature of the villagers, who attempt to circumvent the imposition of taxes in various ways. Since the office of village headman is the corporate holding of the village, election to that office being controlled by the minor lineage of which the headman is a member, the real or potential wealth that might accrue from his position is regulated by the same set of factors that place him in office. In consequence of the diminishing number of material rewards, the prestige formerly associated with village headmanship has been reduced considerably.

In spite of the fact that today far greater possibilities exist for accumulating wealth, mainly because of the broadening effects of the economy resulting from new labour undertakings, socio-economic status between individuals and groups is, on the whole, much the same as in former times. There has not yet emerged anything comparable to a 'wealthy class' in Gurageland; there are individually some wealthy Gurage. The status symbols that are characteristic of the urban Ethiopian, who in many respects resembles other African élite, have not yet been adopted by Gurage men. Socio-economic status is still symbolized by the traditional customs, habits, and forms of material culture, rather than in expensive luxury goods, which in themselves would be incompatible with the surroundings. Most men invest in land. But the possibility of attaining status and prestige through increased land holdings is slight. Virgin land is scarce and most men know this. And they also know that social mobility in Gurageland is becoming increasingly more difficult.

The concerted expressed views of the kin group of an individual and of the community as a whole form a public opinion strong enough to reinforce the cultural values which underlie the determinants of socio-economic status. The sanctions of the community are essentially expressed in the forms of ridicule and accusations of taking on the ways of the Amhara and other tribes, whose customs are abhorrent to Gurage. No man can withstand this for long. One course of action is to leave the tribal land and join the other élites in urban Ethiopia. And many Gurage do just that.

CHAPTER V

The Political System:
Clanship and Ritual

BEFORE Menilek established *pax Aethiopia* over *Yä säbat bet Gurage* in 1889 there was no one leader or one tribe among them with political authority over all; no one could exact tax, tribute or service from all. Gurage had no centralized State exercising legislative, administrative, juridicial, and military functions in the interests of the whole society. Although Gurage tribes frequently united for war against a common enemy, the Amhara, Galla, and Sidamo tribes, not all Gurage tribes could be counted on to join forces at all times. Religious issues especially failed to evoke co-operation, more often than not leading to political dissension. The slave trade was a product of this conflict. The relentless character of enslavement, which was rampant in Gurageland and South-West Ethiopia generally before Ethiopian rule was established, made it increasingly dangerous for any Gurage to enlarge the area of his travel outside his own community, except under the safe-conduct of kinsmen in other clans. And this was not always reliable assurance.

Slavery increased considerably as a consequence of the social and political climate that prevailed in mid-nineteenth-century Ethiopia. In the history of any people, past events of slavery understandably cause much embarrassment, making discussion of it difficult, and denial of its existence commonplace. But moral issues apart, historical accounts of the conditions under which slavery was conducted throw some light on the fragmented nature of Gurage political system and authority structure.

Shoan Ethiopian officials during the reign of Sahla Sellassie apparently adopted a *laissez-faire* attitude towards internecine warfare in Gurageland. The vivid description of tribal conflicts, and the taking of slaves as booty, written by Major Harris in 1844, is one account that indicates the instability of the political system:

Whilst the Galla make constant predatory inroads from without, anarchy reigns within [Gurageland]. A multitude of private feuds animate the turbulent population; and there being neither king nor laws, it is not surprising that every man should stretch forth his hand to kidnap his neighbour. Among the southern portions especially, in the domicile or in the open street, the stronger seizes upon the weaker as his bondsman, and sells him to the greedy Mohammadan dealers . . . and . . . their glittering gew-gaws; the innate love of which induces brother to sell sister, and the parent to carry her own offspring to the market.[1]

Similarly, reports in the journals of Isenberg and Krapf provide footnotes to the above accounts in their lengthy descriptions of village raids and of intrafamilial feuds:

The main reason of this separated state of the Guragueans is . . . the enmity of the people one against the other, and the total want of civil order . . . In general, the Guragueans have no civil authority.[2]

Burton (1856) and Guebre Sellassie (1932) supplement these accounts by the emphasis they place on the weakness of the Gurage political unit to maintain internal social control, and to protect the community against dangers threatening from without. I refer to intravillage strife again with reference to the patterns of Gurage clanship below (p. 147).

THE POLITICAL COMMUNITY

The Gurage political system, it seems, never approximated to a centralized form at the head of which stood a 'king'. While early writings often refer to the political unit as a 'state', or more often as a 'kingdom', the political unit was not a territorial sovereignty having centralized government, specialized administrative staff, and monopoly of the use of legitimate force.[3] Nor were power and authority vested in an institution of tribal chieftainship for the organization of groups of people under a single leader to regulate tax and tribute and modes of production and related services. The Gurage political unit can best be described by the term which

[1] W. Cornwallis Harris, (1844), Vol. III, p. 313.
[2] Isenberg and Krapf, op. cit., pp. 179–80.
[3] I refer above to the definition of State given by Nadel, 1942, p. 69. Gurage also lack 'government' in the way that it is defined by Fortes and Evans-Pritchard, p. 5.

Schapera uses, the 'political community': 'a group of people organized into a single unit managing its affairs independently of external control. Each community also has its own territory and an official head or "chief".[4] The political community implies the largest political unit with internal and external sovereignty, the members of which submit to the recognized form of political leadership. This is the exogamous, patrilineal clan and not the whole tribal society.

The Gurage political community is based on the system of clanship. To recapitulate, the largest genealogical structural unit of the tribe is the non-totemic exogamous patrilineal clan which derives from the nucleus of original ancestors. Clans are built up on maximal lineages whereas a tribal unit is built up on the aggregate group of clans, not necessarily related by a belief in their common descent from one remote tribal ancestor, but by their being in occupation of a continuous stretch of territory, the boundaries of which distinguish the tribal unit from other units and define the area by its tribal name. In addition, there are numerous institutional forms of co-operation and interdependence, political and economic, between different clans of the tribal group, which distinguish interclan relations from intertribal relations. Thus the clan is to be regarded as coterminous with the political community, which in itself can be further defined in terms of consciousness of unity and interdependence. Clans are exogamous and marriage occurs between all clans of the tribal group. These relations establish a close connexion between clans on the one hand, and form an institutional basis for the political structure within the kinship and social structure on the other.

The correspondence between political structure and kinship and social structure can be illustrated by the segments into which Gurage tribes are divided. We have found the terms primary, secondary, and tertiary, as used to define the Nuer system of segmentation, sufficient and convenient terms of definition for the Gurage.[5] Thus, primary tribal section means the largest tribal segment and consists of the clan and related maximal lineages; these are further segmented into secondary tribal sections, that is, major lineages, which are further segmented into tertiary tribal sections; these are minor lineages which we have shown in the previous chapter comprise a number of village communities con-

[4] Schapera, 1956, p. 8.   [5] Evans-Pritchard, 1940, pp. 139–42.

sisting of related homesteads composed of kinship and domestic groups.

In Table IX, primary segmentation of four of the seven Gurage tribes is represented. I can only speak with some accuracy of the Yɜnäkʷamt and Mogämänä primary sections of the Chaha. No attempt to list all sections of the tribe has been made. I have simply endeavoured to indicate the mode of segmentation for a clearer representation of intersegmental relations between tribal divisions.

TABLE IX

Primary Segments of Four Gurage Tribal Divisions

Chaha	Ezha	Ennemor	Gyeto
Yɜnäkʷamt	Šɜrar	Yädɜbɜržära	Bäräsɜyä
Yägäbäreaṭɜb	Nägʸära	Färar	Marawdänyä
Yɜrɜsṭɜb	Qončača	Gɜnäbäke	ɜmfäšä
Mogämänä	Agänna	Yägondär Žara	
Boz		Mʷäbe	
ɜnorgänä		Yätɜwa Gäžära	
Säga			
Yewäṭɜb			
Yägorämarṭɜb			
ɜnnähočä			
Yäwaqesäb			
Aradetṭɜb			
Agrarṭɜb			
Yähoräžära			
Mäzakʷer			

THE GURAGE PATTERN OF CLANSHIP

The clan is a local unit comprising two or more relatively autonomous maximal lineages, which regard themselves, and are regarded by others, as together forming a single unit. But no clan is a self-sufficient unit; it is exogamous and therefore seeks its women from other clans; it is linked with other clans in the inter-clan and intertribal exchange of market goods and services; it acts with other clans in political affairs which concern the tribal unit as a whole; it joins with other clans and tribal segments in common rituals.

These relations form a recognizable pattern of clanship. In secular and ritual affairs within a particular field of clanship there is greater mutual dependence, more frequent and regular co-operation and a stronger solidarity than with equivalent lineages of other clans. There is a regular exercise of mutual privileges and the fulfilment of mutual obligations between constituent maximal lineages of a clan. The region of greatest integration between maximal lineages is formed by the clan, but it is a region not necessarily confined to the social and geographical boundaries of the clan, for these often overlap similar boundaries of neighbouring clans.

The pattern of clanship is also definable by the norms of clanship relations. Clans prohibit intermarriage; the rules of incest formed by the basic kinship unit extend throughout wider units of descent to include the clan itself. Hence, it would be no less abhorent to a Gurage to marry a woman of a remotely related maximal lineage than to take a wife from his village, the minor lineage. Children born of such an incestuous union are said to die during childbirth, or shortly after and the parents themselves are supposed to suffer the discomforts of incurable illnesses. Clans also define the rights and obligations of component lineage segments, and attempt to realign structural ties between lineage segments set apart by breaches of the clan norm. Thus an accepted norm is that clan members should not feud,[6] and that disputes arising between members of the same clan should be settled by peaceful means, preferably through mediation initiated by the Clan Chief and actively conducted by Elders of the respective lineages involved. But acts of hostility between distantly related members over the reclamation of debts are often settled outside the clan council. In former days hostility invariably led to the feud, ending in blood-vengeance and a loss of life.

In spite of the historical evidence shown above of slave raiding between closely located settlements, and even within villages, it is difficult to assess the relevance of such incidents to the principles of clanship. Village raiding is a thing of the past. But a breakdown of relations within clans can occur today over issues of lesser magni-

---

[6] I use 'feud' in the sense of defining extended mutual hostility between clans; 'warfare' was primarily an act of hostility between tribes. 'Blood-vengeance' actually involved close agnatic kin of both sides especially when homicide ensued from feuding. The settlement of a case of homicide is given in an example below, pp. 164–5. The distinctions used between 'feud' and 'blood-vengeance' follow those of Evans-Pritchard, 1940, p. 150, and Middleton and Tait, 1958, p. 21.

tude, as in cases of accidental homicide or serious damages to property, reflecting the principal of structural opposition between clan segments. The Clan Chief and his council are at the pivot of clan political organization but the degree to which they are able to exercise control over constituent elements is theoretically and practically small. In terms of a reconstructed past of Gurage political history, it is conceivable that the widespread social and political disorganization, that was characteristic of mid-nineteenth-century Gurageland, represents a period when the normative principles of clanship had been reduced to their lowest denomination. Clan organization was then no longer an effective means of exercising internal control over its members, nor was it able to guarantee them any measure of security against external forces. But at the present time, although there is no fixed rule, solidarity, co-operation, and mutual dependence are greater between lineages within the clan than between lineages of different clans.

In contrast to the opposition of interclan relations in the field of political and economic rivalry, are clan joking relationships. A familiar form of teasing and prankster joking relations is seen in the behaviour between men of the Mogämänä and Yənäkʷamt clan Gurage, where interclan marriage frequently occurs. With the Gyeto Gurage joking rivalry occurs most often between the Bäräsəyä and the Marawdänyä clans who also commonly exchange women. Rivalry between men having joking clan relations is characterized by some form of joking behaviour that 'lets off steam'.

Even so, in situations of this kind, behaviour must not be pushed too far, since joking relationships are defined within certain limits, and exceeding these limits overrides the function of ridicule. Although 'privileged aggression' seems to occur chiefly between siblings-in-law, no man would take advantage of his brother-in-law, for instance, by attempting to have an affair with his wife, under the assumption that the tenseness arising from his acts could be passed off as a joke. But without permission, a man might 'borrow' his joking rival's goods, provoking merely a mock-fight over seeking their return; whereas a similar 'borrowing' by a non-joking member would be ample grounds for real conflict. In *Šäwa*, on several occasions I have seen a migrant Gurage jokingly refuse to assist a rival, by publicly deriding his plight, as a common condition of all members of his clan. This derision would continue until the person was thoroughly humiliated, and one more word uttered would most certainly lead to a fight. Only then would the accuser end his ridicule, agree to render the favour, and the two men depart as friends. Onlookers at such a spectacle have commented that denigrating a rival clansmen, especially a sibling-in-law, is a privilege of which all Gurage take advantage.

Gurage interclan joking behaviour is less firmly institutionalized than what has been described for the Tallensi, for instance. But similarly, it is a means of reconciling and counteracting tensions of a double-edged social relationship where conflicting interests of structurally opposed groups are bound together by strong ties of obligatory goodwill in another aspect of their social relations.[7] The Gurage rationale for these and other forms of clanship relations is to be found in their myths, genealogical relationships, and the ideology of kinship. Theoretically and fictionally these validate the social structure.

THE POLITICS OF GURAGE CLANSHIP

The Gurage clan is a political unit: any form of socially sanctioned behaviour which, in one way or another, strengthens the unity of the clan and tribal group, through primary and secondary forms of action, is implied in its meaning.

A Gurage clan has political significance. Along with the many functions a clan performs, it fulfills a political function. Political functions take place within the nexus of clanship ties which have structural variability depending on what ties and cleavages are relevant in any given situation. As the largest autonomous grouping, the nexus of clanship, in political affairs, will be referred to here as the 'jural community'.[8] The jural community is symbolized, in one way, in the institution of clan chieftainship. Chieftainship, described in the next section, is vested in a particular maximal lineage of the clan, continuity of office being regulated by the association of the myth of chieftainship with a permanent line of descent and succession. Chieftainship is coexistent with the kinship and lineage system.

Gurage clan chieftainship is hereditary in the senior male line,

[7] Fortes, 1945, p. 91.
[8] Middleton and Tait, op. cit., p. 9: 'the jural community is the widest grouping within which there are moral obligations and a means ultimately to settle disputes peaceably.'

passing from father to son. As a rule the Chief succeeds automatically to his office by right of birth; although cases are known in Gurage history where Chieftainship was usurped, none can be cited of a Chief ever having been elected to office. If a Chief has more than one wife, the eldest son of the first wife has priority to succession over the eldest son of the second wife, and so on for each of his wives and their sons. When no male issue stands as heir within the direct lines of descent, succession shifts to the collateral lines beginning with the brother immediately junior to the deceased Chief.[9] If this brother is also dead and there is no male issue in his line, it passes to the brother next in order of seniority.

The diagram in Fig. 11 shows the rules of succession in a skeleton genealogy of the *Yärgusden* lineage of the Mogämänä clan in which

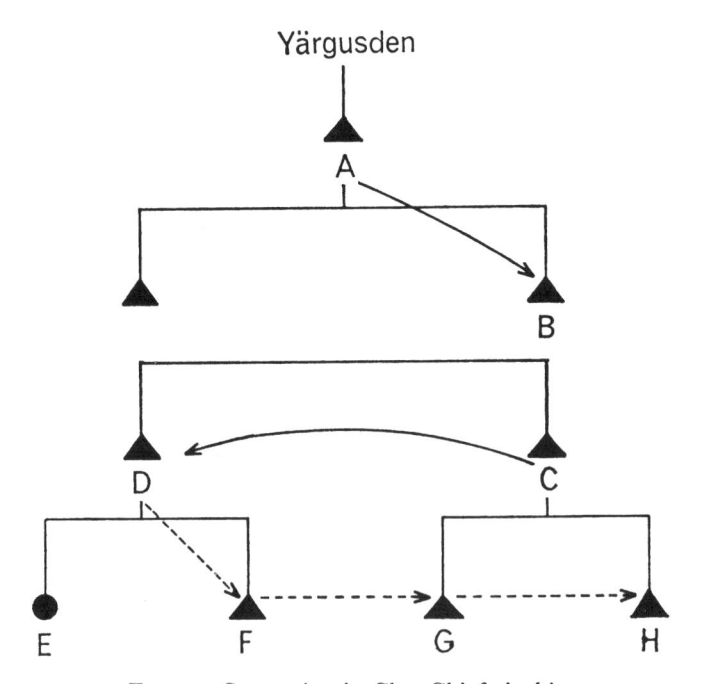

FIG. 11. Succession in Clan Chieftainship.

[9] For example, in 1958 only a girl had been born to Chief Täsämma Amärga; in 1962 when I returned to Gurageland, the Chief had taken a second wife who had presented him with a son and direct heir to Chieftainship.

the present Chieftainship is vested. Individuals are indicated according to birth order corresponding to seniority in succession.

The present ruling line of descent is four generations in depth; succession passed to the former ruler's eldest son A, then to his eldest son B who ruled until his death. Chieftainship should have passed to C and ultimately through his sons G and H. But C, having been mission-educated, had spent most of life outside Gurageland, and held a ministerial post with the Government. After undergoing the customary installation ceremonies, which insured the office in his line, C renounced his rights to Chieftainship in favour of his junior D. Chieftainship cannot be reclaimed by C, but it may pass to his sons should F die without any male issue.[10]

I illustrate further the genealogical relationship between the lineage of Chieftainship to that of other Yärgusden lineages in the diagram below. Berhanä and Gäbru, as with Täsämma, claim relationship to Wərago, though Chieftainship passed to the latter according to the pattern of succession described above and shown in Fig. 11.

The history of several Gurage clans reveals instances of conflict between rival claimants to the succession, even though hereditary seniority is the rule. Of the present ruling Clan Chiefs, several are descended from men who usurped the Chieftainship from the legitimate heir. This often resulted in a split in the clan itself and the founding of a new line. Chieftainship gained in this way remained in the line of the man who actually succeeded,

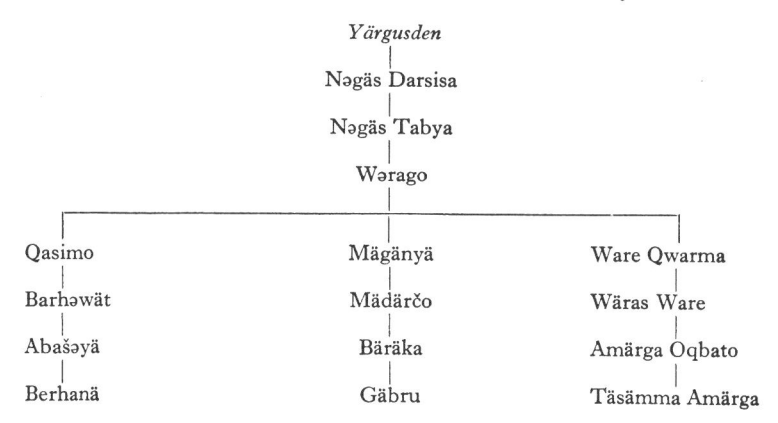

[10] A son (F) has been born to Chief Täsämma by his second wife. See fn. 9 above.

whereas the descendants of the disinherited could only regain the position by force. Failing this, they could accept defeat, or they could beseech the ritual authority, placating him with gifts, not to acknowledge rule by the usurper. The rituals associated with the installation of a Chief, as described in the next section, signify the importance of confirming political ties with those of ritual. Ritual leaders sanction the offices of Chiefs and other representatives of authority and law.

THE RITUALS OF CHIEFTAINSHIP

In all Gurage clans the deaths of Chiefs are announced publicly and this is the signal for the mobilization of the whole tribe. Village headmen are mainly responsible for spreading the news that a Chief is dead. But this is seldom left entirely in their hands, for itinerant traders not only carry news to neighbouring tribes but bring back messages of condolences as well; the exchange of courtesies often extends as far as *Šäwa*. When an important Chief dies, the entire *säbat bet* is represented in the ensuing rites by Clan Chiefs, or their envoys, from each respective tribe; they attend the mourning ceremony and the feast that follows, and many of them remain later to witness the installation of the new Chief.

Clan Chiefs bring cattle, sheep, *äsät*-food, grain, coffee, and when possible, beer to honour the dead Chief. Similar foodstuffs are supplied by the lineage of the deceased in his village as well as from neighbouring villages, all of which are assembled at the homestead of the dead Chief and consumed on a large scale during the thirty-day period of commemoration, *täzkar*, by all who have come to mourn, Chiefs and commoners alike.

Installation of the new Chief takes place as soon as possible after *täzkar* has ended, usually on the same day of the week that the former Chief died. If the heir apparent is not of age, his father's brother exercises the major functions of office, although the junior heir is properly installed as Chief. The fear of disputes arising between brothers over the rights to Chieftainship is avoided partly by the short lapse in time between the burial of a Chief and the inauguration of his successor. Then, on the appointed day, all clan members of the Chief, related clans of the tribe and their leaders and those from other tribes, assemble at the 'special place' for installing political office holders. The ceremony is held at the earth-shrine of the deity *Waq*, in the district of Yabäze, of which the giant *zəgba* tree is the symbol. When a Chief is to be installed a white banner is flown from a staff planted near the shrine. The sacred area is encircled by the number of gathered Chiefs, with those from the tribe of the deceased acting as ceremonial leaders by conducting the secular parts of the inauguration ceremony.

The new Chief is never allowed to set foot on the ground until the installation has formally ended. He is kept secluded from others in the homestead of his father until the moment of presentation to the clan gathering. *En route* to the shrine he is first carried part of the way by servants of his father, and later placed on the late Chief's mule which is customarily named after the Chief. At the shrine the servants lead the Chief around the flagstaff seven times and then carry him shoulder high to the 'Chief's Seat'. This is an elaborately carved throne-like chair, of the three-leg style decorated with embossed linear designs, that a Chief inherits along with the cloak, head covering and other paraphernalia of his office. The Chief's Seat is not sacred although it is inherited from his ancestors, and when it is old and beyond repair, a new Seat is carved by an especially skilled Fuga. At the installation, the Seat is placed directly under the sacred *zəgba*.

Sacred rites of the Chief's installation are conducted by the ritual dignitary known as Yäwäy dämam,[11] and all vessels and vestments used to install the Chief are blessed on behalf of *Waq*. The most important Agäz of the Chief's lineage acts as ceremonial leader in the non-ritual part of the installation. During the ceremony a sheep is slaughtered and a ring made from a tendon is attached to the silver *gʷândär* arm-band, the symbol of Chieftainship. The *gʷândär* and the tendon, after having been dipped in the sacrificial blood, are placed round the right arm of the Chief, whose forehead is also anointed with blood. *Yäwäy dämam* ejects a mouthful of milk and honey into the face of the Chief, then taking the Chief's right ear in his own right hand, he recites a long formula invoking blessings on the new Chief. The ceremonial crowd responds to these incantations with intermittent chants, that alternate from parallel sides of the great circle formed by them. They shrill ululations of joy and shout '*ebo nəgäs*', 'be king'. All those in attendance then pass before the Chief placing at his feet a handful

---

[11] The ritual functions of *Yäwäy dämam* are described more fully on p. 186 *passim* below.

of special grass brought for this purpose. The Chief remounts his mule, rides round the flagstaff seven times and then leads a procession back to his homestead where the installation feast is held. There, the Chief is paid tribute in cattle, money and other gifts by male kin of his mother's clan; her female kin bring butter for preparing the food to be eaten at the feast.

For seven days after the installation the Chief returns each day to Yabäze. There he sits under the shrine of *Waq* in the Chief's Seat where he receives all those who come to pay him courtesy; this often includes presenting him with a gift. On the seventh day, at the principal clan market, he publicly proclaims himself Chief; it is only after this proclamation that he can re-enter the house of his deceased father. Finally, the white banner used in his installation is buried at Yabäze, where the banners of his predecessors have also been buried. From that time onwards the Chief is addressed in terms of respect reserved for him and his mother; anyone failing to address him as *ahu* or 'You' (the polite form, fem. *ax*) is liable to a fine of 15 head of cattle.

During the period of confinement prior to his installation, a Chief is under the tutelage of Elders with knowledge of tribal affairs, who formerly assisted his father. He is advised on the burdens and responsibilities associated with Chieftainship; on the restrictions these bring to his ordinary daily life; on the personal dangers involved in the control and exercising of power; on the demands that will be made on his character and integrity in the handling of situations to enable him to bring about a rightful outcome for the good of the clan and the tribe as a whole. But the ultimate success of a Chief is determined by his political relations with other Chiefs in the interclan politics of the jural community.

A Chief can gain prominence over other Chiefs in several ways and thus win recognition as 'leader' from certain groups within the tribal unit and in certain activities. These factors, now to be described, combined with the political traditions of clans as expressed in their mythology further the meaning of the terms major clan and minor clan, as I have used them, in the context of political leadership.

The first prerequisites a Chief should possess, which add to his qualities of leadership, are those of family tradition and the knowledge of law and custom. These are like assets, the same as wealth, and they are transmittable from father to son, so that within the lineage group the senior line becomes the chief guardian of tradition and its members are responsible for perpetuating them for the benefit of the clan or even the tribal unit.

Wealth is as important as tradition. Historical and social factors make tradition; economic and environmental factors determine the greater or lesser wealth of the Chiefs. Whether a Chief has accumulated possessions through inheritance or through personal effort, the possession of wealth gives him prestige and influence both within and without his clan. Tribute received by a Chief on special occasions and a part of the fines levied on members of his clan at tribal councils become his personal possessions. His ability to offer everyday hospitality, in the form of beer, meat, and *äsät*-food, has a positive value in that it makes his homestead a meeting place for the elders of his own and of neighbouring villages. He can also gain a greater influence over individuals, and aggregates of kin-related groups, by lending them cattle. This practice is known as *wäkya*, 'loan of a cow'; the borrower has the usufruct of the cow, but its offsprings belong to the proprietor. The demands a Chief makes for repayment or reclamation are often considerate, and, in return, the debtor is obliged to praise his Chief and render him small services. Giving feasts on a clan-scale, which requires the slaughtering of many cattle, gains for a wealthy Chief popularity among all his Clansmen. By directing the distribution of meat on these occasions, he can favour those who especially respect and honour him and who can be relied upon to support him in clan matters by accepting his views. Popularity of this nature spreads throughout the tribal area and sooner or later less prosperous Chiefs turn up at these gatherings to receive gifts of food which they apportion to their own clansmen.

Another quality that in the past made for leadership was success in warfare. This not only served as a means of gaining wealth but brought prestige in itself. Every clan has its own history of past Chiefs remembered for their deeds as warriors, and each bearing the title *Agäz* (Amharic, *Abägaz*) signifying that the enemies they have killed number at least one hundred. There were other titles that Chiefs as well as ordinary men could earn for conspicuous bravery in encountering the enemy:

Esehyarb—'one who does not retreat'
Bärdäfärä—'one who attacked the enemy camp'

Bärkäfäta—'one who broke through the enemy line and performed brave deeds'
Wanžätarb—'one who entered the enemy circles'.

The success of a Clan Chief in warfare, especially when the whole tribe or most of its clans was involved, was of considerable importance to the nature of leadership, for such Chiefs were then in an exalted position as tribal heroes. *Agäz* Balčaya of Amya is credited with having led a direct assault against the overwhelming forces of Menilek. *Agäz* Oqbato, said to have led the final assault against Shoan forces at the Uabi River, which Gurage say was 'coloured from the blood that flowed', is especially revered in the history of Chaha. Other Chiefs like *Agäz* Darsamo from Ennemor, who compelled Menilek to placate him with gifts and favours in order to end the rebellions of Ennemor against *Šäwa*, is honoured in a tribal song. I record only a few lines of it here:

> (Menilek) gave you a glass that you may drink from it,
> He gave you a *masar*-plate[a] that you may eat from it,
> He gave you a mule that you may ride upon it
> He gave you a *dak^wä*-cloth[b] that you may put it on:
> All Inaqwam [Yanäk^wamt] has chosen you (as Chief)[12]

Warfare usually involved joint expeditions by several clans, and leadership in fighting more than that acquired in other ways tended to be recognized by several clans, and thus to establish the superiority of one clan over the others. Nowadays, the qualities of leadership which formerly were exhibited in warfare are commonly devoted to litigation with Government especially over land problems and taxation. The long court case fought by Chief Oqbato to reclaim *Chaha Woudema*, the Crown Lands, is frequently mentioned with the same meaning as his exploits at warfare. It is difficult to know to what extent magico-religious virtues were associated with the success of a Chief in warfare, but it seems possible that there must have been at least a modest connexion, because of the ritual blessings bestowed on a Chief at his installation for his successful career of leadership.

Finally, old age is the most general quality that contributes to political leadership. Other things being equal, a Chief older in

---

[12] The remaining text of this song is given in Leslau, 1950, p. 124; (a) hand-carved ivory plate, (b) red cloth used as a saddle cover.

years would be respected and revered more than a young chief; his opinions generally carried the most weight in interclan matters. An older Chief is believed to be a wiser Chief, and all of his actions, and the responses to them, prove that he has this virtue. This is merely an extension of the authoritarian pattern based on age seen at other times in the context of kinship.

The more qualities of leadership a Chief possesses the greater his authority and the wider the scope of his influence outside his own clan. Authority of a Chief is most easily extended throughout the tribe by the distribution of his wealth and formerly by his ability to lead the tribe in times of war. Upon reaching old age, a Chief is believed also to have attained wisdom, and this quality gains for him additional status as an arbiter in legal disputes. Juridical relations, as with political relations, are set within the field of clanship.

THE JURAL ASPECTS OF CLANSHIP: THE CLAN COUNCIL

The primary political function of the jural community is the maintenance of social control. It is through the jural aspects of interclan relations that the principles of group solidarity work in practice. As with most segmentary societies, jural relations operate at several levels of the clan structure. The maintenance of social control at the homestead and village level is of a different order and degree of complexity than that at the level of the maximal lineage and clan; it is different between constituent clans of the same tribe; it is different between tribal groups. The relationships between individuals and small groups at the lowest level of lineage segmentation spread out and involve wider segments of the clan; and the procedure by which these relationships are shaped into a coherent system and graded according to the order of groupings involved, is essentially the function of the clan council. I discuss these jural relations in this section.

The clan council is convened by the Chief. The council is composed of Elders who act as advisors to the Chief, a *danä* or 'judge' of the customary law that concerns the dispute, the village headman who has petitioned the Chief for a council, and the Elders of the village from which the plaintiff comes to demand a hearing for himself or for someone in his homestead. The case has usually been well rehearsed by the litigants long before the council assembles; at informal gatherings, frequently held in an open field, or in the evenings at the homestead of a wise and important elder. As clearly as possible the facts have been ascertained at these consultations, and proceedings at council usually consist of a recital of the facts, interrupted frequently by Elders with interjections about customary legal precedents. Elders not directly involved in the issue act as arbiters between disputing parties. The role of the Chief is essentially that of mediator and he attempts to reach a decision which is determined by, and conforms with, well-established tribal norms. Neither the Chief nor his council are endowed with powers of legislation, this being a jural function exclusive to the intertribal council called *Yä Goka*, next described in this chapter.

The Chief and his council are jurally independent of other clan councils when the dispute is between members of the Chief's clan alone and does not involve clansmen of other constituencies. Disputes between clan members usually arise over common offences, such private delicts as theft of small objects, quarrelling, fighting, slander, or debt, actions which are subject to 'restitutive sanctions'.[13] Appeals are made when efforts to reclaim an object, or to vindicate a wrong, have been resorted to by means of 'self-help' outside the procedure of the council, and have failed. The attempts to secure redress for a common offence by relying upon the unpredictable support a man expects to receive from his own lineage can meet with failure. In consequence, offences of a more serious nature may result in bodily injury or even death. Should this involve another clan, Chiefs of both sides, as well as other Chiefs of the tribe, assemble in council and attempt to reconcile the lineages alienated by the incident, until proper compensation, if any, can be agreed on.

The most serious civil offences (public delicts) are those of murder, arson, and adultery, for which settlement by compensation is rarely possible, and then only after the feud has been resorted to and caused loss of life.[14] Equally important is the fact that such crimes appear as sacrilegious offences, or even 'sins', for which

[13] In the terminology of Radcliffe-Brown on 'Primitive Law', 1956, p. 213.

[14] Cecchi observed a death sentence carried out on a young Gurage slave who had killed his master. When apprehended, the murderer was dressed in the blood-stained clothing of the deceased, the nearest kin of whom was the first to spear the killer (op. cit., p. 42.)

ritual expiation is exacted. It is sacrilegious to destroy a homestead and property by fire, and a Gurage seeks ritual protection against such destruction by placating the Thunder God *Božä*. He and his family are also protected against personal harm by *Däm^{w}am^{w}it*; the faithfulness of his wife is further ensured by placing at his disposal a curse, the invocation of which can bring ritual harm to her and her lover as well. Hence, any one of these offences committed against a Gurage is in fact an act defiling the sacredness of a deity, and before final settlement is reached a ritual agent must intervene. Ritual sanctions strengthen the jural authority of a Chief and his council and also give cohesion to interclan relations.

A Chief has no legitimate armed force at his disposal. His ability to maintain internal order depends upon the strength of his own personality, public opinion, the moral ideas held by his people, and ritual sanctions which ultimately can be applied; these are supported by the Gurage attitude to group solidarity, which itself is expressed in the facts of kinship and clanship. The machinery of social control is based on the principles of kinship; the extension and application of kinship principles give substance to the jural community. A Chief also relies a great deal upon Elders and village headmen to implement the policies of social control, for in most disputes, Elders and headmen are more closely related in genealogical and social terms to the disputants than the Chief, and therefore are at a greater advantage in exploiting the principles of kinship. The only sanction supporting the Chief in his legal decisions is the solidarity of the respective groups in backing them. Whenever the verdict is supported unanimously, or by the great majority of clan Elders, the defendant seldom objects to or appeals against it. If he attempts opposition without support from among his lineage, Elders enforce the verdict by appointing a number of men to exact the proper compensation.

There is more than one course open to the plaintiff who objects to the decision of the council. He can take matters into his own hands, he may appeal against the verdict by taking the case to *Yä Goka*, or have recourse to the spelling of a curse, or seek refuge within another clan district if he is able, through gifts, to persuade an official there to give him protection. If he is successful in this last course, his clan could legally intervene only through the Chief of the clan offering asylum. To evade justice in this manner is always dangerous, since it invariably increases interclan tensions, but in former times, when animosity between clans often led to open hostilities, this was apparently the course taken by many. The final course open to a dissatisfied litigant is to abandon his family and leave the tribal lands for good. And some men do in fact take this step.

RITUALS AND POLITICS OF *YÄ GOKA*

Gurage intertribal political relations are dealt with at the council assembly called *Yä Goka*. In the strictest sense, any meeting at which political heads gather can be so termed; but Gurage consistently reserve the term *Yä Goka*, 'meeting', for interclan and intertribal assemblies of tribal-wide importance. The structure of *Yä Goka* assemblies is different in kind and complexity from commoner meetings of Elders and headmen. At *Yä Goka* the representatives of all *säbat bet*, the Clan Chiefs, meet primarily to enact laws, which, with the passage of time, become customary rules of conduct controlling the behaviour of Gurage between themselves. The political structure of *Yä Goka* is underpinned by the foundations of ritual masonry.

The occasions for *Yä Goka* to meet are unaffected by other social and political events. These meetings are unscheduled and they are not like clan councils, which meet annually, irrespective of specific political and legal demands. *Yä Goka* is held as often as need be to deal with cases arising from unsettled disputes between Gurage of constituent or unrelated clans, which, if prolonged, might go so far as to threaten the peace of the entire *säbat bet*. Of the representative number of Clan Chiefs from each tribe assembled, it is generally the Chief assuming a dominant position over clans of his own tribal group who acts as head spokesman for the group, at the intertribal council.

Any Chief can summon *Yä Goka*. If the Chief and his council have failed to achieve a reconciliation between the contestants, appeal to *Yä Goka* can be made by them, and the Chief is obliged to recognize this appeal. In the customary procedure of appeal, the plaintiff, with a great display of anger, shouts loudly in the midst of the clan council, 'let *Yä Goka* see', 'let the *Waq* rule'. Chiefs are then responsible for informing their own people that *Yä Goka* will 'see the case'. Village headmen principally spread the news, but any person concerned may pass the word along. Since the assembly meets openly, all adult men who care to attend, even strangers, may do so, and take part in the proceedings. Women never attend *Yä Ǧoka* even when they are directly involved in the case; they are represented by their husbands or male kin.

The close relationship between Gurage religious and political institutions is reflected in the ritualization of the structure and organization of *Yä Ǧoka*. *Yä Ǧoka* meetings take place at the shrine of *Waq*, the Sky-god, and the litigation is presided over symbolically by the ritual custodian of the shrine, who is known as the Lord of *Wǻgäpʰäča*. It is sufficient to explain now that according to tradition, *Waq*, a male deity, chooses a woman to be custodian of his shrine. The sacred place where the shrine is located is at Yabäze, in the district of Gumer, where, as we have seen,[15] other important tribal events are held. Other ritual functionaries like *Yäwäy dämam* and *Gʷetakʷəyä* usually attend *Yä Ǧoka* and by their presence the ritual element of the tribal council is strengthened.

The politico-ritual focus of the assembly is the Lord of *Wǻgäpʰäča*. In this and other functions, she, the 'Lord', the chief ritual custodian of the shrine of *Waq*, directly mirrors clanship and ritual ties. On the ground this is manifested symbolically in the seating arrangement of the congregation. Clan representatives sit in a fixed order according to their dominant role in tribal political affairs. The Lord of *Wǻgäpʰäča* sits directly under the shrine, symbolizing the 'entrance'. Other ritual dignitaries sit on opposite sides of the entrance. Then clan Chiefs are seated in order of political seniority, and lesser officials such as headmen and judges are seated last, to complete the circle. This grouping of officials is the centre of a pattern of concentric circles, the outer circles being formed by interested persons, onlookers, and strangers. The placing of individuals according to senior status is customary on all formal political and ritual occasions, and this precedence is followed in the household whenever important guests are present. The guests sit at each side of the entrance to the hut, then senior and junior males of the household form a circular pattern extending from both sides of the entrance, then neighbours, unrelated persons, and women of the household form circular rows reaching back to the rear of the hut.

Yä Ǧoka can also be viewed as shown in the diagram on p. 162 (Fig. 12) which gives a conceptual scheme of the structural relations between tribal units in political affairs. Some indication

[15] pp. 152–5 above.

is given here of how politico-ritual relations and social ties converge to create and maintain interclan and intertribal solidarity. I indicate also both the complementary and the segmentary character of the Gurage political system; mutual dependence as well as interdependence between tribal units function at one and the same time.

One element in the mechanism of social control maintained through the institution of *Yä Ǧoka* is linguistically expressed by Gurage as *ang*. This word may be translated as *justice*, which, as a maxim, has a more profound meaning than a term such as *law*,

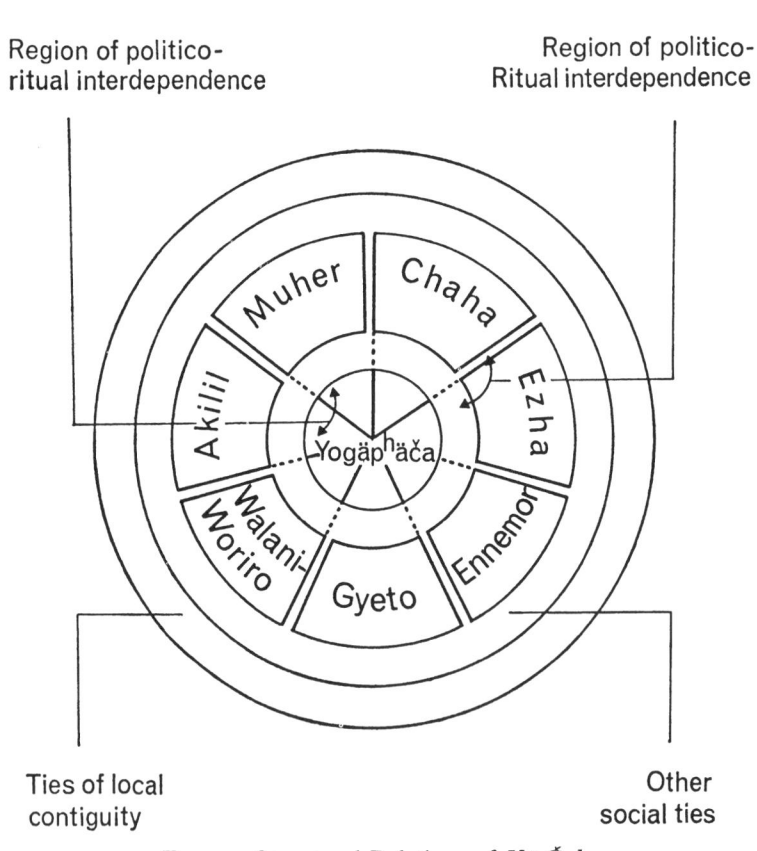

FIG. 12. Structural Relations of *Yä Ǧoka*.

for which the Gurage equivalent is *qʸəǰa*. [16] In one sense the meaning of clan citizenship is contained in the single expression *ang*. Apart from social, economic, and political benefits derived by clan membership, *ang* ensures to Gurage the all-important benefits of security and protection. For the most part, apprehensions of personal harm are intercepted ritually and ritual protection is sought in most instances. Ritual protection is an aspect of equity which does not exclude the thought of others, but rather entertains it, having for its purpose a fair apportionment, an even-handed distribution of what there is; such equity has the elasticity of a spiritual quality. But *ang* has a self-contained quality that inspires confidence by declaration, assuring just compensation when individual rights are infringed. Rules of conduct between constituent clan members as being the same as those between unrelated clan members of wide territorial spacing are conveyed in the concept of *ang*. To a Gurage, *ang* is not circumscribed by genealogical or geographical distances, but overlaps them: it is the basis of a Gurage's egalitarian concept of men, irrespective of rank, age, status, and clan position.

Political equilibrium between minor and major clans is also brought about through the principles of *ang*. These principles, underlying Gurage social and political life, are given practical significance in the area of Gurage ritual life, the strength of which is derived from the great importance attached to the belief in *Waq* and his supernatural powers. The concept of *ang* is thus symbolized in the Lord of *Wågäpʰäča*, whose ritual authority descends directly from *Waq*. Justice handed down, and ritually sanctioned at *Yä Goka*, is supreme, and all decisions are considered to be for the common good.

Further analysis of the functions of *Yä Goka* leads to a discussion of Gurage customary law and legal procedure, the subject of which is complex and exceeds the scope of this study. In a word, Gurage customary law operates side by side with the Ethiopian Penal Code,[17] and only in such cases as an unsatisfactory settlement

[16] I have also heard the term '*qʸəǰa*', used in the same context as *ang*; but the latter translates more nearly to justice which underlies the decisions taken at tribal councils.

[17] See *Penal Code of the Empire of Ethiopia: Addis Ababa*, (1957). The modern penal code is based upon the *Fetha Negast*, a text of ecclesiastical and legal principles and the basic document of Amhara jurisprudence, customary law, and modern legal conventions.

of an issue at the clan council or *Yä Ǧoka*, is Government help resorted to for reinforcement of traditional proceedings. By and large, the vast majority of disputes between Gurage, even sometimes those involving homicide, are dealt with outside Government courts; the legal principles used here, embracing Western concepts of law, cannot be applied easily to Gurage customary modes of handling disputes. The effective maintenance of social control remains in its traditional form and the onus of responsibility is primarily borne by the Chief, his council, and *Yä Ǧoka*.

A final note on the Gurage judicial system can be added by giving a description of the procedure followed in a typical case of homicide that might ultimately be settled at *Yä Ǧoka*. A general impression of the conduct between Clan A, that of the accused, and Clan B, that of the victim, is drawn in the proceedings illustrated below. When the act of homicide is discovered:

Clan A: Immediately expels the accused from the clan district, whether the murder is accidental or intentional. The accused may go to his mother's clan if she is not a member of the victim's clan; he may live in the forests peripheral to another clan until settlement is reached. If he refuses to take one of these courses, Clan B will begin exacting blood-price immediately.

Clan B: Awaits the delegation of Elders of Clan A, to express condolences on behalf of the accused's lineage and to entreat Clan B to withhold feuding, or taking action of any kind, for seven days. Clan B demands that Clan A's lineage leave their homestead if the murder occurred there, or if elsewhere, be banished from the clan's territory until recompense has been made.

Clan A: Elders revisit Clan B after one week, again entreating restraint from feuding; this is repeated seven times.

Clan B: Is presented on the seventh visit with cattle. Elders of Clan A announce 'let us pay these cattle for the blood', that is, for the blood of the victim. If Clan B agrees they receive blood-price later in money; cattle, formerly constituting blood-price, are now used only symbolically.

Clan A: Pays the sum of blood-price fixed by the ritual judge known as *Wåg*, an assistant of the Lord of *Wågäp^häča*, having authority to assess blood-price and the penalties for breach of a ritual covenant.

Clan B: Receives the blood-price from *Wäg*, paid to him by Clan A whose members assume the responsibility jointly. If the amount is considered inadequate, Clan B appeals to *Yä Ğoka*.

The procedure then taken at *Yä Ğoka* is the same as described above.

We have seen that the maintenance of social control among the Gurage depends upon a number of interlocking factors of kinship, clanship, and ritual. There is no one political authority with legislative and juridical functions. Clan Chiefs and their councils are essentially mediators in disputes and decisions pronounced by them may be challenged and ultimately overridden at *Yä Ğoka* tribal assemblies. Here the legal mechanisms of the Gurage jural system operate to establish a standard by which conventional payments considered due to a man who has suffered certain injuries are agreed on. *Yä Ğoka* constitutes an impartial authority to decide the rights and wrongs of a dispute, but there is no organized institutional power in the system to enforce decisions. The law of *Yä Ğoka*, *qʸəċa*, is essentially moral and ritual in nature.

I have also attempted to make clear that the possibility of exercising a right often depends upon one's kinsmen, the strength of force they command and the extent to which they are willing to risk exerting this force to right a wrong. Insistence on a right is to run the risk of homicide and feud. Settlement of disputes to the satisfaction of all concerned depends largely on kinship relations and the relative distances between them in the clan and tribal structure.

I have set forth at some length the view that Gurage political relations are essentially regulated and enforced by supernatural sanctions rather than 'legal' sanctions;[18] Gurage beliefs associated with supernatural sanctions constitute one variable in their system of ideas concerning moral action, unfavourable opinion, and reward and punishment. This has greater meaning in the context of Gurage rituals of contract to be described in the section below, for these, as with decisions handed down at *Yä Ğoka*, are equally functional in the overall system of social control.

[18] Hoebel makes a distinction between 'legal' sanctions and 'supernatural' sanctions; the former are recognized by courts and enforced by political agents (1954, p. 15.)

GURDA: THE RITUALS OF CONTRACT

The system of ideas that constitutes Gurage religious and supernatural interests is significant here since it determines many of their specific courses of action, especially in the behaviour between individuals outside the realm of kinship relations and ceremonial groupings.[19] These relations are formed on the basis of a ritual covenant, which Gurage call *gurda*.

Gurage attribute the vast majority of frustrations, met in the pursuit of their goals, to real or potential ritual afflictions. These are seen in various forms of sickness for which only ritual agents can prescribe effective remedial formulae. Fear of ritual illness is rife; and anticipation of ritual illness is a deep-seated anxiety. Clearly anxieties of this nature overlap those resulting from witchcraft and sorcery. To describe the two without full comprehension of the ramifications of Gurage supernaturalism, of which I confess some ignorance, is not an easy task. Though not entirely for this reason, *gurda* will be separated from the maze of sorcery and superstition, notwithstanding the fact that it is deeply imbedded and intricately interrelated there.

Here I describe chiefly the structure of *gurda* and its implications in relation to the overall system of social control.

Gurda is an institutional form of ritual bond-friendship, which constitutes a life-long association of reciprocal obligations, reinforced by supernatural sanctions. The obligations involved in *gurda* are moral obligations of mutual assistance. *Gurda* ritual covenants[20] are not confined solely to social and economic relations, which in reality have little significance; but they stand as a protection against physical harm, and this is a factor of immense importance. The fear of sudden death as a result of enemy raids, or enslavement in former times, promoted as much anxiety as do

---

[19] The framework of analysis used in describing Gurage rituals of contract is based on the concept developed by Talcott Parsons, that a system of ideas has structural form and that it is part of the total system of action. See Talcott Parsons 1938, p. 655; cf. also Firth, 1948. A more detailed analysis of *gurda* is given in Shack, 1963b.

[20] The distinction between *covenant* and *contract* made by Firth is followed here. A covenant is distinguished from a contract by its voluntary nature; it is an agreement resting on moral obligation. Covenant relations, as opposed to contract relations, are enforced by supernatural sanctions. Cf. also fn. 18 above. See Firth, 1936.

the fear of ritual illness and its discomforts today. Defences against the possibilities of either occurring have been traditionally weak, and though warfare is now extinct, Gurage still harbour apprehensions, from past experience, that physical harm is always a possibility.

The oath-taking ritual performed in establishing a *gurda* is sworn to *Waq*, and it calls upon the Sky-god to punish the offender. An offence is committed by direct hostile action against a *gurda*-brother, or if the idea of such action is entertained. Either is sufficient reason for the suspicious person to seek ritual support for himself; the agent of *Waq* who is known as *Wäg* is consulted. As with other ritual agents, the office of the *Wäg* is passed on in the senior line of his lineage; no other ritual agent within the *säbat bet* can act as arbiter in blood-vengeance or demand supplication of pardon in *gurda* disputes. The person harbouring suspicion is advised by *Wäg* to go to his *gurda*-brother's homestead on seven different occasions and charge him, with the expectation of receiving each time an admission of intended wrongdoings. If confession is not made on the seventh visit, *Wäg* intervenes and invokes the deity to afflict the offender, or the suspected offender, with a ritual illness. Most afflictions begin as mild disorders which become increasingly worse; stomach disorders, diarrhoea, festering sores, even hallucinations and 'bad' dreams are frequent complaints. These illnesses can be remedied effectively only with ritual cures, available upon payment of special fees to *Wäg*, who controls and prescribes pharmacopoeia used in ritual treatment; in this context *äsät* is of unlimited importance.

The strongest ritual sanction imposed is meted out when serious offences against a *gurda*-brother have been committed, such as murder or attempted murder, or the destruction of property and crops by fire. This is the curse of the *Zitänä*; a term which translates as *zit*—'possessed', *änä*—'he who is', literally: 'he who is possessed'.[21] *Zitänä* is a form of 'evil' spirit possession, which results in an illness that usually ends in death. The symptoms of *Zitänä* ritual illness are unmistakable to any Gurage; the swollen limbs, or stomach, or as Gurage sometimes say 'the blood flows down'. There is no cure for the *Zitänä*, he is rejected from his

---

[21] For two other accounts of *Zitänä*, differing somewhat in interpretation and analysis from that given above, however, see Azais and Chambard, 1931, p. 189; Leslau, 1950, p. 58.

lineage and village by his kinsmen who fear ritual contamination of themselves and their land; he joins other ritual outcasts in wandering from village to village, appearing at market gatherings begging for alms. A *Zitänä* cannot be buried in the lineage plot, which is set aside in the *äsät* field, along with his kinsmen, nor can *äsät* leaves be used in the burial rite, an act symbolizing that the association a man has with nature continues even in the afterlife. The property and land of the *Zitänä* cannot be inherited by his kin, for this is given in compensation to the ritual functionary and representative of the deity by the kin group who sacrifice periodically to protect themselves and future generations from the curse.

Gurda-bond relations stand outside the realm of Gurage agnatic and affinal kin relations. *Gurda* is made between distantly related clansmen where the ritual ties of contract span social and spatial distances, such as between maximal lineage kin; they are sometimes made within a village but seldom with members of the agnatic group. Before the cessation of warfare, however, it is claimed that ritual bonds were more often made between men of the same village, than at present. Then the fear of sudden death through enemy raids was more remote than the fear of enslavement by closely located hostile elements, as we have seen. Such fears were also increased considerably by sibling rivalry over scarce land holdings, a feature of Gurage life which is mirrored in clan myths. The fact that Gurage make no distinction between a conceived act of hostility and the act itself, either of which can cause a breach of *gurda* relations, is significant: it points toward an index of normative behaviour that has more than a casual relationship with the system of ideas associated with bond-friendship.

In sum *gurda* has a positive effect in terms of the overall system of social control. It provides a sociological outlet for the *intent* which underlies anxieties brought about by latent hostilities. It provides an aetiology for illness. The diffused linkings of individual associations, though lacking in qualitative aspects, have an overall effect of linking society as a whole. In other ways, such bonds are a means of establishing kin-like relations where none exist, and of strengthening social and economic positions through institutionalized friendship which entails reciprocal obligations; these associations are descriptions of Gurage behaviour. *Gurda* is a moral and ideal construct; in one way a model of the Gurage concept of the good life.

LOCAL POLITY: THE VILLAGE HEADMAN

Traditionally, the village headman is the pivot of the lowest level of political organization. Every village has a headman who holds his position by relative senior status, as reckoned through genealogical claims to the founding ancestors of that village. His position is usually inherited in the senior line of the lineage to which the headman belongs. He is not appointed to office by the Clan Chief or with the consent of village headmen from other areas. But even though the senior son of a headman should automatically succeed to the position held by his father, he must, before entering upon his duties, first be accepted and approved by Elders of the community. The office of headman is the corporate property of the village.

The important changes that have altered the role of the headman have already been mentioned in this and in previous chapters. These alterations have chiefly been in the allocation of tasks, for in general, the mode of recruitment of headmen has not been changed by *Säwa*. The single exception is in the administration of *Chaha Woudema*, where all of the headmen in the eight districts of the Crown Lands have been appointed directly to office, and they are generally referred to by the Amhara title, *chiqa-shum*. Traditional Gurage headmen are known as *quoro*, and unlike the appointed headmen they have direct kinship links with the founder of the village.

The *quoro* has a number of duties attached to his position. He represents his village in the jural community and he is the medium through whom political communications are made to the inhabitants. He acts as judge in local disputes; he attempts to settle issues with a display of wisdom and finesse, but his authority can be appealed against and overridden by a consensus of Elders. All matters affecting the people must be dealt with by him before they are carried further, if need be, to the Clan Chief. The headman must see that his people perform all the duties jointly assumed by the village; chiefly the maintenance of the *wur ema*, the proper sharing of responsibilities over grazing land, and the payment of taxes. He protects the rights of each individual in the community, and in this he normally works together with the village elders. His authority is limited specifically to his village but a majority of headmen from one maximal lineage district can usually present a strong political front at the level of clan politics and influence decisions to favour their own constituencies. The headman is the link between his people and the wider political system.

In both the old and the new systems of provincial administration, tribute and taxes are exacted principally through the office of the village headman. Since 1941, the headman has been responsible to the *Mislane*, the Sub-District Governor, for the collection of tax. But in carrying out the traditional duties of his office, the headman is responsible to the elders of the village and to the Clan Chief.

The village headman of today is placed in a dual position, one part being in conflict with the other part. He is on the one hand a government tax collector; and the villagers hold taxes to be an additional burden from which there are no immediate or long term benefits accruing to the welfare of the community. He is supported by the government in enforcing the payment of taxes, if need be, with armed force. On the other hand, the headman is expected to represent the values of the community and in so doing retain the respect of his people. The goodwill and respect of the villagers tend to waver, whenever the headman tries to implement the collection of taxes, then his relationship with the village becomes brittle. At other times the relationship is tenable. The dilemma of the headman is also the dilemma of the Chief. Both are expected to carry out the policy of the District Governor, the terms of which often alienate them from other Chiefs and headmen. The dilemma of Gurage Chiefs and headmen is the same as that which has been described in relation to Chiefs and village headmen in other parts of changing Africa, where traditional roles of authority are in conflict with new roles established by modern political systems.

I began this chapter by stating that Gurage had no Chiefs with tribal-wide political authority until the coming of Ethiopian domination, and I have tried to show subsequently that the traditional political structure was, and is today, based on descent groups, each having a high degree of political interdependence. I have made no mention of the political role of those Clan Chiefs, who have been appointed to the position of *Mislane*, and at least from the point of view of Government, are expected to assume the role of 'Tribal Chief'. This imposition of tribal chieftainship has had minimal effect on the traditional authority system of *Yä säbat bet*

Gurage. The role of the *Mislane* in instituting Government rule is not comparable to that of the Paramount Chiefs in former British African dependent territories under the system of Indirect Rule.

In the structure and organization of internal political affairs the Tribal Chief (*Mislane*) has no greater authority than any other Clan Chief; his views can be overridden by others; no special sanctions support his decisions. The Tribal Chief acts only when called upon by Government to implement their specific policies and even then the Chief depends upon other political heads and subordinates to carry out the Government orders. Once the required functions have been performed, the authority of the Chief is again limited to his own clan constituency. In principle, there is little fundamental difference between the Tribal Chief of today and the *Agäz*, the 'war leader', of the past. The *Agäz* assumed military authority over all tribes only for the duration of the conflict; afterwards each group disbanded and was once more under the political and military jurisdiction of the respective Clan Chiefs, until such time as another situation confronting the tribes as a whole arose. Thus Gurage political system has traditionally contained elements of elasticity that have allowed the organizational aspects of it to vacillate without effecting radical change in its structure.

But changes have been brought to other areas of the political-ritual system. Religious functionaries who traditionally shared positions of supreme tribal-wide authority now stand in opposition to political leaders who have been forced into position by external sources. In former times, all political leaders depended upon the sanctions of ritual dignitaries, as witnessed in the installation of Chiefs, as a ritual safeguard legitimating their positions of authority. Tribal Chieftainship is supported by Government which has its own body of religious sanctions, alien to many Gurage and especially to the traditional religious leaders. In some ways, but not in all, this has had the effect of reducing the authority of religious leaders. Islam has also affected the traditional character of the authority of Gurage political leaders, as we shall see in the next chapter. All the above factors have sown their seeds of conflict which have grown and, in one way or another in more recent times, have influenced Gurage political affairs.

CHAPTER VI

Religious Organization

I DISCUSS in the pages of this chapter the structure of Gurage religious life. It should, I think, rightfully come at the end of any study of Gurage social institutions, for Gurage ideas about the supernatural and most of their social action which is couched in ritual, form the basis of social relationships in their society. The fact that Gurage participate regularly in religious activities rules out any doubt that religion is important to them; but it is doubtful if Gurage entertain the same concepts about the functional role of religious ideas and ritual behaviour in the shaping of their social structure. Perhaps those Gurage who will read this account of their social life, and perhaps even others will take issue with me on the emphasis I place on the importance of 'sacrificing together', to use Fortes' words,[1] at the *Čəšt*, the *Däm^wam^wit*, and the *Božä* cult festivals, described later. Religious belief and behaviour to the Gurage are things that appear on the ground in everyday real situations; these are not, to the Gurage, variables of a model or construct of social structure. Religion to the Gurage is not a mirror of the form of their society though, to the sociologist a wide range of human experiences are reflected in their belief and ritual systems. This chapter aims at describing the role of religion, the ideas and ritual actions, in the maintenance of Gurage social structure.

RELIGIOUS ASSOCIATIONS

The particular religious calling of the Gurage is as much a determinant of social grouping as membership in the lineage with all its ramifications of social and economic status. Religious associations, which are distinguished by the ritual behaviourisms, ideological beliefs, and linguistic idioms of the aggregate members, cut across those associations based solely on kinship.

---

[1] 'To sacrifice together is the most binding form of ritual collaboration . . . it is totally incompatible with a state of hostility—that is, with an open breach of good relations.' Fortes, op. cit., p. 98.

Every Gurage follows either the calling of his traditional religion, of Christianity (Coptic or other),or of Islam. The active participation of the individual in the rituals of his or her faith, together with the type of head-dress affected, kinds of amulets worn, and the degree of deference shown a religious dignitary of an opposite faith, are overt symbols of behaviour that distinguish the members of various faiths. The presence of a person at a religious gathering cannot of itself be accepted as an absolute indication of his religious belief. Many Gurage converts continue to take part in traditional religious ceremonies, if for no other reason than that such occasions provide for social intermingling, which overrides for them the ritual content afforded to others. Conversely, the absence of Gurage from important religious ceremonies cannot be conclusive evidence of their lack of faith or failure to accept the values of their religious group. This is more particularly true in contemporary conditions that prevent many men from attending important ceremonies because they are away from the tribal lands; but most men put forth an effort to attend great festivals, journeying from several hundred kilometres in order to do so. Of equal importance is the fact that a long history of contact with Christianity and Islam has produced the inevitable result of a Gurage belief and ritual system that is strongly influenced by elements of both religions; Christianity and Islam also have incorporated some aspects of Gurage religion with its basic Cushitic foundation. Wide variations are found in Gurage Christian and Islamic practices giving them more of an indigenous accent and differentiating them from the practices of these religions in other parts of Ethiopia. The practice of *purdah*, which is completely absent among Muslim Gurage, is a case in point; Coptic Gurage often practise polygyny and the levirate.

Religious distinctions are important, and every Gurage makes these distinctions known, but on the whole, Gurage are not fanatical about their religion, at least not today. In market gatherings, for example, members of all religious groups are found side by side. Even though some Muslim Gurage merchants have a monopoly in the trade of such commodities as *ĉat*, I have not heard of any animosity shown toward Muslims or of conflicts arising from religious differences. This seems to be equally true in village relations. Families who comprise a religious minority within the village associate freely with others in the community, indicating that the lineage principles of co-operation are not

weakened by opposite religious views held by individual households. In districts where there is a religious majority of a particular
calling, all lineage groups of the clan usually participate as a ritual
unit; the basic ritual unit is the minimal lineage. The diffusion of
ritual beliefs, practices, and associations within the wider descent
system, which can be seen in clan and tribal-wide religious organizations, begins in the homestead.

Religious practices in most homesteads follow the pattern set
by its head. Other members of the family are expected to follow
his dictates and to take part in the principle ceremonies associated
with his calling. In homesteads where the traditional religion is
practised, women not only participate in ritual observances but
they are also expected to carry out the household duties that are
demanded by the religious leanings of their husband. This often
calls for the preparation of special food in extra quantities on
festive occasions, the baking of *äsät*-bread from the *gwarəyä* plant,
or the preparing of honey, for the husband to pay tribute to his
deity; and women have these duties to perform for their own sake
when the *Däm^wam^wit* festival approaches. Most followers of
Islam make an annual pilgrimage to the shrine of their spiritual
leader, Shaikh Budella. During their absence the division of labour
and authority within the homestead must be reorganized to com-
pensate for the loss of any adult male member. Muslim pilgrims
passing through such a village expect to receive assistance if need
be in food and shelter from a kin or an unrelated follower of
Islam. Most often recognition and needed assistance are freely
given, for a pilgrim is looked up to by some and envied by others.
Islam, especially as propogated through the cult of Shaikh Budella,
has had a far greater impact on traditional Gurage religion than
has any form of Christianity.

Similarly, Christian Gurage have specific religious obligations
and they too follow a pattern of behaviour towards priests and
other dignitaries of the church as set out by the family head. The
Mäsqär festival, corresponding to the Amharic *Mäsqäl* 'Festival of
the Cross', a festival als osignifying the end of the rainy season, is
perhaps the principal religious gathering of Coptic Gurage.
Monthly gatherings called *Mabär* or *Məkyer*, corresponding to the
Amharic *Mahabär*, 'private communion', are also important
rituals to Copts. But unlike *Mäsqär* which is celebrated throughout
Christian Gurageland as well as Ethiopia, *Mabär* gatherings are

confined to the village or parish where a Church is placed and the celebrations are localized in the homestead. This is also true of *Məkʸer* which linguistically reflects the name of St. Michael whose feast is celebrated monthly.[2] Though chiefly a Christian ritual, non-Christians partake in the feasting, singing, and games. Monthly *Məkʸer* gatherings between homesteads function to reconcile temporarily the tensions between village kin groups, for reclamation of debts and the reviving of old quarrels is forbidden on the festival day. Apart from participation in important religious festivals every Christian family should have a 'father confessor'. The priest acting in this capacity expects to receive food and money for providing a family with spiritual blessings, annointing the sick, hearing confessionals at times of life crises, removing evil curses, leading the family in recitation of the psalter, and, in general, ritually cleansing the household.

Gurage in their traditional calling also have ritual observances both as part of their daily life and on ceremonial occasions. The two principal celebrations, *Čəšt* and *Dämʷamʷit*, for men and women respectively, will be described next in this chapter. Other celebrations, unlike tribal-wide festivals, take place at the level of family and village organization. The *Antrošt* feast has already been mentioned.[3] Another festival, *Näqʷä*, is the principal celebration of marriageable girls, those beyond puberty. This yearly festival is characterized by the 'fight' with stones between girls of opposing villages and lineage districts. Victory is gained when one team has forced the other away from the river bank that separates the lineage districts, thereby allowing the victors to 'invade' the territory of the vanquished. This event, like all others concerning *mʷəyät* girls is organized by the Chief *Mʷəyät* in each of their districts.[4]

Finally, there is the annual *Nəpʷär* feast dedicated to *Božä*, the God of Thunder. *Gʷetakʷəyä*, ritual functionary for the deity *Božä*, performs his duties chiefly through his assistants, called *Maga*, who are to be found in every clan district. Throughout the year the *Maga* distribute for profit, the *šənä*, a small strip of wood of a dried tree upon which lightning, a ritual sign of *Božä*'s power, has descended. To visibly display the *šənä* over their land is an act all Gurage, even many of the converted, perform. The *šəna* is usually affixed to the fencing, close to the entrance to the com-

---

[2] See also Leslau, 1950, pp. 66 *passim*.   [3] See p. 128 above.
[4] A short description of *Näqʷä* is to be found in Leslau, op. cit., p. 70.

pound, and the symbol of the cross into which the *šəna* is shaped is well-elevated as a warning to any hostile intruders; some plant the *šənä* in the ground near the entrance to the hut. But wherever the *šənä* is displayed it symbolizes that the land and property is blessed and others respect it for fear of *Božä*'s reprisals.[5]

One week before *Nəpʷär* arrives, the *Maga* perambulate throughout the market in their clan district, making pronouncements on behalf of *Božä*. These entail prohibitions against the cutting of wood, slaughtering of animals, quarrelling or mediating in disputes, as well as the loaning of animals, money or goods, the reclaiming of which might lead to feuding. Some Gurage make a pilgrimage to the shrine of *Božä* at the time of the *Nəpʷär* feast; but others, being unable to attend, give gifts of honey, which the *Maga* use to extinguish 'ritual fires' when *Božä* strikes a house with lightning, his ritual means of taking reprisals; *äsät*-food is also given to the *Maga* who present all these gifts to *Gʷetakʷəyä* on their behalf. In pre-Menilek times the representative of *Božä* was solely a ritual functionary and his role was confined specifically to ritual matters. However, as we shall see later, both the influences of Islam and the struggle for political leadership over tribal affairs have resulted in considerable changes in the structure and organization of the *Božä* cult.

Long before the conquest of Gurage by Menilek, Christianity and Islam were far greater threats to the traditional way of life than they are now. The vigorous campaigns launched against the Gurage by these conflicting religions were attempts to swell their ranks both through proselyte missionary activities and outright capture, and in some cases slaughter, of Gurage who resisted conversion. The decline of religious hostilities is recent in Gurage history. A great deal of intertribal warfare in former days was fought over religious issues which were themselves deeply set in the political turmoil of Ethiopia's past. Gurage changed their religious calling whenever the threat of the sword, Christian or Islam, became dangerously close. Both sides took captives; both sides sold captives into slavery; and both of these acts undoubtedly had far-reaching, serious consequences. The long period of disorganization resulting from this affected all levels of tribal organization.

Nowadays converts are recruited by peaceful methods; little

[5] See p. 109 above; pp. 190–1 below.

dissension takes place now when a man changes his faith, and this discord is usually confined to his immediate family. Religious conversion is often stimulated by the social incentives associated with Christianity and Islam. Young people in particular are concerned with obtaining a formal education and this is made available only through Coptic Priest schools, and Government (Church-State), Catholic and Protestant mission schools. There are no Koranic schools in Gurageland for the education of Muslim-Gurage youths. Formal education and a professed belief in Coptic Christianity are important, but not necessary, prerequisites of social mobility within the wider Ethiopian society. Thus, a large number of Gurage, as with other Ethiopians, nominally profess Christianity because of its obvious social advantages.

Religious distinctions thus share importance with those based on sex, age, and other forms of social groupings. Ceremonials held by the several religious groups, traditional and other, are the principal occasions when aggregates of people outside the minimal lineage group meet. Both Islam and Christianity play an important role in the religious life of many Gurage, but by and large, traditional beliefs and ritual practices are still closely adhered to by the greater number of Gurage, and especially the Chaha Gurage. Missionary efforts of new religious groups have had a twofold effect: they have cut across tribe, clan, and lineage, and they have formed religious factions.

RITUAL STRUCTURE AND ORGANIZATION

The common set of ethical and religious ideas underlying Gurage social relations form an ideological pivot on which aggregate clans revolve. Ceremonial and religious events are expressions of this ideology serving to give moral strength to lineage and clan ties. The cohesion of groups on ritual occasions gives full meaning to the significance of clanship. Of the many ritual ceremonies in the Gurage calendar, two particularly exemplify the principles of ritual cohesion: the annual *Čəšt* festival for Gurage men, and the yearly festival in honour of *Däm^w am^w it*, a ceremony exclusively for Gurage women. Before we examine these ceremonials, it is important that first we consider the characteristics of Gurage rituals: how they overlap clan and lineage characteristics described in the previous chapter, how they stand in juxtaposition and how they complement other characteristics of social structure.

Gurage have no ritual cult bound to one clan or clan segment, or to one tribe to the exclusion of other tribes. They are unlike the Tallensi, who have an elaborate system of politico-ritual segmentation in which 'accessory lineages' of sub-clans are excluded from sacrifices to the founding ancestor of that sub-clan.[6] Gurage have no cult of ancestor worship, exclusive either to any lineage segment or within the tribal configuration of rituals and beliefs. To what extent the absence of ancestor lineage cults can be related to the overall process of ritual assimilation of groups in structural opposition, as in segmentary societies, can only be determined by the comparative method. However, among the Gurage, and this most probably holds good for other segmentary societies as well, there is no ritual discrimination against certain segments of the tribe by virtue of ancestor dogmas. In principle, ritual integration assimilates all segments of the clan and tribe.

Ritual integration is seen in two ways: rituals expressed individually and rituals expressed in collaboration. Sacrifices to a deity can be performed by any man on impromptu occasions according to his spiritual needs since no special esoteric formula held by a ritual functionary is required. Annual celebrations of the great festivals, which Gurage proclaim as '*wåkämya*', 'a great festival', integrate aggregates of clan segments and are expressions of ritual collaboration. The important role of ritual functionaries as intermediaries between the natural world and the supernatural world is shown in *wåkämya*.

The foci of Gurage rituals are the sacred shrines. Gurage shrines symbolize the resting places of their deities, and there important sacrifices are made. The *Čəšt*, and the *Däm^wam^wit* and *Nəp^wär* festivals, in the months of December and February respectively, require the presence at the shrines of all Gurage of each tribal group. The custodian of each shrine is a maximal lineage head in the district where the shrine is located; related maximal lineages of the clan and tribe, and segments of unrelated clans and tribes, congregate at the shrine at festival time.

The structure of ritual congregations is thus comparable with the structure of *Yä Ǧoka* political congregations, which we have already described. The mechanisms of ritual operate both hori-

[6] Cf. Fortes, loc. cit., *passim*.

zontally and vertically, spanning larger tribal groupings and cutting across different levels of segmentation. Ritual relations not only exist between lineage segments linked by agnatic ties, they are also intrinsic in the ideology of *Yä säbat bet Gurage*, even though at times this ideology is politically fragmented. Moreover, ritual relations have a wider dimension than social and political relations, which are of a practical and utilitarian nature; where political relations end, ritual relations having moral interests extend beyond them and become the organizing mechanism of the Gurage social system. In general, the organization of ritual ties corresponds with that of clanship ties; these reinforce each other, and both can be translated into the idioms of kinship and genealogical relations.

The relationship between ritual functionaries and their respective lineages is further exemplification of the complementary characteristics of the ritual and political structure. The maximal lineage in which the principal shrine is located has exclusive ownership of the ritual office. The head of the ritual lineage, as custodian of the shrine, is the focus of the ritual cult. In addition, each other maximal lineage and smaller lineage segment has its private shrine, but there are no offices associated with their guardianship. Any individual or segment of the maximal lineage can sacrifice at these shrines, without the assistance from a ritual functionary or one of his agents, whenever necessary or desirable. Even so, all clans of Gurage and their segments have an interest in the cult head and his office.

Gurage of the same lineage as the ritual dignitary have no closer relationship with the shrine by virtue of contiguity than do distantly related members of the congregation. They are no more obliged to bring him tribute, beyond ceremonial requirements, than are others; they may perhaps bring him tribute even less frequently. For other Gurage often bring tribute in great quantities, especially when personal sacrifices seem to have failed and stronger invocations appear necessary to propitiate the gods. On the other hand, ritual dignitaries have obligations to the congregation to officiate at all rites in the prescribed manner. Furthermore, ritual dignitaries are themselves dependent on the services and provisions of other ritual officials; the installation of one ritual leader can only be performed by another ritual leader, because their power is handed down directly from a deity. But the interdependence of ritual dignitaries extends beyond such practical and utilitarian functions. It is for the common good that animosity should not exist between ritual leaders since schism and conflict at this level eventually affect the political and religious unity of Gurage. One instance to which we have already called attention occurred in the ritual office of the representative of the Thunder God *Božä*. Close bonds of interdependence between ritual leaders strengthen the ideological concept, setting forth explicit moral and ritual principles, adherence to which tends to unite divergent aggregates of the congregation.

I have attempted to provide briefly the background against which the structure of Gurage rituals can be understood according to the principles of Gurage lineage segmentation. The dominant religious conceptions of Gurage men and women are expressed in the cults of *Čəšt* and *Dämʷamʷit*, respectively. Ritual interdictions against association with members of the opposite sex in ceremonial groupings give polarity to the religious structure. This polarity, the opposition of the sexes, has been seen in other aspects of Gurage life to be a fundamental principle of the patrilineal system of Gurage kin grouping.

STRUCTURE OF THE *ČƏŠT* CULT

The cult of *Čəšt* is the central force uniting Gurage men of all tribes. Gurage translate *Čəšt* in terms of its ritual meaning, for there appears to be no etymological explanation for the name of the festival. *Čəšt* is simply the yearly ceremonial in honour of the Sky-god *Waq*. No linguistic elaborations or metaphors are used to describe the function of *Čəšt* in relation to the spiritual benefits derived by the participants. Of this, Gurage merely say '*akäbädäm*', the *raison d'être* is 'to honour'; but *akäbädäm* seems to derive from the term *käpäbäm* often used in the same context as 'honour', and which may be translated as 'surround', a meaning that morphologically describes ceremonial behaviour, for Gurage men physically 'surround' the sacred shrine of *Waq* in paying him honour.

According to Gurage myth, *Waq* is a male deity whose spiritual favours enhance the prestige and valour of tribes who honour him, and respect his supernatural powers. In Gurage mythology *Waq* is akin to a culture hero; symbolically his role in cultural traditions is revalidated annually by the rituals of the cult.

Waq makes his omnipresence known at irregular and unscheduled intervals throughout the year, the prediction of which cannot be determined by any Gurage means of reckoning time and space. The manifestation of *Waq* is a shooting star. Gurage religiously acknowledge *Waq's* presence by reciting a form of words traditionally believed to be especially suited as an appeal to the deity. Conceptually, these infrequent manifestations of *Waq* redefine the upper limits of the Gurage universe. The universe is conceived of as *Yäwaq gän*, that is '*Waq*'s country'. This concept has meaning in Gurage terms of reckoning space, rather than in Western numerical quantities which cannot be translated into their social and cultural notions of time and distance. The concept of the universe is more easily realized by the presence of earth shrines, which *Waq* is said to have chosen sometime in the mythical past at certain heavily-forested areas (*dəbər*) on high mountain plateaux. Many of these shrines are practically inaccessible and few Gurage have ever reached them to sacrifice there; most men remain content with reverently identifying such shrines from afar as resting places of *Waq*. However, the principal shrine of *Waq*, of which the Lord of *Wågäpʰäča* is the guardian, can be approached by all Gurage men. They feel it is their duty to make the yearly pilgrimage to the shrine, and most men do make it.

Each Gurage tribe has its own metaphor by which *Waq* is known, a feature which adds a measure of personification to individual tribal values. Among the Ezha tribe *Waq* is called *Engʸaber*, among the Gyeto as *Yənfaša*, and among the Ennemor Gurage as *Gäbär*. In Chaha, where the sacred grove of *Waq* is situated, he is known as *Ogyät*.[7]

The myth of *Waq* reveals a configuration of themes on the conflicts between him and Gurage women; a variation of the theme is *Waq*'s dependence upon the guilefulness of women, through whom he is interceding, to fulfil his ritual role. In complementary ways the myth gives ritual validation to the structural principle of sex polarity which underlies the male and female cults.

Waq is said to have been vanquished by gods of the Christian

[7] *Waq* appears to be a generic name for the supreme deity among Gurage tribes. The same term is used for the Sky-god among several Cushitic tribes in South-West Ethiopia, linguistically expressed in various forms. Hence, the Galla call their Sky-god *Waqa*; the Hadiya, *Wa'a*; the Kaffa, *Yaro*; the Janjero, *Ha'o*.

tribe of Muher.[8] Death was prevented by the artfulness of a girl from Chaha. Later *Waq* was tricked into capture by a woman from Ennemor, an enemy tribe of the Chaha; this deception and bondage imperilled Chaha who were continually defeated in warfare by the Ennemor and other tribes. Finally, the devious ways of another woman enabled *Waq* successfully to abscond to Chaha, where he landed atop of the tallest *äsät* plant (*Gwarəyä*?) there. He then descended to *Wâgäpʰäča*, selecting this place for his sacred shrine. For custodian of the shrine he chose a woman known as *Yogäpʰäča dämam*, that is, the 'master of the place of *Wâgäpʰäča*'; he selected a man known as *Damo* to represent him as a 'ritual spouse', vesting in him and his lineage the authority to choose succeeding ritual custodians of his shrine.

Thus continuity of ritual custodianship is not prescribed by right of succession in the patrilineage of *Yogäpʰäča*. Ritual custodianship descends patrilineally through the marriage of *Damo* to the woman chosen as the symbol of the 'wife' of *Waq*; the death of *Damo* terminates her tenure of ritual office. The role of 'ritual husband', on the other hand, succeeds patrilineally to the eldest son of *Damo*, who, even if married at the time of inheriting the office, chooses a 'ritual wife' for his exalted position. If there is no male issue in the direct line of *Damo*, his position passes collaterally to his eldest brother; if he is dead it passes to his senior male descendant; if there is no heir in this line, one is sought in that of the brother next in order of seniority; the ritual prescriptions of marriage remain unchanged. Conversely, the ritual position of *Yogäpʰäča* cannot be inherited collaterally either by her eldest sister or by female offspring in the patrilineage of her brother. Either would be in contradiction to the myth which symbolically gives perpetuity to the fertility of the ritual wife. The ability to bear children is a necessary requisite of office, barrenness or an early cessation of fertility has the obverse consequences, bringing an end to *Yogäpʰäča*'s tenure of ritual custodianship. Hence, the *Samər* feast,[9] which all Gurage women hope to celebrate, is given

[8] A more lengthy account of the above myth is given by Leslau, 1950, pp. 53–54. Cf. also the version recorded by Azais and Chambard, 1931, pp. 189–90. It is conceivable that different versions of the myth if told by other tribes would reveal that *Waq* favoured them and not the Chaha as related above. But still a rationale would have to be built into the myth to account for *Waq*'s shrine not being located in their tribal area.

[9] See p. 126 above.

ritual validation upon the birth of her eighth child. For only then is her marriage with *Damo* regarded as permanent.[10] I show these rules of succession and marriage in the ritual offices described below, in Fig. 13.

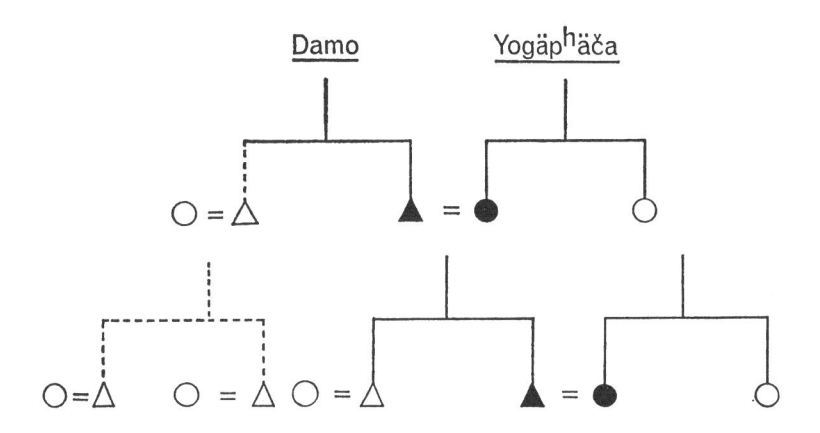

FIG. 13. Succession and Marriage of *Damo* and *Yogäpʰäča.*

In practice, and in the tradition of the myth, *Damo* ceremonially chooses a young virgin for his ritual wife. The ritual selection is signified by 'loosening the hair-dress', of one of a number of virgin girls who have presented themselves for this purpose from the clan of *Mäzakʷər*, which has rights in the ritual office.

The principal function of *Yogäpʰäča dämam* is that of conducting the yearly *Čəšt* festival. But at other times of the year she appeases the god *Waq* upon special request, for which tribute has been brought. She is assisted in her ritual duties by *Damo* and, though he alone cannot propitiate *Waq*, spiritual benefits are requested of *Yogäpʰäča* through him; he often joins her to perform special sacrifices. Dignity and respect are accorded equally to both ritual functionaries, for Gurage see the myth of *Waq* symbolized in their relationship. But the focus of the *Čəšt* cult is *Yogäpʰäča.* As the chief custodian of the shrine, she is the embodiment of Gurage religious values; conceptually, and on the

[10] I am not certain if the present wife of *Damo* has celebrated *Samər.* Cecchi estimated the 'Queen' of *Damo* to be aged 25 and to have given birth by then to seven or eight children, op. cit., p. 84.

ground, *Yogäpʰäča* validates the myth of Gurage ritual structure. However, the ritual position of *Yogäpʰäča* is definable in terms of male secular values and these values underlie the notions Gurage men hold about patrilineality and authority.

Although Gurage women are prohibited from taking part in *Čəšt*, by rigid rules claiming supernatural authority, there are some women present. They belong to the Fuga and are the ritual agents of *Yogäpʰäča*, performing essential ritual functions and services in the organization of the cult. They are in most instances wives or close female kin of Fuga Chief *Mʷəyäts* and their assistants. As ritual agents, Fuga women act as intermediaries between Gurage men and their chief priestess. They frequently conduct sacrifices and rituals on her behalf throughout the year in their ritual districts, the largest being that of a maximal lineage. They distribute amulets, and other ritual paraphernalia, as protection against the evil-eye; they diagnose symptoms of ritual illness, explaining their causes, and prescribe the necessary ritual cures and remedies; they concoct local medicines, increasing their potency by reciting ritual formulae. They have authority to manipulate certain supernatural forces and so they are indirectly responsible for the maintenance of social control. Fuga ritual agents can spell a curse or remove one, and both are religiously and mysteriously feared.

In all ritual activities Fuga women work closely with the Chief *Mʷəyäts* found in every maximal lineage district; the functions and responsibilities of each are directed by the representatives of the male and female deities. At the *Čəšt* festival, female Fuga ritual agents bring together all Gurage men of their maximal lineage district, leading them in procession to the sacred grove of *Waq*; at the head of the procession is *Damo*. Once there, they gather the tribute which has been brought to *Yogäphäča*, assist in sacrificing, and in the ceremonial singing and dancing and worship of *Waq*. The manifold differentiation of their ceremonial roles, in general, corresponds to their positions in the hierarchy of ritual assistants. This, as with the *Mʷəyät* organization, is similar to the segmentary structure of clans and lineages.

Three aspects of the *Čəšt* cult can be restated in terms of Gurage social structure. First, the mythology of the cult furnishes certain supplements by which the cosmological and cultural values of the Gurage world view can be comprehended. Second, the religious character of the cult provides specific repetitive experiences regrouping segments of the tribe in common ritual expression thereby realigning and re-establishing tribal values. Third, the focus of the cult, the Lord of *Wâgäpʰäča*, reconciles the antagonism of the sexes, by ritually expressing the importance of woman as sexual partner and procreatrix, of which the fulfilment of these roles furnishes the social dominance of men with a legitimate outlet.

STRUCTURE OF THE *DÄM^W AMWIT* CULT

The focus of religious activities for Gurage women is the cult of *Däm^wam^wit*. The characteristic features of its structure and organization are the opposite of those of the male cult of *Čəšt*. At the pivotal position of the cult, which is hierarchically structured, is the female deity *Däm^wam^wit*, whom no Gurage male or female has ever seen. The Gurage concept of *Däm^wam^wit* is realized in the manifold expressions of her supernatural power to inflict harm; the consequences evoked if anyone fails in his or her social and ritual duties are epitomized and manifested in the ritual illness of the *Zitänä*. *Däm^wam^wit* can be called a 'guardian spirit', devoting herself to looking after the welfare of the Gurage and increasing their tribal solidarity. Guardian spirits have a dual role, producing contrary phenomena, good and evil, life and death; they create a model of the good life. The good life is also guarded by *Däm^wam^wit*, and men and women can achieve this only by upholding her moral and ritual decrees, which set a standard of behaviour of one Gurage to another. Social behaviour is linked with ritual behaviour; thus in order to carry out social duties, that is, to behave in a moral way, ritual assistance is often required. In the continued performance of these duties, Gurage as a whole, and especially their women, intercede through the representative of *Däm^wam^wit*, whom they call *Yäwäy dämam*. The ritual duties and obligations of Gurage women are linked directly to *Yäwäy dämam* through his assistants, the Fuga Chief *M^wəyät*.

The origin of *Däm^wam^wit* appears to be obscure in Gurage oral traditions. Tribal folklore contains no myth of her origin, to parallel the numerous tales concerning the origin of *Waq*. But Gurage myths seem to be man-made, and the cult of *Däm^wam^wit* is essentially a female cult with which men have no direct concern and which they often tacitly consider contemptible. Moreover, the good life is mainly a prerogative of males, and failure to achieve it is attributed to the maledictions of *Däm^wam^wit*. It seems reasonable to assume that the system of ideas concerning socio-ritual adversities of life, though not crystallized by mythological explanations, is maintained by repetitive ritual phenomena of an explainable nature.

Yäwäy dämam forms the core of the *Däm^wam^wit* cult. 'Collector of honey' is the literal meaning Gurage give of his title, for traditionally, the 'master (*dämam*) 'of honey' (*wiyä*) demands tribute in honey, amongst other things, for keeping away sickness.[11] His ritual office is the exclusive property of his maximal lineage, the clan of which, *Yäwaqesäb*, is one of the primary tribal sections of Chaha. His position descends patrilineally according to the rules of primogeniture, or, failing a suitable male issue in his direct line, it passes collaterally to the brother senior to him and his lineage, and so on. The heir to the office of *Yäwäy dämam* must be without physical blemish; this rule is rigidly enforced here, more than in the inheritance of other ritual or political offices. The chief representative of *Däm^wam^wit*, by virtue of his position, symbolizes the moral and physical perfection inherent in the ideals of the cult; a physically or mentally defective ritual functionary would be contradictory to these ideals. As to his marriage, there is no preferential or prescribed form, though generally *Yäwäy dämam* is polygynous. The only women permitted to enter his homestead in any circumstances are his wives and female servants. This interdiction is one aspect of the female impurity complex which also extends beyond the range of mankind to include the animal world as well.

For at the homestead of *Yäwäy dämam*, in the district of Yäbitara, even female mules and goats, held to be impure, are kept from his compound.[12] When wives or servants attend to his meals, none is allowed to speak during the course of his eating, or touch his food or utensils after he has been served; if the food or

---

[11] *Yäwäy dämam* is said by some Gurage to be also a rainmaker, but I have no evidence of this being one of his ritual duties. This probably was a duty that has now virtually ceased to exist.

[12] This taboo is commonly associated with Ethiopian monasteries. For instance, Alvarez noted: 'no females enter [monasteries], that is to say, neither women, nor she-mules, nor cows, nor hens, nor anything else that is female', op. cit., p. 35.

utensils are touched, fresh food must be served and the utensils must be replaced. When he receives an audience of males, they must conceal themselves behind the wall of his guest house within speaking distance of the entrance, and *Yäwäy dämam* sits on the outside in front of the entrance in his specially carved, sacred, throne-like chair; because of the fear that one of the men might have been contaminated by contact with a woman, and so pollute the entire audience, they cannot sit in the same enclosure with the ritual dignitary. For similar reasons, when travelling, *Yäwäy dämam* never enters the homestead of a Gurage; instead he seeks shelter and seclusion under a tree, and all who pass acknowledge his presence by maintaining a respectful distance. Men often show even greater deference by kissing the ground three times before they approach *Yäwäy dämam*; after this form of greeting he may converse with them. Women are forbidden absolutely ever to see his face or to speak to him; upon pain of death women must prostrate themselves respectfully with their faces well hidden until *Yäwäy dämam* is out of sight.

A woman is considered as being impure at all times. This is a consequence of her sexual and reproductive functions, which appear at irregular, but always repetitive intervals, especially during her menstrual period; a woman is held to contaminate a homestead. Unless she performs the necessary rituals of cleansing after childbirth, menstruation, and particularly after sexual intercourse, a woman can pollute the men of her household as well as other men with whom she may have contact. The interdictions of contact with *Yäwäy dämam* thus function as double-edged ritual safeguards; they prevent a woman from offending *Däm^{w}am^{w}it* by confronting her representative in an unclean condition and reduce the possibility of her being penalized for having committed an offence by forcing her to avoid the dignitary. Apart from the annual festival, there are no other circumstances in which these interdictions may be transgressed. *Yäwäy dämam* comes into contact with Gurage men mainly at *Yä Ğoka* assemblies or at other politico-ritual gatherings, which presupposes that proper ritual conditions are prevailing in accordance with the nature of the event.

In the description of the initiation of girls,[13] we have seen that *Yäwäy dämam* sets up in each maximal lineage district Chiefs of

[13] See pp. 132–4 above.

$M^w\partial y\ddot{a}t$. Their principal function is to organize the ritual activities of girls who are beyond puberty, and of adult women, seeing to it that they perform their ritual duties, and to penalize those who are negligent. The culmination of day-to-day ritual activities is expressed annually when the several Chief $M^w\partial y\ddot{a}t$ lead their groups to Yäbitara for the festival in honour of $D\ddot{a}m^wam^wit$.

Gurage women from all tribes partake of the $D\ddot{a}m^wam^wit$ festival. Apart from the abstention of girls who have not yet reached puberty, all other females are under ritual obligation to participate, age and marital state notwithstanding. Women are not absolved from making the pilgrimage to Yäbitara, and consequently from intermingling with others, even during menstruation. In performing the necessary rituals of sacrifice, praise, and atonement, women expect to receive the maximal benefits that the deity can supernaturally bestow. By paying tribute they expect to be cured of all sickness that has occurred within the year or that has lingered from previous years with no signs of diminishing. Most of these discomforts are held to affect the capacity of a woman to bear children, the consequences of which prevent her from achieving the ideals expected of a wife, and so affect the stability of her marriage. Some completely sterile women expect to renew their fertility and thus, in some cases, enable themselves to make a second marriage. Young unmarried girls, in hoping to strengthen their fertility, have expectations of a different kind which are linked with additional spiritual requests that will bring prestige to their family through a suitable early betrothal. Apart from presenting tribute, each of the women supports her spiritual petition by bringing flowers and a thin stick of *lumčä*-tree, which is used in the sacrifice and obtainable only from the Chief $M^w\partial y\ddot{a}t$ upon the payment of special fees.

During the festival, each Chief $M^w\partial y\ddot{a}t$ leads his group of women in the *Fedwät* songs and the dancing in honour of $D\ddot{a}m^wam^wit$. He has the privilege of striking with his *lumčä*-stick any member whose misbehaviour during the dancing causes disorder or whose violent agitation becomes passionately uncontrollable. Some say that even if a Chief $M^w\partial y\ddot{a}t$ kills a Gurage during the festival, no punishment is imposed, for it is believed

[14] It would be of interest to know how far this was actually practised in the past since it is a rationale for 'ritual homicide', with Chief $M^w\partial y\ddot{a}ts$ as agents being employed to avenge a death, for which compensation was not satisfactorily settled at *Yä Ǧoka*. There is some evidence of this having occurred but I gained no more of it than mere hearsay.

to be an act of *Däm^wam^wit*.[14] On the other hand, women are also given temporary reprieve from many of the restrictions that, in the normal course of familial relations in the homestead, govern their behaviour towards men. They need not obtain permission to take part in the festival; they may neglect their household in preparation for the occasion; they may assume an authoritarian position in relations with male kin or unrelated men in their village or elsewhere. Such privileged behaviour is sanctioned by *Däm^wam^wit*, and no man in his right mind would attempt to interpose his own authority during festival time.

At Yäbitara, the Fuga Chief of all *M^wəyät*, known as *Səmam^wä*, collects all the tribute on behalf of *Yäwäy dämam*. Most of the tribute is honey, grain, cloth, and coffee, and on this occasion a woman needs no permission to take tribute from the homestead; women from more prosperous homesteads might bring money as well, others might bring a male sheep. When the ceremonial dancing and chanting reach the peak of their frenzy, *Səmam^wä* announces the approach of the ritual dignitary, which symbolizes the descent of *Däm^wam^wit*; and when *Yäwäy dämam* appears, having incorporated the deity in his person, all the women prostrate themselves, covering their faces in fear of the ritual reprisals for breaking this taboo. After all the women have assumed the ritual posture, *Yäwäy dämam* recites prayers to *Däm^wam^wit*, which collectively present the spiritual petitions of the faithful. Following the recitation, the remaining tribute is collected and *Yäwäy dämam* returns to the seclusion of his compound. Women are then allowed to uncover their faces and to resume their dances and chants which last throughout the day. As dark approaches, *Səmam^wä* terminates the festival and his Chief *M^wəyät* lead the separate groups of women back to their respective districts. The ritual privileges of women are thus at an end for another year.

The *Däm^wam^wit* cult mirrors the conflict between Gurage men and women, which in the mundane aspects of their society is manifest in the polar opposition of the sexes. The structure of male–female relations is formed on the basis of this polarity, and sex antagonism is the form in which the range of moral and social evils believed to be inherent in women is crystallized. Men are capable of irrational acts, which affect the order and stability of society, but Gurage women seemingly are predisposed to irrationality. As a Gurage male might see this, it is mainly as a consequence of the actions of women, or merely of their sex, which in itself symbolizes immorality and unrighteousness, that antagonisms are aroused. Thus, one view of this conflict points towards a morality upheld and guarded by men, the equities of which must be fulfilled in order that they may achieve spiritual rewards; and women potentially threaten this. The periodic ritual cleansing of women is one way by which they can be uplifted to the moral plane held to be achieved by men.

The cult of *Däm^w am^w it* provides an outlet for this conflict by opening up to women a path for good ritual action. Yet the ritual resolution of sex antagonisms is of a temporary nature; the polarity of the sexes is continually manifested in conflicts over authority, kinship position, morality, and the potential instability of women in domestic life and marriage; all of these are institutionalized structural features of Gurage society. However, on certain occasions, the religion of the cult provides the mechanism for steering and releasing those strong social tensions which are aroused by conflict between different structural principles when they are not controlled in distinct secular institutions.[15]

THE *BOŽÄ* CULT: RITUAL SEGMENTATION AND POLITICAL CHANGE

Before summarizing the political–ritual structure of Gurage society in the next section, I now describe changes in the structure and organization of the cult of the Thunder God, *Božä*; these changes bear upon the structure of the tribal system as a whole. The representative of *Božä* has traditionally shared equal ritual authority and prestige with leaders of other ritual cults. No former head of the *Božä* cult had ever achieved political prominence before Menilek's rule was established over Gurageland.

I have said above that the ritual functionary of the Thunder God, *G^w etak^w əyä*, has the sole authority to exact tribute from subjects in all tribes in the name of *Božä*. For this tribute Gurage receive ritual protection against the destruction of their property

---

[15] The conclusions drawn here have obviously been shaped by the analyses made by Gluckman and Nadel respectively of Zulu and Nupe rituals and their relationships to certain institutional forms of male–female conflicts. See Gluckman, 1954 and 1949; and Nadel, 1954, p. 275.

by lightning, the principal manifestation of the deity.[16] He also provides ritual safeguards against theft; and the sacred paraphernalia, the *šənä*, used for protection against fire and theft, is distributed throughout Gurageland by his ritual agents, the *Maga*. Like all other ritual dignitaries with comparable powers, the *Gʷetakʷəyä* extends his tribal-wide authority over the entire *Yä säbat bet Gurage*.

At some time before the Ethiopian domination of Gurageland had been completed, the representative of *Božä* became a convert to Islam. How the conversion actually came about and for what exact reasons, we do not know. In view of later political developments, it is reasonable to assume that Islamic conversion was part of that same general pattern of shifting religious faiths set by many Gurage Chiefs who sought protection under the cloak of Islam.

Religious conversion segmented the hereditary lineage which has vested rights in the ritual position of representing *Božä*. The office of ritual functionary shifted from the senior line which adopted Islam, to the junior collateral line which kept to its traditional calling. The role of *Gʷetakʷəyä* was inherited by the junior brother, but many old followers of the former senior functionary held strong beliefs in his powers to mediate with *Božä* and they carried their spiritual allegiance over to him by adopting Islam as he had done. The splinter group led by the elder ritual leader gained followers, since he still maintained a close association with *Božä*, and under his name plus that of Allah, special sacrifices were still performed and ritual protection offered. As Islam soon came to be used as a means of evading the exactions of Ethiopian rule, not only was the ritual prestige of the new cult and its head increased, but its political influence was also established. The gap between traditional and Muslim believers in *Božä* was even further widened. Today, *Gʷetakʷəyä* heads the junior lineage conducting most of the traditional rituals on behalf of *Božä*; the head of the senior line, now only loosely associated with *Božä*, has assumed a prominent role in Gurage politics. In this he is known by various names, the most general terms of respect being '*Šehotč*' and 'Abba Ramus'. Gurage sometimes refer to him simply as *Šeq*; but to all he personifies a prophet.

[16] 'Ritual protection' functions in two ways: it can be bought to protect property against lightning or other fires; it can be a means of retaliation in the feud. By making payments to agents of *Gʷetakʷəyä* vengeance can be ritually exacted against an enemy.

Political and religious leadership of *Šehotč* has increased in the past two decades. During the Italian occupation *Šehotč* symbolized resistance against European aggression by offering leniency in his Muslim court (*Qaḍi*) where matters were dealt with according to the *Shari'a*, an attraction not only to Muslim Gurage, but to Gurage of Christian and traditional leanings as well. Following the restoration, many Gurage held that *Šehotč* would also prevent Ethiopian occupation of Gurageland. The *gäbbar* system was not restored, as we have seen, but this was not because, as many Gurage believed, of any supernatural powers commanded by *Šehotč*.

One legend relates that *Šehotč* gained authority over Gurage Chiefs by putting to them a challenge to undergo a ritual ordeal, the survivor of which was to be acclaimed the leader of all Gurage. The ordeal is said to have consisted of drinking a poisonous potion containing 'snakes'. All the Chiefs, except *Šehotč*, refused to take part in the ordeal; he drank the potion and survived, which signified that he still had command of the supernatural powers of *Božä*. Chiefs reverently submitted to his leadership, showing regard for him with acts of salutation, and addressing him in terms of respect. The superior position *Šehotč* holds in tribal politics is further indicated by the way in which his presence alters the structure of *Yä Ǵoka*; the seating arrangement shifts and *Šehotč* is at the pivot of the assembly. He occupies the senior place under the sacred tree and only after he is seated do other dignitaries take up their positions. He opens the discussions and concludes them according to his will and gives final sanction to any decision that is taken by the total council. The sanctions of *Šehotč* are never overridden.

Two other factors have contributed to the rise to political and religious prominence of *Šehotč*: his recognition intertribally as a spiritual leader, and the increasing religious importance of the annual pilgrimage to his village to celebrate *Mulid*, which to Gurage and other Muslims in South-West Ethiopia is as important as is the *Hadj* to Muslims elsewhere. Intertribal recognition of *Šehotč* as a politico–religious leader is an outgrowth of the spread of Islam in South-West Ethiopia which increased in the late nineteenth century. In recent years, the Sidamo, Gudella (Hadiya), Jimma-Galla, and some Harari, have joined with Gurage Muslims in making the pilgrimage to the shrine of *Šehotč*, at Yäbrite.

Alliances with the Jimma-Galla were established by the father of
Šehotč with the Sultan of Jimma, Abba Jifar II, during the reign
of Menilek. Abba Jifar had then given protection to the *Tijaniyya*,
an Islamic dervish order that was spreading throughout South-
West Ethiopia. The revelant features of the *Tijaniyya* order are its
propagandist zeal, its scant attention to religious teaching, and its
aim of increasing the political authority of its leader, a *Šeq*, by
channelling all power through his hands. This new movement
swept over the older *Qadiriyya* dervish order, which had only a
weak foothold in Gurageland and the neighbouring Sidamo states.[17]

The Gurage–Jimma-Galla alliance was further strengthened by
the marriage of the daughter of Sultan Abba Jawbir, grandson of
Abba Jifar, to *Šehotč*, as his second wife. The propagation of the
Tijaniyya movement throughout Gurageland and neighbouring
regions has been successful, in part it seems, because of the
'political marriage' between the Gurage and Jimma-Galla. With
the increasing religious importance of *Šehotč*, the seat of the new
dervish order shifted from Jimma, the former nineteenth century
stronghold of Islam in the South-West, to Gurageland. The
migration of *Tijaniyya* Muslims to other parts of Ethiopia, holding
unwavering devotion to *Šehotč*, also must be considered a missionary
factor that converts Muslims of other orders to their movement.

Šehotč is a prophet fulfilling Messiah to his followers who have
a fanatical adoration of his saintly person. Unlike other Muslim
prophets in Ethiopia such as the immortalized Shaikh Ḥusain in
Harar, who were elevated to the status of sainthood only after
death, *Šehotč* has achieved the attributes of sainthood while still
alive. His village at Yäbrite is held to be a shrine and the annual
celebration of *Mulid* attracts pilgrims from all regions of South-
West Ethiopia who join with Gurage in bringing tribute and
receiving spiritual blessings. Pilgrims often return with samples of
the earth collected from around the shrine, and especially from
where *Šehotč* has walked, or his sacred white mule has trotted.
This earth is held to be sacred. A potion said to have special
spiritual and curative powers is made from the sacred earth and is
drunk on occasions when a spiritual uplift is needed.

Šehotč can be compared with the prophets of the Nuer.[18] The
Gurage prophet is considered possessed by reasons of his heredit-

[17] Trimingham, op. cit., pp. 233–56. See also E. Cerulli, 1932, pp. 24- 25.
[18] Evans-Pritchard, 1940, pp. 184–9.

ary connexion with *Božä*, and powers thus acquired having been assimilated with Islamic beliefs; he has achieved greater sanctity and wider influence than any other person in Gurageland. He is a tribal figure, but his influence extends beyond tribal boundaries. This appears to be directly related to the conflict between Islam and Christianity over the domination of Gurageland, and latterly to the eventual conquest of the Gurage under Menilek. *Šehotč* symbolizes in a spiritual and institutional form the unity of the *säbat bet* in opposition to Ethiopian domination. This no other Gurage political or religious leader has ever been able to achieve. Like the Nuer Prophet, *Šehotč* is a 'pivot of federation' personifying the structural principle of opposition in its widest expression.

The rise of *Šehotč* must be seen in retrospect with the spread of Islam in South-West Ethiopia and among the nation as a whole. Islam has not provided a basis for ethnic and cultural unity in Gurageland, as it has done elsewhere in Ethiopia and Africa, for a basis of this kind was never needed for the Gurage. However, Islam has provided a basis for political unity, a measure of centralized political stability, albeit on a religious foundation, to the traditional opposing segmentary character of Gurage political structure.

Long term predictions as to the trend this new political–religious form will eventually take are fruitless. A great deal depends upon the extent to which a 'messianic' movement, such as *Šehotč* leads, becomes institutional; it depends upon the extent to which diverse religious groups of the tribe are assimilated under its ideology; it depends upon the relative rate at which this is done and the extent to which this persists over generations. A great deal also depends upon the external forces that have created the conditions that gave rise to *Šehotč*; his position is politically and religiously important only so long as those conditions remain unchanged.

THE POLITICAL-RITUAL STRUCTURE OF GURAGE SOCIETY

I

I have set forth in this chapter and in the preceding one, the characteristic features of Gurage institutions of authority and religion. The total pattern of interrelationships between individual

Gurage and between groups of Gurage, defined in terms of these institutional sets of behaviour, forms the political and ritual structure of Gurage society; the summary features of it are re-examined in this section.

The territorial structure which provides the framework for the political organization has been defined as the clan district. One of the principal functions of the Gurage clan, which occupies that territorial framework, is the maintenance or establishment of social order by the organized exercise of authority. The nature of Gurage political authority is primarily moral; it is backed by ritual and supernatural sanctions. As the largest territorial and political unit, the clan has been identified as that group which forms the structure of the political organization. By definition, the political organization determines the boundaries of the political community. This community is the largest politically autonomous segment of the Gurage tribe.

There are similarities as well as differences between Gurage ritual organization and the political organization. Ritual authority is delegated to special ritual dignitaries who are to be found only in specific clans. The vital principle from which this authority is thought to spring comes directly from a deity. The ritual organization is dissimilar from the political organization in that the congregations of its cults draw upon Gurage from all tribes honouring the deity. All Gurage sacrifice together irrespective of descent, local grouping or tribal affiliation, and in doing so present a sharp contrast to the political community formed on the basis of membership in descent groups and local contiguity. There is no segmentary cult of worship associated with the lineage system.

The Gurage religious system, including the variables of ideology and ritual behaviour, cuts across the political structure at all levels of descent grouping. On the following page (Fig. 14) a scheme similar in structure to that of the diagram in Chapter V (p. 162), illustrates the total political and ritual structure of the Gurage tribes. The focus of the structure is *Waq*; the core of tribal integration. The widest field of tribal integration is formed by the *Čǝšt* cult which overlaps the political and territorial boundaries of tribal groups. The features of a common religion and a common mythology and a common set of rituals conceptually form an ideological field which circumscribes *Yä säbat bet Gurage*.

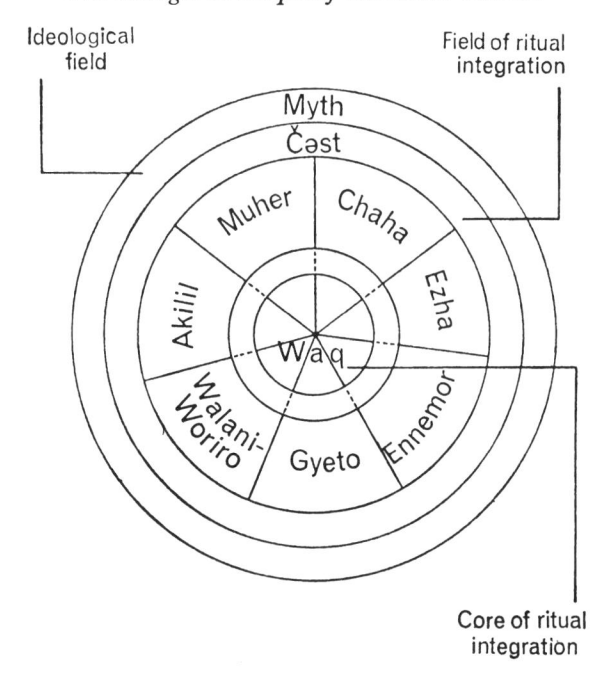

FIG. 14. The Political and Ritual Structure of Gurage.

II

It has often been pointed out that there is a close correspondence between the form of religion and the form of social structure, and that religious rites reaffirm and strengthen the sentiments on which the social order depends.[19] The analyses and interpretations given above of the *Čəšt* and *Däm^wam^wit* cults in relation to Gurage social order support this; and one step further has been taken. It has been stated that one of the dominant structural principles of Gurage society is the polarity of the sexes, this cleavage being overcome periodically through religious observances and circumscribed ritual behaviour. A second structural principle, the dispersal and segmentation of lineages, has also been dealt with. We have seen that a degree of stability and of structural persistence, mainly due to the lack of centralized and continuous political authority, is achieved and maintained through the mechanisms of the ritual system. The dispersal and segmentary features of groups

[19] Radcliffe-Brown, 1952, p. 169.

who maintain some degree of corporate identity with, yet are independent of, other corporate groups are common in African political systems of the non-centralized type, and there are no fundamental differences of principle in the Gurage system from that found in other segmentary societies having similar structural form. Now we turn to the first principle of the social structure, the polar opposition of the sexes, and see how this is reflected in the Gurage religious system.

For greater clarity, the main actors in Gurage ritual cults and their interrelated roles are presented in diagrammatic form. In Fig. 15, below, the cult deities, their chief representatives, assistants, and congregations, are each indicated with reference to sex and role. The functioning of the ritual process bifurcates the total society into male and female ritual organizations. In turn the structure of each ritual group is horizontally cut at intermediate levels by ritual functionaries and their assistants. The sex and role of each functionary are opposite to those of the deity, and the sex

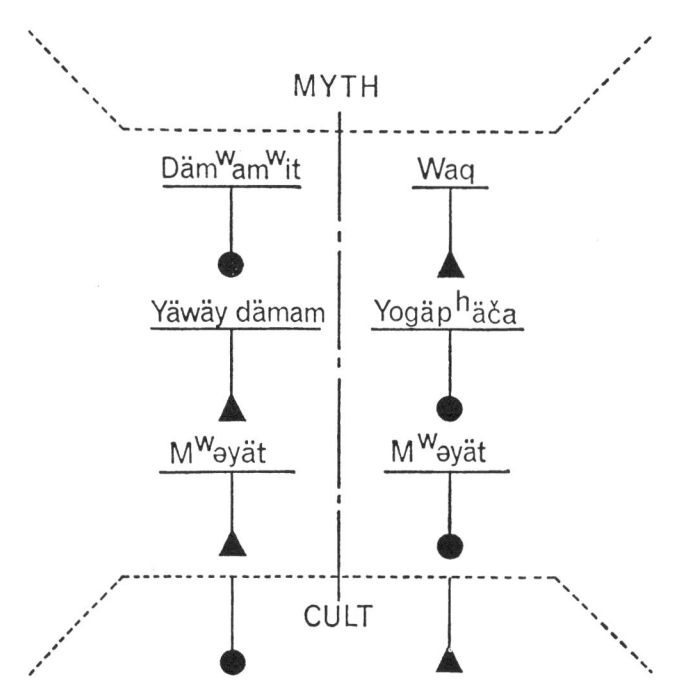

FIG. 15. The Polarity of the Sexes in Cult Rituals.

of their respective congregation; Gurage men and women are placed in a cross-sexual ritual relationship with the deity honoured by them. In short, the male sector of Gurage society is ritually bound to a female representative of a male deity: a female deity is the focus of the ritual cult for Gurage women for whom a male functionary intercedes.

The *Čəšt* and *Däm^{w}am^{w}it* cults are ritualizations[20] of organizations based on sex membership. Ritualization gives validation to the structural principle of sex polarity in Gurage society by the association of deities of the sex opposite to that of their following. The bilateral aspects of the cult association is reflected in other aspects of the social structure, of which the bilateral structure of the kinship system is one form in which this is manifested. These cults also serve to stabilize the inequalities between male and female Gurage which result from conflicting structural principles inherent in the patrilineal system of descent. At a conceptual level, ritualization functions to achieve an equilibrium between groups which by reasons of descent are structurally at polar extremes. The mundane values held by each ritual group can only be realized by sacrificing to the deity of its respective cult who symbolically represents the group to which each, on the ground, is in structural opposition. The form of ritualization in Gurage society maintains social cohesion and structural opposition at one and the same time.

[20] I am following Gluckman's usage of 'ritualization' here: 'a stylized ceremonial in which persons related in various ways to the central actors, as well as these themselves, perform prescribed actions according to their secular roles; and that it is believed by the participant that these prescribed actions express and amend social relationships so as to secure general blessing purification, protection, and prosperity for the persons involved in some mystical manner which is out of sensory control.' (Gluckman, 1962, p. 24.)

CHAPTER VII

Conclusions

OUR concern in this study has been with a descriptive analysis of the social institutions of an ensete cultivating people. It remains for us to consider more broadly the factors of social and cultural change which have influenced Gurage tribal life, and the stability and cohesion of the tribe, as a consequence of Ethiopian rule. The effects of Western customs and technology, in a word, 'civilization', on Ethiopia as a whole and on the Gurage in particular have been relatively superficial. The historical and political factors by which this can be explained, in terms of Ethiopia maintaining its political independence during the nineteenth-century European scramble for Africa, are well documented and need not be reviewed here.

As a nation, Ethiopia is a multi-tribal society in which the customs and values of the politically dominant Amhara tribe form the core of what might be called the 'national' social and cultural system. Coptic Christianity has been the most effective medium through which Amhara culture has spread, especially among the Central Plateau peoples and in lesser degrees among tribes in the Ensete Culture Area. The national language, *Amharic*, has also been an important agent in the diffusion of culture, whereas the consequences of Amhara political and military exploits have been only incidental. Until Menilek established Addis Ababa, the developing Amhara national social and cultural system had no fixed geographical centre of diffusion.[1] Traders, Coptic priests, soldiers, and adventurers have, for centuries, been the chief agents of Amhara culture, among the Gurage and other Ethiopian tribes.

Trade and warfare have been the principal mechanisms of change in Gurage tribal life. Hence, it was Gurage men who chiefly introduced new manners of dress and new forms of speech, but the preference shown for their own forms of material culture has

[1] From 1520 to 1890 Ethiopian kings moved about the country, having no permanent capital. European observers have described the 'captial' as a shifting city of tents. See Alvarez, 1881; also Pankhurst, 1961.

tended to preserve the distinctive features of it. In all aspects of life, even in speech and dress, Gurage women have been less affected by outside influences than men.

The impact of Amhara domination was less severe on Gurage social and cultural life than on their political life. The aims and policy of the Government never proposed making radical changes in Gurage life. Ethiopian rule was not concerned with uprooting 'pagan' customs and supplanting them by Christian Amhara culture. The doctrine of Amhara rule embraced no creed of having precepts of a 'civilizing mission' to perform. Missionary activity was not the veil for concealing political activity. It was in fact the reverse of this. Ethiopian rule relied upon maintaining an effective system of political control by the expedient of religious conversion. Hence, Gurage traditional modes of subsistence, land tenure (except for land expropriated under the *gäbbar* system), and forms of social grouping, remained unaffected by the veneer formed by a nominal inclination some Gurage made towards new religious beliefs and practices.

The function of Government in Gurage tribal life is primarily administrative. In this, its effectiveness as an agent of culture change is greatly diminished, for it has little or no opportunity or real desire, to reveal an 'improved' way of life which could stand as a challenge to Gurage customs. Tribal administration consists solely in the implementing of new laws, in imposing penalties for their breach, and in instituting new judicial courts and methods of procedure. On the other hand, economic development programmes and health services are lacking. Government has neither encouraged cash-crop farming, attempted to regulate production, nor sought means to extend the flow of cash through the tribal economic system, a practice common in former dependent African territories. Techniques employed in cash-crop production are crude.[2] The cash return from farming, never great at the end of any season, cannot be considered so important a factor of change that it has affected all aspects of Gurage life. As we noted in Chapter III, the use of currency is not a recent innovation in Gurage economy. Health, education, and welfare are also the concern of the Gurage. Apart from the limited health facilities

[2] For a comprehensive report on farming techniques and their implications for cash-crop production, see *The Agriculture of Ethiopia*, I, 1954. Staff report of the Point Four Agriculture Mission to Ethiopia.

provided by the Protestant Mission,[3] no other medical services exist in Gurageland. The Gurage practitioner must still be relied upon for healing chiefly through ritual and magical cures, and with the indispensable medicines concocted from *äsät*. Labour migration, like other aspects of tribal life, is independent of Government control. The high tide of labour migration is in no way comparable to the low ebb of currency flowing back into the tribal land.

Gurage technology and modes of production have maintained the level of subsistence to provide economic and social stability for kinship and other social groupings. Techniques of agriculture and animal husbandry have not been affected by a now more extensive use of money and an increase in purchasing power. The extension of cash-crop farming has made no change in the cultivation of *äsät*. The traditional division of labour is also maintained, and domestic industries are still the primary source of supply for Gurage hardware. European articles are rarely seen;[4] they have not supplanted the need for potters, weavers, or the arts and crafts of the Fuga. In fact, the business of the artisan as a whole has improved as a result of an increase in the flow of currency. Similarly, there has been no rise in a new class of specialists either in the crafts, or in agriculture, due to formal education. On the other hand, the pattern of responses to obligations and expectations of the traditional kinds of service from others remains unchanged. The economic system cannot be marked-off into 'traditional' and 'modern' structures as a consequence of Ethiopian rule. In sum, economic change in Gurageland is primarily at a potential existing in the expansible nature of the wants of the members of the society.[5]

The impact of mass education in Ethiopia has produced no currents of change in Gurageland. Only a fraction of the eligible school population receive formal training; family restrictions prevent more than a few girls from attending school.[6] Adult

[3] See Chapter II above.

[4] There are no cars and bicycles in Gurageland. One lorry makes a weekly visit to Endeber during the dry season to collect *qanča*-fibres; an occasional land-rover may arrive at this time. In 1957–9 there were perhaps no more than half a dozen wireless sets in the districts in which I worked.

[5] A useful distinction between the 'potentials' and the 'actualities' of social change has been made by Firth, 1959, p. 342. The actualities of social change depend on where the control of resources lie, and on the differential responses to new opportunities.

[6] In 1962 only one Gurage girl, to my knowledge, had gone beyond primary school training. See also Shack, 1959.

literacy, evaluated in terms of the reading and writing of Amharic, is a skill acquired only by a few Chiefs, headmen, clerks, and traders. There is no literature available in the vernacular.[7] Government publications, periodicals, and other media of communication seldom penetrate tribal boundaries; no regular communication exists between Gurageland and the outside world.

But Gurageland economic and social systems have maintained themselves within the bounds of some overall constancy. The striking stability of the systems raise questions of two different orders: whether some social structures are better able to survive under situations of contact than others; and what are the social, economic, and political characteristics of the contact situation itself? We address ourselves to the second question.

Ethiopia can be compared in some ways, but not in all, with other African states. It is similar in that formerly independent tribes have been brought under the authority of a central government; it is different in that urbanization and industrialization, which followed in the footsteps of European penetration elsewhere in Africa, have not yet emerged to any marked degree in Ethiopia. The economic and social structures of Ethiopia are supported largely by a subsistence level agricultural economy. The machinery of industrialization has yet to be put into high gear, and it cannot be concluded that urbanization, given its full sociological meaning, has developed in Addis Ababa solely on the basis of ethnic heterogenity and geographical size. In Redfield's terms, Addis Ababa is a 'folk society' based on a market economy; socially and economically it is undifferentiated from any other large market town in Ethiopia. Thus the question is not to what extent an urban industrial system has influenced a tribal system like the Gurage's, but to what extent one social system, whose economy is based on the land, has affected another social system having a land-based economy. Stated in a slightly different way, we are dealing here with the effects of 'Amharaization' on a non-Amhara people, not with the effects of 'urbanization' or 'westernization' on a tribal society.

Apart from structural modifications in Gurage political institutions and changes in the religious beliefs of some Gurage, the Amharaization process has been superficial. In the first instance this is directly related to the character of Ethiopian rule, as I have

---

[7] The only publication in *Guraginä* is a Catholic catechism printed in the Chaha dialect during the Italian occupation.

shown. But social distances as well as physical contiguity between Gurage and Amhara are important; social interaction is a mechanism of change. Of enormous importance are the ethnic and cultural factors which, having shaped the pattern of the Ethiopian domination of the Gurage now influence the process of their assimilation into the wider society. The adoption of Amhara customs and values is not necessarily a vehicle of assimilation. A Gurage is still a Gurage, notwithstanding the extent to which he may become Amharaized. And not only that, a Gurage wants to be only a Gurage and nothing more. Socio-cultural integration of the Gurage into the larger Amhara-Ethiopian society is at its lowest level.[8]

The Ethiopian–Gurage socio-cultural relations compare favourably with the Zulu–White socio-cultural relations as analysed by Gluckman.[9] A 'distinctive cleavage' (to use Gluckman's phrase) exists between the dominant Ethiopian and the subordinate Gurage systems. The conflict is expressed in an internalization of the customs and values of each group, which tends to emphasize the independence of each group; this is a manifestation of the values of their cultural differences as well. This cleavage is sustained by the maximization of conflicting cultural values. The Ethiopian–Gurage socio-cultural situation supports Gluckman's hypothesis that 'when the dominant cleavage in a changing system is into culture groups, each group also tends to set a value on the other groups' culture as distinguishing the other group from itself'.[10]

The viability of the Gurage system has been maintained by this socio-cultural cleavage. Gurage themselves make the best of both worlds: they are economically integrated into the wider society through wage labour and cash-crop farming, and the economic benefits thus obtained are invested in maintaining the social and cultural traditions of the Gurage way of life. But how long can their system remain viable under such conditions? The magnitude of the economic system is too small to allow the Gurage to continue to exist as a quasi-independent economic group.[11] But so

[8] I am using here the socio-cultural dichotomy as it relates to the 'concepts of levels of socio-cultural integration'. See Steward, 1955, p. 61: '[It] . . . is a conclusion about culture change only in the sense that there appear to be phenomena which cannot be explained by any other frame of reference.'

[9] Gluckman, 1958, p. 64.   [10] Ibid., p. 66.

[11] Cf. also, Firth, op. cit., pp. 346–7, where adjustments must be made in the Tikopia subsistence level economic system to accommodate itself to social change.

long as Gurage economy remains at the subsistence level, never falling below it, their system can no doubt endure. Their mode of production is crucial in this respect. For although the subsistence system is based primarily on a single crop, *äsät* can effectively support their social system even under extreme conditions of density. The economic and social systems can, however, be strained beyond the point of efficiency in spite of their apparent stability. Villages have already reached their maximum capacity of density, land shortage restricts further expansion, and only through seasonal migration is relief brought to the situation. Ecological factors of the environment, poor farming techniques for cash-crop production, and the deeply-rooted Ensete Culture Complex, together act as an erosion slowly wearing away the structure of the system. Land is the viable factor in the Gurage system but this factor also contains elements of dissolution.

At the time of this writing, the Ethiopian social system, based on a land economy, lacks the dimension and complexity for integrating other land systems, such as the Gurage; it provides no social or economic security and offers few incentives for change. Gurage tribal cohesion and stability can persist only so long as the nature of their economic and political ties with Ethiopia remain, as they do, relatively unchanged.

Appendix I

AN HISTORICAL NOTE ON THE
GURAGE HOUSES

For historical interest, the organizational changes in the political grouping of the Gurage houses deserves to be mentioned. No adequate records exist concerning these changes, and the accounts of Guebre Sellassie, and Beckingham and Huntingford, chiefly deal with the forming of new territorial divisions after the conquest of Gurage in 1889; and with these writers there are even differences of fact.[1] These notes contained here, based on information obtained from Gurage Chiefs and Elders, summarize their views on this issue.

There is a consensus of opinion that before 1875 the Chaha, Muher, Gyeto, Ennemor, and Ezha tribes formed a tribal federation then known as the *aməst bet Gurage*, the Five Gurage Houses. Other tribes such as Gumer, Akilil and Walani, geographically contiguous to this political grouping (see Map 4) maintained loose economic and military links with the *aməst bet*, these ties being underlined by the common interests held in the trade in war captives. Sometimes after the complete submission of Gurage in 1889, the *säbat bet* came into existence.

Exactly when the Seven Gurage Houses were formed is a question, however, that gave rise to long hours of debate among informants when discussed with me. Some maintain that the federation occurred during the reign of Menilek, others claim that the Italian occupation was responsible, while still a few traditionally-minded Elders tend to ignore the existence of the *säbat bet* and consider the original Five Houses as the only political group of any consequence. The question remains unsettled. Whatever the actual date, it is generally agreed that at some definite stage Akilil and Walani were combined with the *aməst bet*, and that former small independent groups were combined territorially and politically with larger tribal units, presumably for administrative purposes. War leaders of the *aməst bet* at the time of Menilek's conquest of the Gurage were:

[1] Beckingham and Huntingford, 1954, p. lxx: 'In 1875 the country [of Gurage] was conquered by Menelik and divided into five *nagarit* or drum districts.' Cf. Guebre Sellassie, 1932, p. 124: '*Déjà, au mois de mai 1875, Menelik y avait fait une expédition et s'était emparé cinq districts, mais la soumission complète du Gouraguie ne fut guère acheveé avant 1889.*'

Chaha   —*Agäz* Amärga
Ezha   —*Agäz* Bange, and
        Agäz Andəta
Ennemor—*Esehʸarb* Namada
Gyeto   —*Agäz* Andena
Muher   —*Agäz* Səbəta

The internal politics of the *säbat bet*, notwithstanding these changes, are dominated by the senior group of five tribes; the Akilil and Walani are relegated to a junior political status. In the main, the expansion of the Gurage houses, politically and geographically, has had little effect on the structure and the function of the group.

Appendix II

LINEAGE SEGMENTATION OF THE *YəNÄKᵂAMT* CLAN

The two major clans of Chaha, Mogämänä and Yənäkᵂamt, which have figured prominently in the discussion of Gurage political and ritual systems, are genealogically related. In clan mythology, *Arab* was father of the two sons, the apical ancestors of the clans that bear their names. The illustration on the following page is included to show the principal segments of the Yənäkᵂamt clan, thereby completing that portion of the tribal genealogy diagrammed in part, in Figure 10, in the text.

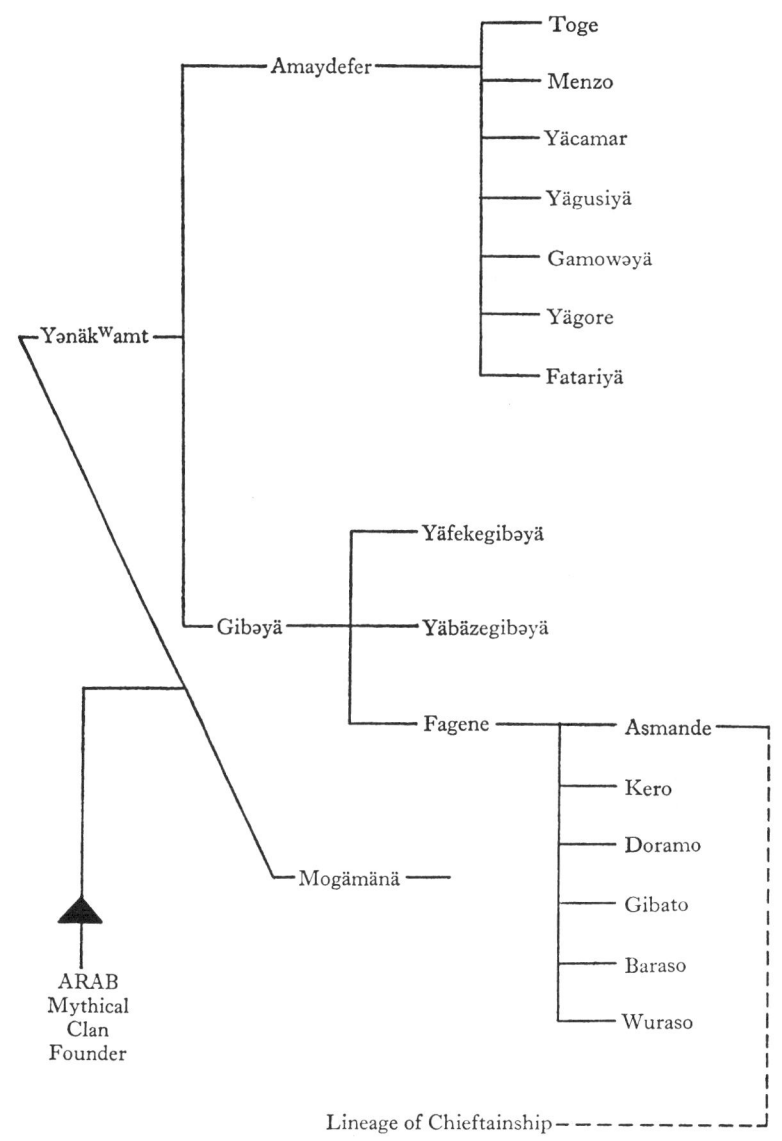

FIG. 16. Lineage Segmentation of the *Yənäkʷamt* Clan.

Appendix III

GURAGE DIVISION OF LABOUR BETWEEN
MEN AND WOMEN

	Men	Women
Cultivation and Cattle keeping	Clearing land, tilling soil, planting and harvesting *äsät* and other crops; breeding livestock, slaughtering, no herding.	Weeding, manuring, harvesting bush crops, preparation and storage of *äsät* and other crops; drying meat.
Other Productions	House construction, weaving; no domestic work.	Domestic work, basketry, pottery, matting, beer-making.
Political work	Totally men's work.	
Religious work	Ritual specialists, practitioners of medicine, wisemen, male congregates.	Ritual specialists, practitioners of medicine, female congregates.
Specialized work	*Fuga*, woodworkers; $Näf^w rä$, smiths, $Gəžä$, tanners; *Fuga* cut wood for all purposes, ritual specialists and assistants in female ceremonials, circumcision, hunting.	Ritual assistants in male ceremonials, some craft work.
Trade	Cash-crops, livestock, crafts, itinerant traders.	Non-cash-crops, cash-crops, domestic products, crafts.
Wage labour	Seasonal migration as wage labours; some permanent migrants.	Some migrate with their husbands temporarily; others are permanent emigrants with their families.
Young people	Herding cattle, collecting dung, fetching water, assisting fathers.	Herding cattle, collecting dung, fetching water, assisting in domestic work, watching infants, aiding the aged and infirmed.
Old people	Idling, watching infants, giving special knowledge of tribal affairs, judges, wisemen, training young boys.	Idling, watching infants, care of sick, training young girls for marriage, 'nose mothers' at birth.

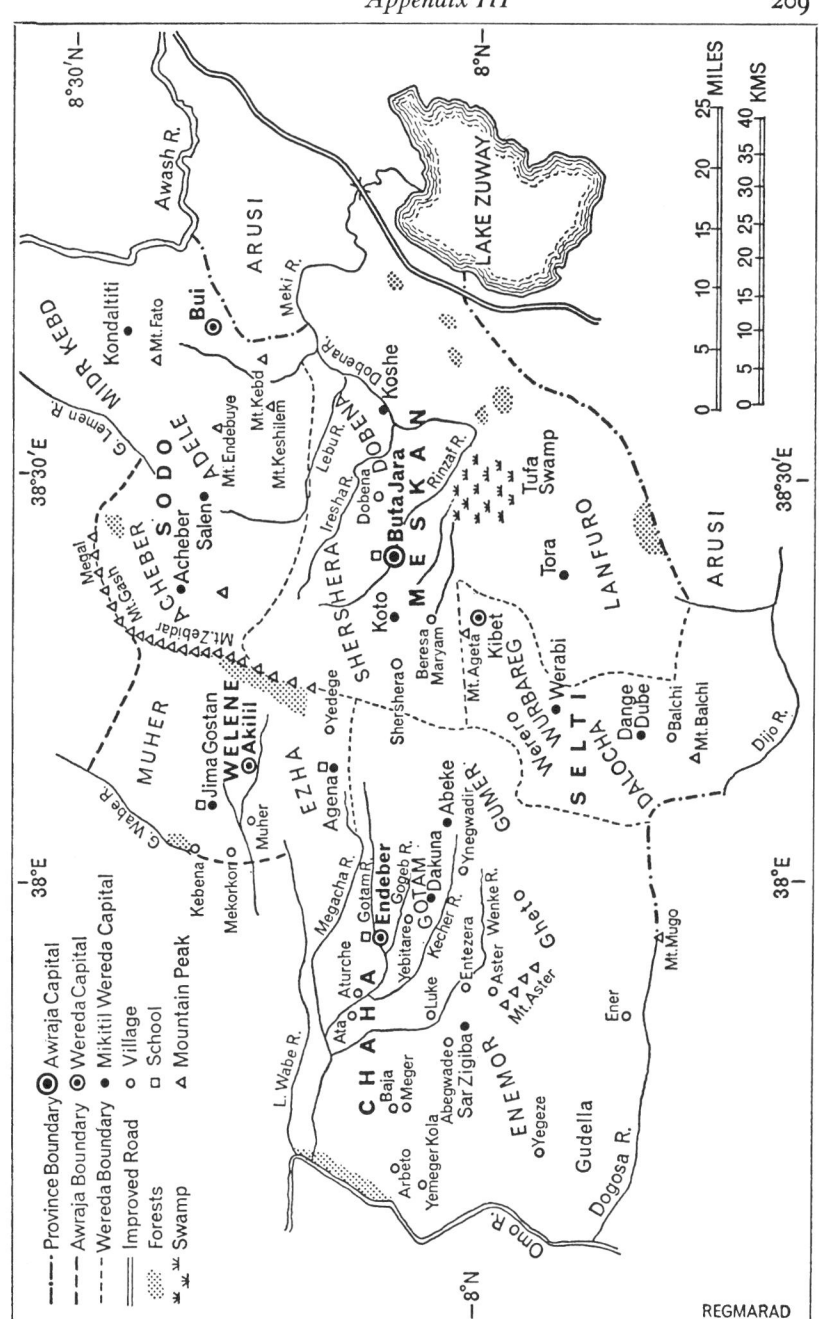

MAP 4. Gurage Awraja: Shoa Province.

Bibliographies

A. A BIBLIOGRAPHY FOR THE GURAGE

d'Abbadie, Antoine. *Géographie de l'Ethiopie*. Vol. I, Paris, 1860.

Azais, R. P. 'Le paganisme en pays Gouraghé,' *Revue d'ethnographie et des traditions populaires*. Vol. VII, 1926, pp. 21–27.

Azais, R. P., et Chambard, R. 'Notes sur quelques coutumes observées en Gourague,' *Revue d'ethnographie et des traditions populaires*. Vol. VIII, 1927, pp. 39–44.

——*Cinq années de recherches archéologiques en Ethiopie*. Paris, 1931 (pp. 147–98).

Baetemann, J. *Dictionnaire Amarigna-Français*. Dire-Daoua, 1929 (p. 1026).

Basset, René. *Histoire de la conquête de l'Abyssinie*. Paris, 1897 (pp. 222–4).

Bianchi, Gustavo. *Alla terra dei Galla*. Milano, 1884 (pp. 283–302).

Cecchi, Antoni. *Da Zeila alle frontiere del Caffa*. Vol. II, Rome, 1886 (pp. 76–109).

Cohen, Marcel. 'Rapport sur une mission linguistique en Abyssinie,' *Nouvelles archives des missions scientifiques*. Paris, nouv. série, fasc. 6, 1912, (pp. 39–50).

——*Etudes d'Ethiopien méridional*. Paris, 1931 (pp. 77–103).

Conti Rossini, Carlo. *Storia d'Etiopia*. Milano, 1928 (pp. 282–4).

——*Etiopia e genti d'Etiopia*. Firenze, 1937 (pp. 132–5).

——'Sui Guraghe e su loro consuetudini prima della conquista Scioana,' *Rivista de Diritto Coloniale*, 1938, pp. 393–406.

DeLuchon, P. Pascal. 'Le mariage chez les Gouraghes (Ethiopie),' *Annali Lateranensi*, 9, 1945, pp. 213–17.

Esteves Pereira, F. M. *Chronica de Susneyos, rei de Ethiopia*. Vol. II, 1900 (pp. 302–3).

Guèbrè Sellassié. *Chronique du régne de Ménélik II, Roi des Rois d'Ethiopie*. Paris, 1932.

Jensen, A. E. *Im Lande des Gada*. Stuttgart, 1936 (pp. 247–87).

Leslau, Wolf. *Ethiopic Documents: Gurage*. Viking Fund Publications in Anthropology, 14, New York, 1950.

Mondon-Vidailhet, C. *La langue harari et des dialects éthiopiens du Gouraghe*. Paris, 1902 (pp. 77–81).

Shack, W. A. 'Some Aspects of Ecology and Social Structure in the Ensete Complex in South-West Ethiopia,' *Journal of the Royal Anthropological Institute*, Vol. 93, 1, 1963a, pp. 72–79.

Shack, W. A. 'Religious Ideas and Social Action in Gurage Bond-Friendship,' *Africa*, Vol. XXXIII, 3, July 1963b, pp. 198–206.

——'Notes on Occupational Castes Among the Gurage of South-west Ethiopia,' *Man*, 1964, 54.

Taye, Aleqa. *History of the Peoples of Ethiopia*, in Amharic. Asmara, 1927 (p. 49).

——*The Gurage and Their Social Life*. The Gurage Exhibition Committee. Addis Ababa. N. D.

Traversi, L. 'Estratto di lettera sul viaggio nei Guraghi,' *Bolletino della Società Geografica Italiana*, 1887, pp. 277–90.

——'Lettera del dott. L. Traversi al conte Buturlin sul viaggio nell 'Urbaragh,' *Bolletino della Società Geografica Italiana*, 1888, pp. 122–4.

——'Lo Scioa ed i paesi limitrofi,' *Bolletino della Società Geografica Italiana*, 1889, pp. 718–21.

B. WORKS CITED IN THE TEXT

Alvarez, Francisco. *Narrative of the Portuguese Embassy to Abyssinia During the Years 1520–1527*. Tr. and ed. by Lord Stanley of Alderly. London. Hakluyt Society, Series 1, Vol. 64, 1881.

Beckingham, G. F., and Huntingford, G. W. B. *Some Records of Ethiopia: 1593–1646*. Hakluyt Society, London, 1954.

Blundell, H. W. *The Royal Chronicle of Abyssinia: 1769–1840*. Cambridge University Press, 1922.

Bohannan, Laura. 'Political Aspects of Tiv Social Organization,' in *Tribes Without Rulers*, (ed.) J. Middleton and D. Tait, London, 1958.

Bruce, James. *Travels to Discover the Source of the Nile, in the Years 1768, 1769, 1770, 1771, 1772, and 1773*. 5 vols. Edinburgh, 1790.

Bryan, M. A. 'A Linguistic No-Man's Land,' *Africa*, Vol. XV, 4, 1945, pp. 188–205.

Buxton, D. R. 'The Shoan Plateau and its People: An Essay in Local Geography,' *Geographical Journal*, Vol. CXIV, Oct.–Dec., 1949, pp. 157–72.

Cerulli, Enrico. *Folk Literature of the Galla of Southern Abyssinia*. Harvard African Studies III: Varia Africana III. Cambridge, Mass., 1922, pp. 11–228.

——*Etiopia Occidentale*. Vol. I, 1932; Vol. II, 1933. Roma.

Cerulli, Ernesta. *Peoples of Southwest Ethiopia and its Borderland*. Ethnographic Survey of Africa: Northeastern Africa, III. International African Institute. London, 1965.

Clark, J. D., *Prehistory of the Horn of Africa*. Cambridge University Press, 1954.

Cole, Sonia. *Prehistory of East Africa*. London, 1954.

Crawford, O. G. S. *Ethiopian Itineraries, ca. 1400–1524.* Hakluyt Society, Cambridge, 1955.

Economic Handbook. Ethiopia: Ministry of Commerce and Industry. Addis Ababa, December 1958.

Ethiopia Observer. 'The Land System of Ethiopia,' Vol. I, 9, October 1957, pp. 283–301.

Evans-Pritchard, E. E. *The Nuer,* Oxfod, 1940.

——*Kinship and Marriage Among the Nuer.* Oxford, 1951.

Fallers, L. *A Bantu Bureaucracy.* London, 1956.

——'Some Determinants of Soga Marriage Stability,' *Africa,* Vol. XXVII, 2, 1957, pp. 106–21.

Firth, R. 'Bond-Friendship in Tikopia' in *Custom is King,* (ed.) L. H. Dudley. London, 1936.

——'Religious Belief and Personal Adjustment.' *Journal of the Royal Anthropological Institute,* 1948.

——*Social Change in Tikopia,* London, 1959.

Fortes, Meyer. *The Dynamics of Clanship Among the Tallensi.* Oxford, 1945.

Fortes, M., and Evans-Pritchard, E. E. (ed.) *African Political Systems.* Oxford, 1940.

Gebre-Wold-Ingida-worq. 'Ethiopia's Traditional System of Land Tenure and Taxation,' (trs. Mengesha Gessesse, *Ya Ityopya Maretna Gebir Sim*). *Ethiopia Observer,* Vol. 4, 1962, pp. 302–39.

Gluckman, Max. *Economy of the Central Barotse Plain.* Rhodes Livingston Papers, No. 7. Manchester, 1941.

——'The Role of the Sexes in Wiko Circumcision Ceremonies,' in *Social Structure,* (ed.) Meyer Fortes, Oxford, 1949.

——"Kinship and Marriage Among the Lozi of Northern Rhodesia and the Zulu of Natal,' in *African Systems of Kinship and Marriage,* (ed.) Radcliffe-Brown and Forde, Oxford, 1950, pp. 166–206.

——*Rituals of Rebellion in South-East Africa.* Manchester, 1954.

——*Analysis of a Social Situation in Modern Zululand.* Rhodes-Livingstone Papers, No. 23. Manchester, 1958.

——(ed.) *Essays on the Ritual of Social Relations.* Manchester University Press, 1962.

Harris, W. Cornwallis. *The Highlands of Ethiopia,* 3 vols. London, 1844.

Hodson, A. 'Notes on Abyssinian Lakes,' *Geographical Journal,* Vol. LX, 1, July, 1922, pp. 65–72.

Hoebel, A. E. *The Law of Primitive Man.* Cambridge, Mass., 1954.

Hoernle, A. W. 'The Importance of the Sib in the Marriage Ceremonies of the Southeastern Bantu,' *South African Journal of Science,* Vol. 22, 1925, pp. 480–91.

Honea, K. *A Contribution to the History of the Hamitic Peoples of Africa.* Acta Ethnologica et Linguistica, 5, 1958, Universität Wien.

Huntingford, G. W. B. *The Galla of Ethiopia: The Kingdoms of Kaffa and Janjero:* Ethnographic Survey of Africa: Northeastern Africa, II. International African Institute. London, 1955.

Jensen, A. E. *Im Lande des Gada.* Stuttgart, 1936.

——(ed.) *Altvölker Süd-Äthiopiens.* Stuttgart, 1959.

Krapf, J. L., and Isenberg, C. W. *Journals of the Rev. Messrs. Isenberg and Krapf, Missionaries of the Church Missionary Society.* London, 1843.

Leslau, Wolf. 'The Influence of Cushitic on the Semitic Languages of Ethiopia: A Problem of Sub-stratum,' *Word*, 1, 1945, pp. 59–82.

——'An Ethiopian Argot of a People Possessed by a Spirit,' *Africa*, Vol. XIX, 3, July 1949, pp. 204–12.

——'The Influence of Sidamo in the Ethiopic Languages of Gurage,' *Language*, Vol. 28, 1, Jan.-Mar., 1952, pp. 63–81 (1952a).

——'A Footnote on Interlingual Taboos [Gurage and Amharic],' *American Anthropologist*, Vol. 54, 2, April–June, 1952, p. 275 (1952b).

——'The Arabic Loanwords in Gurage,' *Arabica*, 3, 3, Sept. 1956, pp. 266–84.

——'Taboo Expressions in Ethiopia,' *American Anthropologist*, Vol. 61, 1, Feb. 1959, pp. 105–6.

Lewis, I. M. *A Pastoral Democracy.* London, 1961.

Luther, E. *Ethiopia Today.* Oxford, 1958.

Messing, Simon D. 'The Highland Plateau Amhara of Ethiopia.' Unpublished Ph. D. Dissertation. University of Pennsylvania, 1957.

Middleton, J., and Tait, D. (ed.) *Tribes Without Rulers.* London, 1958.

Montandon, G. *Au pays Ghimirra.* Neuchatel, 1913.

Murdock, G. P. *Africa: Its People and Their Culture History.* New York, 1959.

——'Staple Subsistence Crops in Africa,' *Geographical Review*, Vol. XLX, 4, October 1960, pp. 521–40.

Nadel, S. F. *A Black Byzantium.* Oxford, 1942.

——'Land Tenure on the Eritrean Plateau,' *Africa*, Vol. XVI, nos. 1–2, 1946, pp. 1–22, 99–109.

——*Nupe Religion.* Oxford, 1954.

Pankhurst, R., and Eshete, E. 'Self-Help in Ethiopia,' *Ethiopia Observer*, Vol. II, 11, December 1958.

Pankhurst, R. *An Introduction to the Economic History of Ethiopia.* London, 1961a.

——'Menilek and the Foundations of Addis Ababa,' *Journal of African History*, Vol. 11, 1, 1961b, pp. 103–17.

——'Primitive Money in Ethiopia,' *Journal de la Société des Africanistes*, Vol. 32, 2, 1962, pp. 213–47.

Parsons, Talcott. 'The Role of Ideas in Social Action,' *American Sociological Review*, Vol. 3, 5, 1938.

Penal Code of the Empire of Ethiopia. Addis Ababa, 1957.

Perham, M. *The Government of Ethiopia*. London, 1947.

Perruchon, J. 'Histoire des guerres d'Amda Syon,' *Journal Asiatique*, Série 8, 14, 1889, pp. 271–7; 327–63; 441–83.

Radcliffe-Brown, A. R. *Structure and Function in Primitive Society*. Glencoe: The Free Press, 1956.

Radcliffe-Brown, A. R., and Forde, Daryll, (ed.) *African Systems of Kinship and Marriage*. Oxford, 1950.

Read, M. *The Ngoni of Nyasaland*. London, 1956.

Richards, A. I. *Land, Labour and Diet in Northern Rhodesia*. London, 1939.

Schapera, I. 'Kinship and Marriage Among the Tswana,' in *African Systems of Kinship and Marriage*, (ed.) Radcliffe-Brown and Forde, Oxford, 1950, pp. 140–65.

——*Government and Politics in Tribal Societies*. London, 1956.

Scott, Hugh. 'Journey to the Gughe Highlands,' *Linnean Society*. London, 1948–49.

Shack, W. A. 'Organization and Problems of Education in Ethiopia,' *Journal of Negro Education*, Vol. 28, 4, Fall, 1959, pp. 504–20.

Simmonds, N. W. 'Ensete Cultivation in the Southern Highlands of Ethiopia; a Review,' *Tropical Agriculture*, Vol. 35, 1958, pp. 302–7.

Simoons, F. *Northwest Ethiopia*. University of Wisconsin Press, 1960.

Smeds, E. 'The Ensete Planting Cultures of Eastern Sidamo, Ethiopia,' *Acta Geographica*, Vol. XIII, no. 4, 1955.

Steward, J. *Theory of Culture Change*. University of Illinois Press, 1955.

Tait, D. 'The Territorial Pattern and Lineage System of Konkomba,' *Tribes Without Rulers*, (ed.) Middleton and Tait, London, 1958, pp. 167–202.

The Agriculture of Ethiopia, Vol. I. U.S. Operations Mission to Ethiopia, January 1954.

Trimingham, J. S. *Islam in Ethiopia*. Oxford, 1952.

Tucker, A. N., and Bryan, M. A. *The Non-Bantu Languages of North-Eastern Africa*. International African Institute. London, 1956.

Ullendorff, E. 'Gurage Notes,' *Africa*, Vol. XX, 4, October 1950, pp. 335–44.

——*The Semitic Languages of Ethiopia*. London, 1955.

——*The Ethiopians*. Oxford, 1960.

Walker, C. H. *The Abyssinian at Home*. London, 1933.

Watson, W. *Tribal Cohesion in a Money Economy*. Manchester University Press, 1958.

Wilson, M. *Rituals of Kinship among the Nyakyusa*. London, 1957.

Winter, E. *Bwamba: A Structural-Functional Analysis of a Patrilineal Society*. Cambridge, 1956.

——'The Aboriginal Political Structure of Bwamba,' in *Tribes Without Rulers*, (ed.) Middleton and Tait, London, 1958, pp. 136–66.

Index

Abyssinia, *see* Ethiopia
Ab emänä, see Trade
Abar, dry season, 32
Abba François Markos, xi
Abba Jawbir, 193
Abba Jifar II, 193
Abba Ramus, *see Šehotč*, Shaikh
Sayyid Budella
Addis Ababa, 27, 29f; Gurage migration to —, 81f; $M^w e\lambda ät$ groups in
—, 135(fn.44); urbanization in —,
202
Adultery, 125; judge of —, 138, 159;
see also Danä
Agäz, war leader title, 24, 106; young
initiates awarded —, 132, 138, 156;
see also Clan Chief
Agäz Amärga Oqbato, of Chaha, 24;
burial of —, 129; honours of —,
157; *see also* War leader
Agäz Andena, of Gyeto, 207
Agäz Andəta, of Ezha, 207
Agäz Balčəya, of Amya, 156
Agäz Bange, of Ezha, 207
Agäz Darsamo, of Ennemor, 157
Agäz Səbəta, of Muher, 207
Agänna, market village, 70; *see also*
Markets
Age-organizations, absent among Gurage men, 131; ritual — of women,
132ff; *see also M^wəyät*
Agriculture, Gurage, 1, 33, 45; *see
also Äsät, Ensete edulis*, Ensete Culture Complex
Agnatic kinship, basis of society, 2; —
in structure of household, 83, 89
(fn.7), 95; domestic group organized
around —, 107; — in notion of
unilineal descent, 91ff; — in clan
genealogical fiction, 94ff, 97, 101f;
— defines rights in land, 91f; *see
also* Lineage
Aksum, invasion of 'Aksumites' from
—, 5, 6
Amda Syon I, invasion of Gurageland
during reign of —, 14ff, 103
Aməst bet Gurage, Five Gurage
Houses, 205

Amhara, tribe of, primitive hunters
among —, 8; character of — political system, 13; — Ethiopian rule,
15, 18; — land system in Gurageland, 21f; — military colonies in
Gurageland, 22f, 25; — post-Italian liberation government, 27f;
— attitudes towards Gurage, 34ff;
— system of land use, 45; — marriage practice, 87; — cognatic kin
ties, 88; 143; — cultural system,
199; — influence in Gurageland, 200
Amharaization, mode of cultural assimilation, 81, 202ff
Amharic, language, influence on
Guraginä, 8; — as a *lingua franca*,
29; — as an agent of culture change,
199
Amya, Chaha clan district, 98, 103
Ancestors, in genealogical record, 94,
98, 101
Animals, taboos on hunting and eating
certain —, 9; trophies of — as
symbols of bravery, 136
Antrošt, mother's festival, 128, 175
Arab, mythical clan founder, 103 208
Arabs, as traders, 48
Arson, ritual protection against —,
159, 175ff, 191; *see also Božä,
Maga, Sənä*
Arussi, Galla tribe of, 4, 18ff, 28
Äsät, Gurage staple food, 33, 42ff,
50ff; — culture complex, 52f; —
plant disease, 33; — used in pharmacopeia, 53; ritual attitudes towards —, 53ff; — cultivation, 57ff;
status indexed by —, 63, 138; trade
in —, 69, 74; labour migration and
— cultivation, 80; — as cash-crop,
67f, 82; burial in — field, 114, 129;
204, 209 *see also Ensete edulis*,
False banana
Asfa Wasan, Crown Prince of Ethiopia, 23
Authority, of elders, 40, 72f, 93f, 98,
108; — of Chiefs, 145, 148, 160,
164; — of ritual dignitaries, 176,
184f, 186f, 190ff, 195f

Magic, 9

Mahabär, feast, 174; *see also Mäbär*

Malkanya, Sub-district Governor, 25, 27; *see also Dejazmach, Mislane*

Mambwe, the, 78(fn.27)

Manjo, 8ff; *see also Fuga, Midgaan, Tumaal, Watta, Wayto, Yibir*

Markets, women in, 69; inter-tribal —, 70f; clan control over —, 72; — items of transaction, 69f, 74f; social functions of —, 75ff

Marriage, factors effecting stability of, 89ff; age of —, 108; selection of — partner, 121; — season, 122; — and concubinage, 122; — feast, 123; lineage hostility preceeding —, 123; ritual legitimation of —, 126; step-mother in —, 127; *see also* Bride-wealth

Mäsetäna, bride's best-friends, 123

Mäsqäl, Amhara feast of the Holy Cross, 174; *see also Mäsqär*

Mäsqär, Gurage feast of the Holy Cross, 128, 174; *see also Mäsqäl*

Mäzakᵂər clan, 183

Menilek II, Emperor, 14; — conquest of Gurage, 14f, 15(fn.27), 18; policy of —, 24; *pax Aethiopia* under —, 143, 191ff, 193, 205

Megacha River, 40f

Məkʸer, feast, 174f.

Messianic movement, Islamic, 193ff

Məze, groom's best-friends, 121, 123(fn.33)

Middleton, J., 2(fn.4), 101(fn.18), 147(fn.6), 149(fn.8)

Midgaan, primitive hunters among Somali, 8; *see also Tumaal, Yibir*

Mikital Wereda, Administrative sub-district, 37ff

Minority groups, general position of, 8ff

Mislane, Governor's Deputy, 21, 25, 27ff, 170ff; *see also Dejazmach, Malkanya*

Missions, Christian, 35, 172, 201

Mogämänä clan, 24, 98; lineages of —, 99; origin of —, 102ff; 119; — primary segment of Chaha, 146; — lineage of chieftainship, 150ff; 208

Mohammad Gran, wars of, 16, 40

Mother's brother (*mwena*), 85ff, 89, 117

Muher, tribe of, 4; — tribal boundaries, 40

Mulid, pilgrimage to, 193

Murdock, G. P., 5(fn.7, 8, 9), 6(fn.11), 50(fn.1), 85(fn.1)

Mᵂəyät, girl's ritual age-organization, 132ff; — in Addis Ababa, 135 (fn.44); — tribute to ritual leader, 140, 175

Nadel, S. F., 12(fn.25), 45(fn.16), 144(fn.3), 190(fn.15)

Näfᵂrä, caste of blacksmiths, 11, 209; *see also Fuga, Gəžä*

Näqᵂa, festival, 93, 134, 175

Nəpᵂär, festival, 175ff, 178; *see also Božä, Gᵂetakᵂəyä*

Ngoni, the, 1(fn.1)

Nuer, the, 52(fn.5), 76(fn.20), 89 (fn.7), 145(fn.5), 147(fn.6), 194 (fn.18)

Nupe, the, 144(fn.3), 190(fn.15)

Nyakyusa, the, 89(fn.8)

Plains of Atat, see Crown Lands

Political community, defined, 144ff; *see also* Clan, Clanship

Political structure, clanship and —, 149ff; — ritual, 195ff

Polygyny, 67f, 87f; — and co-wife behaviour, 111ff

Prester John, *see* Lebna Dengel

Purdah, 173

Qabena, muslim state, 20; market of —, 69; 104

Qadi, court of, 192

Qadiriyya Dervish Order, 193

Qänazmač Amärga Oqbato, *see* Agäz Amärga

Quoro, village headman, 24, 63, 72, 76, 93; tribute received by —, 140ff; — in tribal politics, 162; — in local politics, 169ff

Radcliffe-Brown, A. R., xii, 92(fn.12), 130(fn.41), 159(fn.13), 196(fn.19)

Rain-maker, 186(fn.11)

Ras Dargie, armies of in Gurage wars, 19(fn.41)

Ras Gobena, armies of in Gurage wars, 23

Ras Mulugetta, District Governor of Gurageland, 23